22.50

D0204689

Between Struggle and Hope:
The Nicaraguan Literacy Crusade

Also of Interest

†*Nicaragua: The Land of Sandino*, Second Edition, Revised and Updated, Thomas W. Walker

†*The End and the Beginning: The Nicaraguan Revolution*, Second Edition, Revised and Updated, John A. Booth

Demographic, Economic, and Resource-Use Trends in Seventeen Caribbean Basin Countries, Norman A. Graham and Keith L. Edwards

Unfinished Agenda: The Dynamics of Modernization in Developing Nations, Manning Nash

Development and the Politics of Administrative Reform: Lessons from Latin America, Linn Hammergren

†*Managing Development in the Third World*, Coralie Bryant and Louise G. White

Change in Central America: Internal and External Dimensions, edited by Wolf Grabendorff, Heinrich-W. Krumwiede, and Jörg Todt

†*Revolution and Counterrevolution in Central America and the Caribbean*, edited by Donald E. Schulz and Douglas H. Graham

†*FOREIGN POLICY on Latin America, 1970–1980*, edited by the staff of *Foreign Policy*

Colossus Challenged: The Struggle for Caribbean Influence, edited by H. Michael Erisman and John D. Martz

†Available in hardcover and paperback.

Westview Special Studies on Latin America and the Caribbean

Between Struggle and Hope:
The Nicaraguan Literacy Crusade
Valerie Miller

In July 1979, Nicaragua began a process of profound structural transformation to redistribute power and wealth in order to redress past societal inequities. This book critically examines the planning and implementation of one of the first programs of national transformation—the Nicaraguan National Literacy Crusade, an educational effort directly involving almost one-fourth of the country's population. International experts praised the program as an exemplary model for national development and unanimously chose the campaign to receive UNESCO's 1980 grand prize in literacy.

A vivid combination of anecdote and analysis, *Between Struggle and Hope* is a study of policymaking and institution building within a revolutionary society. Written by an international adviser to the program, the book provides an insider's look at educational planning and political formation. A critique, it combines the human story of the struggle to create the literacy campaign with a detailed evaluation of program results, both positive and negative. Unique in the literature, it allows the reader to follow firsthand the behind-the-scenes development of an educational campaign designed as part of a national plan of structural transformation and to share the personal concerns, criticisms, and analysis of the program planners. *Between Struggle and Hope* offers a rare opportunity to examine the process of political change through education and to probe the internal dynamics of revolution.

Valerie Miller has studied and worked in Central America since 1964. Beginning her career as an educational specialist for the Peace Corps in rural Panama, she has been involved in area development and education programs ever since. Dr. Miller has worked with projects of the United Nations, the U.S. Agency for International Development, the Organization of American States, the Central American Institute of Business Administration, the U.S. Congress, and Catholic and Protestant church organizations. She received her doctorate in international education from the University of Massachusetts and worked on the executive staff of the Nicaraguan National Literacy Crusade for one year. Dr. Miller presently serves as director of Central American programs for the Foreign Policy Education Fund of Washington, D.C.

Between Struggle and Hope: The Nicaraguan Literacy Crusade

Valerie Miller

Foreword by Carman St. John Hunter

Westview Press / Boulder and London

Westview Special Studies on Latin America and the Caribbean

Published in 1985 in the United States of America by Westview Press, Inc., 5500 Central Avenue, Boulder, Colorado 80301; Frederick A. Praeger, Publisher

Library of Congress Cataloging in Publication Data
Miller, Valerie.
  Between struggle and hope.
  Bibliography: p.
  Includes index.
  1. Literacy—Nicaragua. 2. Education and state—
Nicaragua. I. Title.
LC155.N5M55 1985   370.19′4′097285   84-11984
ISBN 0-8133-0081-9
ISBN 0-8133-0082-7 (pbk.)

Printed and bound in the United States of America

10 9 8 7 6 5 4 3 2 1

To Enoc and *compañeros*,

To all those who have challenged me to question inequity,
given me the strength to persevere,
and helped me understand the poetry and power of people,

To all the many Nicaraguans who have shared their dreams
with me and made this work come alive,

To Fernando and Kay,

These many pages belong to you.

Contents

Foreword

With the publication of *Between Struggle and Hope: The Nicaraguan Literacy Crusade,* educators and social scientists all over the world will owe Valerie Miller a large debt of gratitude. Much has been written about other famous literacy campaigns, but this is the first time we have been privileged to go behind the scenes to join responsible leaders in their daily struggles and decisions. We know something about the Tanzanian, Chinese, and Cuban successes, but we do not know how those responsible for them assessed their own work. What went right? What went wrong? If they could start again, what would they do differently? What issues were most debated? Which ideas were considered and discarded?

It was Father Fernando Cardenal, the director of the Nicaraguan crusade, who understood this need for detail. He invited Valerie Miller to assume the role of an inside-outsider, a knowledgeable participant-observer and critic, with the task of documenting the crusade from its very beginning and assisting in the evaluation. Father Cardenal's wisdom, both in issuing such a invitation and in choosing this particular adult educator, is amply proved by the book that has resulted.

There appear to me to be at least three levels on which this book merits study and appreciation. First, adult educators will find in it a challenging account of the way in which many familiar, practical situations were met and resolved or, in some cases, not resolved. Although both the problems and the successes may appear larger than life, this incredible story is valuable on the level of information about the planning, administration, and implementation of any major educational initiative.

On another level, students of social and political history will find here a case study of a people who, having triumphed over the oppressive forces of a powerful dictatorship, began the process of constructing a more inclusive and democratic state. Why did China, Cuba, and now Nicaragua choose a literacy campaign as the first step toward the creation of a new society? What were the political and educational decisions involved? And why is it that the most successful literacy campaigns have been those that followed a dramatic social and political change? We get some insight into the urgency felt by leaders to act quickly and decisively against ignorance and poverty. We can also appreciate how such political pressure may conflict with the need for careful planning and logistic precision.

Third, the unique value of this document, however, is not that it provides a blueprint for others to follow; it does not. Nor is its chief importance the fact that it is a detailed case study of political change. Rather, its significance lies in the fact that it is the first concrete model of the interaction between political theory, educational methodology, and the acquisition of literacy skills and that it is accompanied by the reflections of those responsible. Many people have written with considerable heat on these matters, but our thinking has been based on conjecture from experience with small-scale models. This crusade was both government sponsored and national in scope.

Dr. Miller, in an excellent section outlining the changes that have occurred in recent decades in the understanding of the social and political context of literacy, quotes from the statements of a large number of international agencies. There is increasing acceptance of the fact that the question of who is literate and who is illiterate in any society has more to do with relations of power than with technical reading skills. Illiterate people everywhere are the poor, the marginal, the excluded. The deepest shame is not their inability to read and write but that they have no hope for their future in the society into which they were born. Their situation does not automatically change when they acquire reading and writing skills. Literacy is a basic right, not a privilege, but it is meaningless without the right, also, to use the skills for one's own benefit and for one's family and community. Unless there is the intention to open more than the printed page to literacy learners, the skills are the route to a dead end. A literacy campaign must create new options and build hope. It must be both a symbol and a foretaste of a future that calls forth and rewards the best that each can contribute to the common good.

From the beginning, the Nicaraguan experience was intended as a political action with educational implications. In this sense, although literacy was a central objective, this objective was to serve the larger purpose of promoting the growth and development of the learners as full, participating members of the society. As we follow the decisions and events of this crusade, we can see the way in which the objectives, intentions, and priorities of those responsible for literacy campaigns— or any educational program—affect even the seemingly most unimportant decisions and, thus, the outcomes.

In view of the commitment of Nicaraguans to literacy as part of the liberation process, some of the difficulties they encountered have particular significance. The persistent struggle to engage the learners in dialogue illustrates just how hard it is to move from an authoritarian to a participatory stance. In the same way, the debates about the inclusion or exclusion of the design for community research and about the strategic importance of integrating literacy and community organizing are also instructive. These activities and the use of sociodrama, art, and learning games were seen by some as detracting from the "central purpose," the teaching of reading and writing. Yet the central purpose had been defined from the start as more inclusive than technical skills.

What is at stake here is deeper than methodology. Teaching methods, like political strategies, are a structured way of acting out one's basic attitudes toward society and toward people. When participatory methods are seen as expendable, it is quite possible that the goal they serve may also have a low priority despite rhetoric to the contrary.

Issues such as these are present in any literacy action, just as they are present in any political movement. The fact that they are made very visible in the Nicaraguan story gives us a better understanding of their impact. In this account, actions or intentions are not presented as good or bad, right or wrong. They are simply set forth as they happened. This is essentially a human document that depicts a mixture of pressures, emotions, tragedies, courage, and the triumph of hope. After observing all of this, we are better able to appreciate and understand the assessments made by Valerie Miller and the other leaders.

We can see with them that whenever people were able to form bonds of friendship and trust and to express freely their own creativity and imagination, there was greater success on all levels of the crusade. When methods were consistent with the overall purposes of the crusade, the results fulfilled these purposes. Both staff and learners not only gained technical skills but achieved a deeper understanding of their own capacities and were able to act on these.

As we celebrate the Nicaraguan success, we are challenged to re-evaluate our own goals, our criteria for success, and our appreciation of the complexity and the cost of working toward human liberation. This book enlightens both our struggle and our hope.

Carman St. John Hunter
Author of *Adult Illiteracy*
in the United States

Preface

This book is intended to raise questions for people who are concerned about problems of illiteracy and inequality. During the past five years of writing, I have been challenged to examine my understanding of these issues and of those of my profession—education, development, and international relations. It is my hope that people who read this study will be challenged in a similar way. The preface is written to give the reader an understanding of the experiences that led me to write the book and that have influenced my judgments about the campaign and the problems that it attempted to address. Three different periods of history and professional involvement have shaped my understanding of Nicaragua and the issues examined in this book: one, as a development specialist under the Somoza dictatorship; two, as a participant in the Nicaraguan literacy campaign during the first years of the revolution; and three, more recently, as a member of congressional fact-finding missions to Central America. This study was conducted with the full cooperation of the campaign's director, Father Fernando Cardenal, and his staff. It was written completely independently of government supervision and financed by university, foundation, and development agency grants. As in this preface, personal experiences and analysis are woven together throughout the book in order to give meaning and life to the study's conclusions. For those readers who especially enjoy the human side of these endeavors, stories and quotations are frequent and reveal most vividly the progress, problems, and significance of the campaign.

• • •

I first arrived in Nicaragua in 1971, wide-eyed and rather cocky, ready to tackle poverty head-on. With Peace Corps service and political science studies behind me, I considered myself somewhat of an expert in development. At the time, solutions to the problems of poverty seemed obvious to me, and I wanted to be involved in working on them—

agricultural cooperatives, education, health care—those development programs that would lead to a better life for the poor. So I took on a variety of jobs. I became a paramedic for a Baptist clinic program, a research consultant for a Central American graduate school of business, and on weekends, an adviser to a Catholic rural development organization.

My energetic idealism was mixed with a certain sense of political pragmatism. I reasoned that if misery were lessened and opportunities for the poor expanded, then U.S. foreign policy goals of stability and trade would be better served. The challenge facing countries like Nicaragua was to organize dynamic programs of national development, for if increasing numbers of people could earn adequate salaries and participate in decisions affecting their own lives, the need to rebel would disappear and stability would be assured. With ever greater purchasing power on the part of a growing majority, trade could even expand. It was only common sense. Some of my friends in the U.S. embassy thought so too and pointed to the millions of dollars that the United States was putting into economic development projects with the government there for those same reasons. Yet in my work, I found a different picture. During the two years I spent there, I watched people grow increasingly impoverished and children die of malnutrition, their parents too poor to provide them with a proper diet or prompt medical attention. For them, the development model was not working.

The memory of one child and his mother never quite leaves me. One day I held a baby in my arms, an infant weak from hunger and malnutrition; two weeks later the child was dead. His mother was an active member of the church health program for which I worked, a young woman who inspired everyone with her smiles and enthusiasm. After her infant son's death, she told me about her hopes and dreams, her desire to get a basic education, to become a paramedic like me. As she spoke, tears gathered in her eyes, but she held them back somehow. She wanted to be brave, she said; at home, four other small children still depended upon her. She told me that her husband worked every day as a laborer in the rice fields, but that he and the other laborers on the plantation had not been paid any wages for four months. His employer was one of the dictator Somoza's business partners, a Cuban exile, and one of the beneficiaries of U.S.-supported development projects.

This woman was one of the best students in my health classes; she could recite the nutrition chart by heart. But knowing the chart did not help her feed her son when there was no food. With no income, food was scarce and an adequate diet impossible. The result was the loss of her child. What difference could our health program make when faced with such poverty?

There were some attempts to respond to these problems, yet when one village priest tried to start a food production cooperative, its leaders were arrested by Somoza's National Guard. The dictator worried about priests organizing the poor and peasants exerting leadership, but food wasn't a problem for him at that time. A devastating earthquake had destroyed Managua, the capital city, and aid was pouring in from around the world. Somoza and his associates were selling the donations of food and medicine on the black market and profiteering off the massive amounts of international generosity. One day, three months after the earthquake, I took a child to a nearby public hospital only to find that no medicine was available there and that, despite all the international aid, the hospital had not received any. Yet, throughout wealthy neighborhoods, well-stocked pharmacies had opened up overnight in the big garages of National Guard officers. From these experiences, it was clear to me that corruption was growing, and that, increasingly, wealth was becoming concentrated in the hands of a few. After the earthquake, rumors circulated that a small armed group called the *Frente Sandinista* was active in the mountains, occasionally attacking isolated National Guard outposts. Revolution seemed only a matter of time.

The lessons that I learned from all this were painful. They went against all that I had believed in. Economic aid did not necessarily assist the poor and, in fact, could easily lead to greater inequalities and instability. It all depended on who distributed it and how. Moreover, with distribution so unfair, education and health care didn't help much either. Development programs only helped a tiny minority. As long as U.S. foreign policy supported governments that did not address the basic problem of equitable distribution, our development assistance programs would contribute to greater disparities, eventual instability, violence, and maybe even revolution.

Questions robbed me of sleep. I wondered what peaceful choices remained for countries like Nicaragua and what we gained by buttressing up corrupt and greedy governments. Change would come, but did it have to come with U.S. opposition, at the end of a gun? Wasn't hunger a form of violence as devastating as the violence wrought with guns? And since the United States had placed Somoza in power and supported his family regime for over forty years, what responsibility did we bear in this situation? What would be our nation's response to future changes there?

I left Nicaragua in 1973 for doctoral studies and other consulting work in Latin America. When I returned seven years later, the dictator had been toppled, and the hard part of the revolution was just beginning. People whom I had worked with before in church projects were now heads of government—cabinet ministers, agency directors, and technical advisers. Programs we had once dreamed about were now being planned and implemented. The *Frente Sandinista* had come down from the mountains as heroes, bringing together a broad spectrum of the population in a massive movement for change. Everything seemed possible. The spirit was contagious.

I remember the two young children of a friend, eleven and fourteen, working one Sunday after mass on a new public housing project for the poor. They, along with other neighbors both young and old, had responded to a government call for volunteers to help at odd jobs around the community on the weekends. The brother and sister, their clothes and faces streaked with dirt, were hauling bricks in a rickety wheelbarrow for a volunteer construction crew. They made a game out of it, laughing as they piled the bricks higher and higher. Stacking and carting, loading and unloading, they were a tireless twosome, despite the many bumps and bruises on their hands and arms incurred during their labors. When a priest friend came by and asked them what they were doing—if, maybe, they were helping to build a house—the young girl looked up at him, grinning widely, and said, "No, Father, we're working on building a country. Do you want to help?" Against tremendous odds, yet with enormous enthusiasm, people were working together to create a new model of development and new systems of distributing power and wealth so that individuals could take responsibility for solving their community problems more effectively and fairly.

The questions they wanted to tackle were awesome and encompassed the most basic of their country's problems: how to overcome misery and underdevelopment; how to build a better, more equitable society; how to get at the root causes of poverty—the extreme imbalances of power and wealth—knowing that such an effort would be resisted by a small, wealthy elite with vested interests in the status quo; how to bring about the needed redistribution in the economic and political system to benefit the majority of the population; and how to involve that majority—the poor and disenfranchised—in the development of their own future.

Finding answers to these questions was the challenge that drew me back to Nicaragua. They were the same kinds of questions that I had found people struggling with throughout Latin America—development experts and peasant leaders alike. The difference in Nicaragua was that a new generation of leaders had become the government and, as such, was committed to engaging an entire country in a program of redistribution and national development. Because of my graduate studies in adult education and long experience in Latin America working with the poor, I was especially interested in how they planned to organize the development and education programs for adults with little or no formal schooling. What intrigued me most was how those programs could help such people, who had been kept so long at the margins of society, to become active participating members of both their communities and country.

News about the literacy crusade first reached me while I was finishing a study on Nicaragua for the World Council of Churches and the United Nations Commission on Human Rights. My colleagues shared my enthusiasm about the campaign and encouraged me to return to Nicaragua in order to participate in its development. I was eager to work in the program and, perhaps, one day write about the experience because I knew that the lessons gained from such a national effort, whether a success or failure, would be invaluable. I knew, too, that books on the subject were scarce and that those few that existed were usually written long after programs had been completed by people who were never present during the actual operations. As a result, such studies, although useful for a broad understanding of programs, lacked an insider's perspective and were limited by the fading memories of planners and participants who, over time, tended to forget all but the most poignant personal vignettes. The hard, detailed lessons about planning and organization were often lost.

In designing Nicaragua's campaign, the director, Father Fernando Cardenal, found this assessment about the scarcity of analytical information to be frustratingly accurate. He could find no critical analysis of a national literacy program that could help him or his team address or predict the staggering problems that awaited them. Because of this experience and the indebtedness that he felt to the international community for their financial contributions to the campaign, he wanted to see that the lessons from the Nicaraguan program, especially the problems, would be well documented and analyzed by someone who knew about adult education and literacy. He wanted to be sure that others could learn from Nicaragua's effort and could avoid the errors that the campaign would inevitably make along the way. Throughout the program, he reminded the staff repeatedly to keep track of their problems and mistakes so that an accurate record of the crusade could be written.

When Father Cardenal asked me to take on this task of historian and critic, I was both honored and delighted. It was an opportunity to participate directly in a historic educational event and to document such a program's development critically so that its lessons could be saved and used by others. The interest of international organizations allowed me to accept the position. The Canadian foundation World Literacy[1] provided me with a grant to do my research in Nicaragua, and later, the University of Massachusetts, Center for International Education, awarded me a research fellowship from the United States Agency for

International Development to continue my writing in Washington, D.C. I am deeply indebted to all of them and also to friends in Texas and Minnesota who provided the final support for the completion of this project.

During the first days of the campaign, however, I had serious doubts about the feasibility of my work. Everyone was so busy that no one had any time to talk, except for the library personnel and the UNESCO adviser from Cuba, who began most days by reading poetry to the staff on his way to his office. I expected politics from him and got poetry. I wondered if I should be suspicious. During my weeks there, I became friends with a young library volunteer, a shy freckle-faced Nicaraguan woman who looked more Irish than Latin. One day, at lunch, she quietly told me how much she missed her boyfriend; he had been killed in the last days of fighting against Somoza. Her uncle had been killed fifteen years earlier by the National Guard. As we talked together in the noon heat, we watched a group of students from a nearby high school walk by the campaign offices, serenading the staff with the crusade's theme song. The hot dusty wind blew at their clothes as they went along, but didn't seem to affect their enthusiasm at all. I, on the other hand, could hardly breathe.

Despite my initial doubts, I was soon immersed in the life of the campaign. Training workshops were being mounted across the country and since national supervisory staff was in short supply, I was temporarily drafted to help. When I arrived at my assigned site, an isolated church retreat center outside Managua, I found that the workshop coordinators were completely frazzled and about to lose their tempers. The staff person in charge of supplies hadn't stocked any food, the woman in charge of cooking for the 180 participants had not arrived yet, and the provincial supervisor was lecturing, then interrogating the workshop leaders about the quality of their revolutionary zeal. As he was the same person who had forgotten the food, they didn't take him too seriously, but his attitude made them furious. He was fired a week later. Father Cardenal did not have to worry—finding problems to analyze was going to be easy.

Much has happened since that time. Almost five years have passed. Recently, I returned to Nicaragua where I ran into my friend whose children used to spend their Sundays carrying bricks in order, as they had once said, to help build a country. His son, Miguel, is now somewhere in the northern mountains of Nicaragua, exact location unknown, in charge of an antiaircraft gun. He's stationed on the front lines of defense against the groups called the *contras*—Nicaraguans, trained and, until recently, financed by the U.S. Central Intelligence Agency (CIA), fighting under the military command of Somoza's former National Guard to overthrow the present government.

Miguel volunteered for army service when these U.S.-backed forces began escalating their killing of community leaders and development specialists—schoolteachers, nurses, doctors, agronomists, and church activists. He was among the smartest in his high school class; now he is the youngest in his battalion. He was a stubborn kid, as I remember him in 1980, determined against all odds to serve as a literacy teacher, even though he was under the minimum age requirement of twelve. Undaunted he badgered government authorities so persistently with letters, visits, and petitions that he was finally granted special permission at age eleven to become a volunteer. When he came home from the literacy campaign, he talked about becoming an agronomist or maybe a doctor. School had new meaning for him. His father, mother, and sisters worry about him constantly now, hoping that he is safe, but they're proud of his decision to defend the country. When I talked to them last, they hadn't received a letter from him in over three weeks.

I also know several people on the *contra* side. Their experiences reveal another view of the problems that affect development and education in Nicaragua. One man, with whom I had worked at the graduate school of business during my first stay in Nicaragua, became a member of the nine-man ruling board of the CIA-backed group in Honduras. Disenchanted with the Sandinista government, he felt that they were ruining the country by becoming a Soviet puppet state and believed that they had to be removed from power. I remember him in 1973 as a sadly bitter man, cynical and beaten down by the Somoza dictatorship, with no hope in the future. A former priest, he ended up selling cars. Recently, I read that he had been dismissed from his position with the *contras* because of internal disagreements over the role of the CIA. He opposed certain sections of a handbook (written by the CIA for his group) that called for political assassination and evidently, like many others, he objected to growing corruption within his organization and the CIA's control over the group's internal operations.

At present, lives are being lost in Nicaragua and development and education efforts crippled. Because of the war, the country's defense costs have skyrocketed and young boys have become soldiers. The follow-up program to the literacy campaign has been severely affected by increasing defense expenditures and resulting cutbacks in social programs, but the worst effect of the war has been the loss of life. In the last few years, some 150 elementary schoolteachers and adult education coordinators have been killed by the CIA-backed groups.[2]

Because much of the Reagan administration believes that the present Nicaraguan government is a totalitarian state, it has tried to cast the conflict solely in terms of the East-West struggle in order to justify its policy of covert war. There is a tendency among many administration members to equate revolution automatically with Soviet domination and conspiracy. This categorization provides a convenient explanation as to why everything being done by the Nicaraguan government must be discredited and destroyed, including education programs. However, my experience doesn't lend support to such arguments.

In three out of the four congressional delegations that I have accompanied to Nicaragua, the U.S. ambassador and high-level embassy officials have disagreed with President Reagan's assessment of the situation there. These U.S. officials demonstrated concern about Nicaragua's military buildup, press censorship, and the presence of Cuban advisers but refuted administration claims that Nicaragua was a totalitarian state and expressed a surprising respect for the revolution's development programs and for Sandinista concern about improving the lives of the poor. Although questioning the government's future direction, these same officials also said that they thought Nicaragua's elections would be free and honest, but that the incumbent Sandinista administration would have unfair advantage over the less organized parties. In mid-1984, these embassy officials were transferred and new ones appointed who more closely share the president's views.

My work in the campaign revealed many Nicaraguan government successes and many problems as well, some that the embassy staff had mentioned—problems of bureaucracy, inefficiency, inexperience, occasional dogmatism, cultural insensitivity, and concerns about press censorship. However, what always impressed me was the basic sense of pragmatism and openness to new ideas that prevailed in the face of such problems. Creativity and responsive problem solving were characteristics of development personnel throughout the Nicaraguan administration. The Sandinistas were a mixed group, a blend of nationalism, socialism, Marxism, and Christianity, committed to developing and transforming their society. As such, they welcomed international experts from around the world to assist them in planning and management work—people of different beliefs and faiths from Western Europe, the United States, Latin America, and Canada, as well as the Soviet bloc nations. Programs were enriched by the resulting broad exchange of views and experiences. But Nicaraguans, I found, are proud people, and if international advisers tried to impose their ideas or demonstrated disrespect for national values or religious traditions, those advisers were asked to leave, regardless of their country of origin—East or West. In the Managua offices of the campaign, one Canadian, one Cuban, and one Colombian were dismissed for such reasons. Contrary to the Reagan administration's view, my experience revealed that while the Nicaraguan government sought international assistance and advice, the nation's leaders also wanted development programs to reflect the uniqueness of their own country and did not want any outsiders deciding policy for them.

In trying to understand these discrepancies in information and viewpoint I think that the CIA, through its documents and the groups that it trained, reveals more accurately what is behind the administration's opposition to the Nicaraguan government. According to the agency's handbook and pamphlets written especially for counterrevolutionary groups, *contra* forces have been instructed to sabotage and eliminate Nicaraguan government programs and their personnel.[3] Over the last several years, these *contra* groups have attacked government development projects—burning down clinics, cooperatives, kindergartens, and schools and killing or kidnapping the people who serve in them.

What is most threatening to U.S. administration officials about Nicaragua is its potential example as an alternative development model. The administration's concern is merited, for despite internal inefficiency and abuses and the problems of war, the Nicaraguan government has had impressive successes in health, education, agriculture, and urban development. Although in 1984 Nicaragua's rate of economic growth fell significantly in large part because of increasing *contra* destruction, in 1983, according to United Nations' studies, Nicaragua was the only Central American country to show any significant growth, a healthy figure of 5 percent.[4]

If Nicaragua's approach to development and education can prove itself to be viable and productive, such a model will have enormous appeal to people in other nations facing similar problems. If this should happen, the U.S. development approach would lose considerable legitimacy. U.S. officials would then have to question some of their basic premises about development, and the U.S. government would face the probability of relinquishing what power and influence it holds over such nations and of redefining its relationship with them. The real issues at stake reach beyond Nicaragua or the United States: whether peoples of different cultures and ideologies can coexist and learn from each other's experiences in confronting inequality and repression and whether countries of the North and South, the rich nations and the poor nations, can negotiate new, more equitable relationships with each other.

The experiences of thousands of U.S. and Nicaraguan citizens who have participated in fact-finding missions and exchange programs between their countries over the past five years demonstrate that coexistence and mutual learning is not only possible but sought after. Nevertheless, our two nations' histories make the formation of new relationships difficult. For almost 130 years, the United States has dominated the internal politics of Nicaragua. (For example, U.S. citizen William Walker set up a coalition government in 1855 and in 1856 declared himself president of Nicaragua, declared English the official language, and ruled Nicaragua until 1857.) The long pattern of domination is not an easy one to break nor is that form of power easy to relinquish. If, however, the U.S. administration is not willing to examine new relationships with Third World countries like Nicaragua, then it naturally will seek to discredit and destroy those development experiments that challenge the status quo. But what is gained by destroying them?

No development model has been completely satisfactory in responding to problems of poverty, hunger, and repression and, as a result, in countries across the world, countless numbers of parents watch helplessly as their children slowly weaken and die. Alternative development approaches that address these problems are scarce. Above all, we need to encourage variety and apply the collective wisdom of many experiences in order to find positive solutions to such violence and misery. If future experiments in development are destroyed before they are proven or disproven as viable, our capacity to learn from them will be severely curtailed. The base of knowledge upon which we can draw in order to solve problems will be restricted and our ability to address the important issues of our time will be limited. If experiments are suppressed and answers not found, problems and tensions will increase, only to give rise to ever-worsening conditions that will then demand more drastic and extreme responses. Millions of people will be relegated to lives of hopeless misery and some may even be killed in attempts to suppress the alternative development programs in which they are working. Central America is a prime example of this dilemma.

We need to examine carefully what is at stake. The literacy campaign was the first major development program tackled by the Nicaraguan government. As such, it revealed a great deal about the direction of the country's revolution and future development priorities. These are the kinds of programs now under attack, and the lessons and experience gleaned from them may be lost. The question for people who are concerned about solving the problems of illiteracy and poverty is whether the world can afford to lose such experiences.

For almost fourteen years, both before the revolution and after, Nicaragua and its people have challenged me—sometimes with tears and other times with laughter—but always with questions that lead me to examine my understanding of the world more deeply. This challenge has never been easy. The questions have been probing, painful, and on occasion, inspirational, seeming to touch the very core of human spirit, for Nicaragua's history arouses enormous passions, and its people inspire great admiration. More than anything else, they have taught me how much we have to learn from one another and how important our learning is if we are to address the problems of our nations with intelligence and compassion. Yet, recent events demonstrate how difficult that is. We are people of different cultures and ideologies. I hope that we can overcome the stereotypes and misperceptions that limit our understanding of one another and our ability to respond constructively to the challenges before us. Our times demand nothing less. Our future demands the best of us as does the next generation.

And so my closing words are directed to Caitlin, Rich, and Josh, to David Alejandro, and Martina José, to the future generations of North and South. May you learn from our mistakes and from our moments of greatness; may you never have to take up arms against one another; and may you do better than we did in understanding each other and in challenging your generation to ever higher standards of justice and excellence. Our unfinished struggle and stubborn hope will soon be yours; we are counting on you to give them meaning.

Valerie Miller
Washington, D.C.

Notes

1. World Literacy is a nonprofit foundation that receives grant monies for education research from the Canadian government and private donations.

2. Central American Historical Institute, *UPDATE*, July 25, 1984, Vol. 3, No. 25 (Washington, D.C.: Georgetown University).

3. Tayacan [pseud.], *Psychological Operations in Guerilla Warfare*, translated by Congressional Research Services, Language Services, October 15, 1984 (Washington, D.C.: 90 pp.).

4. Jaime Belcazar, director of United Nations Development Program, interview, May 10, 1984, Managua, Nicaragua.

Acknowledgments

In special gratitude to all those people who helped see me through this challenge: Thank you, each and everyone, for your support, your friendship, and all the questions and comments that you made along the way that have enriched the pages of this book and its author immeasurably.

Writing has not come without pause or doubt. Trying to convey the complexity of revolutionary change with any kind of balance and integrity is a difficult task. To assist me in this, I sought out friends and colleagues—international experts from the fields of literacy, adult education, political science, economics, and development, people with extensive experience in programming, planning, and evaluation—who during this time have served as critical sounding boards for my thinking and analysis. Thank you for your insights at midnight and all the other many times we have debated and discussed Nicaragua and its campaign. To Suzanne Kindervatter, Deborah Barndt, Paul Mhaiki, Budd Hall, Marcos Arruda, Carmen Diana Deere, Sue Thrasher, Carman St. John Hunter, Dan Lyons, Brian McCall, Myles Horton, David Macharia, Margaret Schuler, Deborah Golub, Juan Aulestia, Arthur Gillette, David Evans, Michael Conroy, Ed Killackey, John Ryan, George Urch, Susan Carpenter, and John Gaventa. And a special thanks to Lisa Veneklasen, Mary Fran Doyle, Amy Brodigan, and the staff of Westview Press, for enthusiastic proofreading and final editing.

In this book, I teli the history of the literacy program and analyze its developments by combining my experience and critique with those of the planners and participants themselves. Interestingly enough, all the issues and critical questions that I felt were important to raise were also raised at one time or another by staff members of the campaign. Nevertheless, the emphasis and degree to which such issues are dealt with in this book were my decisions, and mine alone.

This book is a tribute to the program staff and participants who so generously shared their time and ideas with me and whose story this book tells. Thank you for your openness, your patience, and your sense of humor. And special thanks to Father Fernando Cardenal, Francisco Lacayo, and Father Xabier Gorostiaga, whose support, insights, and enthusiasm were invaluable to me in understanding the campaign and in completing the study, as were those of other colleagues in Nicaragua: María Suarez, Dr. Gustavo Parajón, Martin Santos, John McFadden, Rita Delia Casco, Milú Vargas, René Nuñez, Juan José Mercado, Marta Tanenhaus, Peggy Healy, Alonso Cano, Deborah Barry, Molly Dougherty, Betsy Cohn, Beverly Trueman, Charles Roberts, and my dear friends Kay Stubbs and Reynaldo Diaz, whose patience with me and my stacks of paper, which grew to cover their entire dining room table for weeks on end, deserves special merit.

Other people also inspired me along the way and kept me going when writer's block threatened my equanimity. They all share a special place in this book. Thank you all and especially my parents, at ages seventy and seventy-one, who have always instilled values of community service and equality in their sometimes stubborn daughter, and who continue to do so; to Dad, who coordinates Meals-on-Wheels rain or shine, a proud Republican; and to Mom, who last year began teaching literacy, a proud Independent. Thank you for your maddening questions, your constant example of giving, and your love of people and of me.

V.M.

A Twentieth-Century Challenge

*If we want the darkness to flower, if we hope to establish lands of dignity and integrity with the millions of people who still have not learned to read or write . . . lands where all people can live in light and justice . . . then our guiding stars must be struggle and hope.**

—Pablo Neruda, 1971
Nobel Prize Acceptance Speech

The Challenge from a Nicaraguan Village

The afternoon shadows filled the dusty yard and nearly covered the cornfield beyond. In the twilight, a one-room house of wooden slats leaned precariously against a fence. It, like the rest of the houses in the village, had no electricity, water, or plumbing and looked like it might blow down in a big wind. A rusty can filled with yellow flowers hung from the open window.

Concerned about the approaching darkness, five people sat around a crooked table outside the house, taking advantage of the last rays of sun. Every minute of light had to be rationed carefully if they were to finish their lesson, for that day there was no money to buy kerosene for the lantern. The members of the family painstakingly copied words into notebooks—a grandfather, deeply wrinkled by years of work in the sun; his two daughters, tired after a long day of washing at the river three miles away; one of their husbands, hair curly with sweat after ten hours behind the plow; and a child of thirteen, eager to learn but illiterate because the village had never had a teacher, the nearest school being two hours over the mountain.

Chickens scratched the earth at the students' bare feet. Curious children surrounded them, the littlest ones, without clothes, watching the movement of the pencils, tugging occasionally at their mothers' knees; the

---

*All quotations that were in Spanish, whether written or verbal, have been translated by the author except when they are taken from secondary sources and already translated.

older ones sitting on a nearby bench scribbling onto scrap paper with tiny discarded pencil stubs. Their faces and bodies were smudged with dirt. Water was always scarce during April, and a fine blanket of dust covered everything. Beyond the table, the grandmother, eyesight blurred by a lifetime of cooking smoke, stirred a pot of rice balanced carefully on three stones over the open fire. Dinner would be ready soon, but she refused to join the class, pleading sore eyes and old age. "It's too late for me," she said. "My head's too hard; my eyes no longer see."

A teenager stood over the group, giving directions and encouragement, pointing occasionally to a chart of syllables tacked to a tree. The girl bent down to help guide the efforts of a young mother who was balancing an infant at her breast. The baby sucked away noisily while the mother used her free hand to write words onto a small rubber blackboard. The teenage teacher smiled, as did the visiting journalist and education supervisor who watched behind her. Inexperienced, but earnest and hard working, the young girl lectured more than she intended. The visitors made her nervous. Her students listened attentively and sometimes spoke, usually responding to her questions only after long moments of unsure silence.

When asked why they wanted to learn, the grandfather responded first by waving his arm at the children and saying, "To be an example." One daughter, hesitating for a moment, searching for words, replied, "So when I go to market I won't be cheated ever again." The other daughter remained quiet, but her husband answered, smiling at his newly printed letters on the page before him: "To defend myself, . . . to learn about farming, and so I never have to suffer humiliation like before when they made me use my thumb to sign papers. Now," he said proudly, "now, I can write my own name for all to see." The child, when asked the same question, stopped for a long moment, looked up shyly, and said in a soft voice, halting as she spoke, "So someday . . . well someday . . . so maybe I can learn how . . . to fly."

During the Nicaraguan National Literacy Crusade, scenes like this were repeated over and over again throughout the country. They were scenes that affected all who witnessed them. The planners who designed the campaign felt joy and a certain humility and wonderment at the sight, knowing the extraordinary problems they had faced in mounting the program. Most Nicaraguans felt inspiration and an enormous sense of pride and accomplishment; a small wealthy sector of society felt threatened. International development and education experts marveled at the dedication of the participants and the overall organization of the program. Even cynical journalists were struck by the excitement that the effort generated. Those who were not personally witness to the campaign sometimes found such accounts hard to believe, but skeptics and supporters alike could agree on two things. What was occurring in the villages and towns of the country challenged Nicaraguans to rethink how they saw themselves, their neighbors, their nation, and their place in the world and provided a challenging example to other countries facing similar problems of illiteracy and poverty.

Illiteracy Beyond Nicaragua's Borders

The world map of poverty is also the world map of illiteracy. Within nations, the illiterates are the most desperately poor. They are the hungry, sick, abused and powerless.

—H. S. Bhola

The Nicaraguan experience is part of a broader challenge confronting people far beyond one Central American nation's borders. While a grandfather and his family learn basic literacy skills in a remote village, millions in other parts of the globe do not. In less than ten years, an estimated 1 billion people will be illiterate (Udaipur 1982). However, the problem is not confined to the Third World. In the United States the magnitude of illiteracy reaches alarming dimensions. Although researchers caution that precise statistics are unavailable, some figures suggest that from 25 to 60 million people in the United States do not have the fundamental literacy skills to function effectively in society (Harmon and Hunter 1979).

In the final decades of the twentieth century, illiteracy is a problem of disturbing proportions, a problem that has a close correlation to poverty and inequity (Bhola 1981, UNESCO 1975b). Considered a serious obstacle to national development, illiteracy contributes to the exclusion of significant sectors of a population from economic and political participation and from sharing in the full benefits of society (UNESCO/UNDP 1976). Even in a country like the United States, proud of its democratic tradition, illiteracy has been used as a means to prevent the poor, especially blacks, from participation in the political system by requiring proof of reading ability in order to be eligible to vote. Part of a vicious circle, illiteracy becomes both a source and a product of inequality (UNESCO 1975b).

The dimensions of the world problem are complex, rooted in unequal social structures that favor powerful elites and discriminate against the poor. Nicaragua's heritage of illiteracy and inequity is typical of countries of Asia, Africa, and Latin America. Reports from international organizations document the complexities of the problem.

> Existing social structures in some countries do not favour equality of opportunity; education has often been misdirected with undue emphasis on the training of elites and the adoption of standards inappropriate for the participation of the general population, and even reforms have led to new structures favouring elites. Social/economic situations still exist in which literacy is not required. . . . In many countries land reforms and attempts at income redistribution have not yet been undertaken. [UNESCO 1975a, 6]

Fundamentally a problem of poverty and power, the challenge to overcome illiteracy often becomes part of the larger challenge to overcome inequity and to create more egalitarian social structures through which the poorer members of a society can participate in the exercise of both economic power and political decision making.

Although the percentage of illiterates in the adult population is slowly decreasing, statistics developed by the United Nations Educational, Scientific, and Cultural Organization (the UN institution in charge of promoting education, science, and culture in member nations) indicate that the absolute number of illiterates continues to grow steadily (UNESCO 1975b). In the 1990s, with close to 1 billion people over the age of ten not knowing how to read and write, major portions of the world's population will be prevented from participating and sharing equitably in the development and benefits of their nations (Udaipur 1982). Their contributions to society will be limited. Despite international and domestic efforts to address this problem, educational programs have met with, at best, isolated success. Frequently, despite the availability of technical expertise, developing nations have paid only lip service to the challenge of illiteracy and have not provided the financial and political support necessary to combat it effectively (UNESCO/UNDP 1976).

Increasingly, major theorists and practitioners of adult education are recognizing that political will and organizational structure are the principal determining factors in whether a country develops and implements effective literacy programs and whether those programs actually are aimed at increasing the economic and political participation of the illiterate population (Bhola 1981, ICAE 1979, UNESCO/UNDP 1976). The presence of a strong political commitment and an effective organizational framework seems to be directly related to a government's desire to bring about profound changes in its nation's economic and social order, changes specifically geared toward favoring the poor (UNESCO

1978). Certain exceptions do exist, however, such as Brazil, which has invested considerable resources in adult literacy (Bhola 1981).

The most successful national literacy programs, therefore, are generally found in nations whose governments are involved in profoundly restructuring society (Bhola 1981). In these environments, literacy efforts frequently mobilize a nation's human and financial resources on a massive scale, not only to eradicate illiteracy but to develop the personal attitudes, values, skills, and behaviors that are fundamental for participation in the new society—the political culture and ideology emerging from the program of transformation. As such, these literacy efforts attempt to build a solid national consensus for the consolidation of the structural changes that are being implemented (Fagen 1969, Gillette 1977, Lorenzetti and Neys 1964).

Characterized by inequity and illiteracy, many nations have experienced abrupt societal changes either through revolution, such as Cuba, or colonial independence struggles, such as Algeria, Guinea-Bissau, and Tanzania (ICAE 1979). In their attempts to rebuild their countries after years of violence or colonial domination, they have faced extraordinary development and educational challenges. To meet these challenges they have espoused goals and programs (Fagen 1969, Freire 1978, Gillette 1977) that are designed specifically to

1. create more equitable societies in which the former sociopolitical and economic systems are transformed,
2. develop national consensus, cohesion, stability, and legitimacy,
3. prepare the citizenry for participation in the new society and its structures by eradicating illiteracy and promoting skills appropriate to the new context, and
4. transform the national political culture by instilling and nurturing attitudes and values reflective of a new society.

One means of accomplishing these varied goals has been to initiate nationwide educational campaigns (Bhola 1981). Although the full extent to which countries have been successful in these endeavors is the subject of continuing debate, the importance and significance of the development and political challenges they have attempted to address through these programs are undisputed. Illiteracy rates have decreased, in some cases quite dramatically. In the process citizens have gained a new appreciation of their nation's problems and challenges, become acquainted with national development programs and affirmed attitudes and values conducive to change.

But even when literacy campaigns are seriously attempted, many obstacles hamper their successful completion:

> . . . lack of human and material resources; social structures which place
> the illiterate majority at a disadvantage, an unrealistic content to literacy
> materials; bad communications; lack of transport facilities; scattered pop-
> ulation groups; multiple language situations; problems of choice of language
> for instruction; lack of written material; lack of trained teachers. But
> perhaps the most important of all, the "lack of literacy environment," i.e.,
> the social structures and facilities geared to the uses of literacy. [UNESCO
> 1975b, 25]

In countries undertaking major social transformation another problem inherent to such a process also arises. Strong vested interests that are threatened by structural change respond by attempting to undermine and disrupt the transformation program, sometimes with violence (Fagen 1969).

If a literacy effort manages to surmount these many difficulties and the desired results are achieved, new challenges emerge, especially in the case of intensive, short-term literacy campaigns that are designed as part of overall sociopolitical transformation processes (Freire 1979). New educational expectations and demands are generated, pressures on the system mount at an accelerated pace, and effective responses need to be found quickly in order to consolidate the skills and understandings acquired and to move beyond the elementary levels attained. If groups opposing the transformation continue to fight against the changes, as can be expected, their activities, especially if violent, can also seriously affect the overall scope and future of the follow-up learning program.

A History of Literacy Programs

Priorities and Purposes

During the first half of the twentieth century, the challenge of adult illiteracy was largely ignored. Most literacy programs were small, conceived and conducted by private voluntary organizations and religious groups, and unable to meet national learning needs (Kahler 1978). Few governments saw adult literacy as a development priority. Mexico and the Soviet Union, at the beginning of the century, were exceptions, as were the governments of Vietnam and China in the 1940s and 1950s. In these countries, literacy programs were part of a revolutionary nation-building process, which attempted to redress historic inequities while creating and consolidating new social systems (Walker 1982, Bhola 1981).

It was not until 1960 and the World Conference of Adult Education in Montreal, Canada, that the issue of adult illiteracy received international recognition. Challenged by this meeting, member governments asked

UNESCO to compile information and develop plans that would assist them in overcoming the problem. This effort would later become known as the Experimental World Literacy Program (EWLP). Independent of this international undertaking, Cuba launched its own national campaign in 1961, and within one year, dramatically reduced its rate of illiteracy. However, despite a highly favorable UNESCO evaluation of the program (Lorenzetti and Neys 1964), UNESCO never disseminated its report on the Cuban effort, nor were the program's lessons considered in planning the EWLP. At the 1965 World Conference of Ministers of Education on the Eradication of Illiteracy held in Tehran, Iran, for example, the accomplishments of Cuba's literacy campaign were not taken into account in the official forums. The report was ignored until the Cubans themselves published the evaluation (Ferrer 1980).

The Iran conference, however, did serve as an impetus for the UNESCO-sponsored EWLP program, which continued to take form throughout the sixties. The Tehran meeting provided the international effort with a basic program focus and definition—functional literacy—the thrust of which became the development of skills and knowledge to increase economic productivity. Officially launched in 1967, the eleven-country EWLP effort lasted until 1973 and included the nations of Algeria, Ecuador, Ethiopia, Guinea, India, Iran, Madagascar, Mali, Sudan, Syria, and Tanzania. Selective in approach, the program targeted specific priority populations and geographic areas within participating countries and involved some 1 million adults, of whom reportedly 120,000 attained literacy during its six-year period of operation (UNESCO/UNDP 1976).

The UNESCO experiment, while not as successful as some people had hoped, did increase international awareness of the massive dimensions of illiteracy and raised important questions for future planners and activists (Kahler 1978). Serious debate over the concept of functional literacy was generated, and critical reflection over its relationship to development was undertaken. One of the most basic issues that emerged from this discussion was also part of a larger international debate occurring throughout the world over the consequences of development. The debate can be summarized by the question, Who benefits from what kind of development? With regard to literacy, the issue was formulated on a more general level: What literacy is "functional" for what development? (UNESCO/UNDP 1976).

The concept of functional literacy was fundamental to the EWLP, but the related underlying question regarding development remained unasked by most planners until the program's conclusion: What kind of development orientation was reflected in functional literacy? Essentially, the functional approach of the EWLP was an attempt to combine the teaching of literacy and numeracy with vocational skills in order to better prepare a nation's potential work force for productive labor. According to UNES-CO's own thoughtful evaluation of the effort, *The Experimental World Literacy Programme: A Critical Assessment* (UNESCO/UNDP 1976), one of the major program weaknesses involved flaws in conceptualization. The concept of functional literacy emerged from the beliefs that economic growth is the major force in development and that nations are under-developed in large part because the majority of their people are under-developed and unskilled. Education and literacy, therefore, were con-sidered vital to stimulating growth and, hence, to development. According to the critique presented in the UNESCO report, this widely held position overlooked several important truths about the nature of the development process. Underdevelopment, the authors reasoned, is not simply the result of an uneducated populace; it is partially related to inequities in the economic system when distribution of benefits is highly unequal. Moreover, the process of development, they argued, is not exclusively a technical one based on economic growth and increased production. It also depends upon social change and opportunities for citizen par-ticipation.

Basic flaws occurred in the problem conceptualization and the program design, for the EWLP planners mistakenly thought that literacy was a purely technical problem and overlooked these other important factors. The authors of the study pointed out that as a result, the program's reasoning too narrowly defined the problem as well as the response. Since the problem was considered basically technical, the solution offered was also technical—the creation of a new technique to increase literacy. The UNESCO report challenged this thinking and concluded that the definition of *functional* needed to be broadened and related to an expanded concept of development. "Indeed, it would seem that literacy programmes can only be fully functional—and development contexts can only be fully conducive to literacy—if they accord importance to social, cultural, and political change and economic growth . . . enhancing popular participation" (UNESCO/UNDP 1976, 122). In their final deliberations, the team of experts coordinating the EWLP research emphasized that without the mobilization of the hearts and minds of people, there can be no sustained development or literacy work. Change and participation are key components of the process.

The report questioned some of the premises of the reigning theory of development—the trickle-down model—in terms of both productivity and motivation. It challenged the assumptions that illiterates hinder development and production because of their lack of education and pointed out that lack of "opportunity structures" might be the more fundamental reason. If society does not provide the basic structures for people to use their skills in order to improve their lives, then literacy is a meaningless exercise. If increased production or new skills are not going to result in real, perceived benefits and opportunities for people, why should they participate in either educational programs or development efforts? Timidly raised in the form of a question, the report indicated that for participation to occur, profound changes were needed in the social structures.

During the same period, and independent of UNESCO's program, a Brazilian educator, Paulo Freire (1968, 1973, 1978), was quietly revolutionizing educational thinking. Brought up amid the extreme inequities of northern Brazil, Freire believed that the massive poverty and illiteracy of his nation stemmed from structural problems that were directly related to the unequal exercise of power in society. To overcome these problems meant that oppressive social structures had to be broken and transformed. As part of this transformation process, Freire conceived of adult education and literacy work as "cultural acts of freedom," as a process of *concientización*—expanding people's capacity for social analysis, political action, and commitment to the common good. Accordingly, his view of literacy was not hemmed in by narrow economic definitions of growth or occupational sectors but, rather, touched every aspect of life and involved people in critical discussion and action. Freire considered literacy to be not just the reading of words or the repeating of information. For him, it was a conscious act of liberation—reading the world in order to transform it.

Freire focused on the uniqueness of the human species. He argued that through literacy, dialogue, and participation, human beings can affirm their unique nature as active creators, by understanding the social context in which they live and by developing the critical skills necessary to transform oppressive structures and relationships present in their societies. Indeed, he believed that human beings lose their essential humanity when they are deprived of their creative and transforming capacities, when they are prevented from participating actively in decisions affecting their lives. What is human is a person's ability to act upon the world, to create, to improve, and to excel. The purpose of education, therefore, is social transformation—human participation in society. For Freire, adult education and literacy in a context of oppression become a means to question the established order and a potential tool and resource for social change (Mashayekh 1974). As his work extended from Brazil in the sixties to Chile and Guinea-Bissau in the seventies, Freire increasingly emphasized the political nature of education and the need for political organizing to bring about social change.

During the same period, mass literacy campaigns were designed and took form in such countries as Somalia, Iraq, and Brazil. Tanzania and Ethiopia also developed national programs, building upon the EWLP experience, and the initial groundwork was laid for other campaigns in Kenya and India. Julius Nyerere (1967), president of Tanzania, became a prominent voice in the development and education debate at this time, pointing out the importance of people's participation and structural change as the foundations for development. For Nyerere, as for Freire, authentic development and education meant a political struggle for human liberation. Despite Tanzania's involvement in the EWLP, Nyerere was a proponent of the campaign approach to literacy, and he believed that national programs were vital to a process of equitable development (Mhaiki 1982).

During the 1950s and 1960s, a group of southerners in the United States, under the auspices of the Highlander Center in Tennessee, developed a regional education program based on philosophies and analyses that were strikingly similar to those of Freire and Nyerere, which directly linked literacy to political participation and social transformation (Adams 1975). In the South, literacy had been used to make voter registration especially difficult for poor, unschooled blacks. As part of the civil rights movement, therefore, a network of "citizenship schools" was organized to teach not only the skills of literacy but also those necessary for transforming structures of inequity—problem solving, leadership training, and political organization and planning (Tjerandsen 1980). For Myles Horton, the director of the Highlander Center, the program's goal was to keep "your eyes on the 'ought to be'—human dignity, brotherhood, democracy" on all levels of society, the economic as well as the political, in order to create "the world we would like to live in" (Horton 1971, 288). On occasion, the center was raided by police, closed down by the courts, and burned by the Ku Klux Klan for its promotion of integration and political participation by blacks.

Recent Trends

On the international scene, the seventies marked a change in how literacy programs were defined. The particular focus on economic productivity was abandoned for a view that supported literacy as a strategy for liberation and social change. The influences of Paulo Freire and President Nyerere were clearly felt; those of Myles Horton and the Highlander Center were unknown on the international level but involved a similar strategy. In the 1975 International Symposium for Literacy in Iran, UN experts, government officials, and educators from around the world unanimously agreed that

> literacy . . . [is] not just the process of learning the skills of reading, writing, and arithmetic, but a contribution to the liberation of man and to his full development. Thus conceived, literacy creates the conditions

for the acquisition of a critical consciousness of the contradictions of society in which man lives and of its aims; it also stimulates initiative and his participation in the creation of projects capable of acting upon the world, of transforming it, and of defining the aims of an authentic human development. [The Declaration of Persepolis, quoted in FAO 1975, 43]

The symposium members maintained that successful literacy work depends upon addressing the full range of human needs and stressed the fundamental importance of the need for people to participate effectively in decision making. "Literacy is effective to the extent that the people to whom it is addressed . . . feel the need for it in order to meet their most essential requirements, in particular the need to take part in the decisions of the community to which they belong. Literacy is therefore inseparable from participation, which is at once its purpose and its condition" (UNESCO 1975a, 45).

On an operational level, the director-general of UNESCO set out some preconditions for effective government efforts and indicated that the challenge of literacy is best addressed when it is seen in the context of social change. "There is clear evidence that whenever a government has tackled the problem because it was a precondition of other social change, the results have been favorable" (M'Bow 1978, 4).

There continued to be debate about the priority of literacy and development into the eighties. Some educators (Verner 1974, Crone 1979) advocated a "development first" policy rather than specific educational programs for literacy. They argued that the skills and information necessary for development can be acquired by means other than literacy, through creative nonformal education methods, and that illiterate adults may feel that concrete marketable skills such as carpentry or improved agricultural techniques are more immediately useful. These writers concluded that since adult illiterates do not usually have an urgent use for literacy skills, they lack the motivation to become literate. According to this thinking, once other needs are met and concrete development information is communicated to illiterate adults through nonprint forms of media, the desire to attain literacy will be generated.

The proponents of adult literacy (Jeffries 1967, Hall 1980, Bhola 1981) argue that literacy cannot wait. Educational programs must include the achievement of literacy now, for literacy is . . . not merely a vehicle for development information, but a potent partner in development" (Bhola 1981, 21). Bhola further argues that "literacy and nonformal education without literacy are not merely two different instrumental approaches to promoting development; they constitute a choice between two different epistemologies . . . , between two different processes of formation of individual identities and structural relationships" (Bhola 1981, 21).

Justifying the "literacy now" argument, Bhola points to a myriad of effects—cognitive, affective, and structural—that are necessary for a society's development and that can occur as a result of literacy learning. According to this position, reading and writing foster an expansion of an individual's mental processes and an affirmation of self. New status is bestowed upon the people who become literate, personal expectations are expanded, confidence is gained, and skills are developed that can generate changes in economic and power relationships. New structures and values can also be reinforced, and a sense of individual and collective empowerment be gained. When programs are conceived of as being part of an empowerment and transformation process, organizing literacy programs can generate development by creating and strengthening local channels of participation (Cardenal and Miller 1981). Such efforts can enhance a society's sense of purpose, foster a national spirit of community service, and affirm attitudes of empathy, sacrifice, commitment, and cooperation that are conducive to social change.

More recently, the debate has led some educators to call for the implementation of national campaigns in order to respond to the challenge of illiteracy: "The magnitude of the problem in many countries calls for massive efforts. Only specific campaigns with clearly defined targets can create the sense of urgency, mobilize popular support and marshall all possible resources to sustain mass action, continuity and follow up" (Udaipur 1982, 1). The 1980 campaign in Nicaragua gave new impetus to this movement, as did a 1982 conference in India sponsored by the International Council for Adult Education, the West German Foundation for International Development, and UNESCO that was attended by educators from around the world. In the closing statement, the conference participants stressed the importance of the campaign approach as part of an integrated strategy for development and justice. They concluded that citizen participation was fundamental.

> Literacy campaigns succeed and realize their liberating and development potential when they are avenues for popular participation in all phases. . . .
>
> A literacy campaign must be seen as a necessary part of a national strategy for overcoming poverty and injustice. . . . An effective campaign is part of a comprehensive and continuing effort to raise the level of basic education [and] . . . is a potent and vivid symbol of a nation's struggle for development and commitment to a just society. [Udaipur 1982, 2]

Questions from Nicaragua

How do nations respond to the problem of illiteracy in the context of massive inequity and what can be learned from their experiences? Nicaragua provides one example. Designed as part of a larger sociopolitical transformation process, the Nicaraguan program provides a rare opportunity to examine a national campaign closely from its inception to its completion and beyond, a campaign with all the major prerequisites for success—an organizational network founded on popular participation, a strong government commitment, and evolving socioeconomic structures that reward and depend upon the ability to read and write.

The uniqueness and significance of this opportunity becomes more evident in light of the fact that leading educational institutions such as the International Council for Adult Education, the International Institute for Educational Planning, and UNESCO have praised the Nicaraguan National Literacy Crusade for its contributions to the field of literacy programming and have pointed out the importance of studying its operation and achievements. Experts have called it an "exciting experiment from both an ethical and pedagogical perspective" (M'Bow 1980) and a "challenge to educators and politicians everywhere" (Hall 1980). In 1980, as a measure of these views, an international panel of judges unanimously awarded the Nicaraguan campaign the annual UNESCO grand prize for literacy achievement, and in that same year, members of the British Parliament nominated the director of the program, Father Fernando Cardenal, and the crusade for the Nobel Peace Prize.

When examining the Nicaraguan campaign, a variety of questions come to mind about how the program was planned, what problems it confronted, what mistakes were incurred, and what successes were achieved. This book tries to respond to some of these questions, especially those that relate to certain educational aspects of the campaign—curriculum, methodology, and training—and their relationship to the fulfillment of program goals. Specifically those questions include:

- What were the principal educational components of the crusade and what was their relationship to the overall accomplishment of the program's intended goals for both personal development and social transformation?
- What were the major obstacles confronting the educational aspects of the program, what strategies were designed to overcome them, and how effective were those strategies in responding to the problems?
- What have been the results of the campaign and the perceived effectiveness of its educational components?

- What are some conclusions emerging from the Nicaraguan experience that may provide insights for educational planners, specifically in regard to issues of content, method, organization, and training?

In this study, the crusade's effectiveness has been assessed in terms of the expressed goals of the program planners and the goals of transformation envisioned for the new society—especially those related to participation and redistribution.

Questions about other components of the crusade, such as political philosophy, organizational structure, management style, and staff evaluations, will be addressed in order to provide an overall picture of the context in which the campaign was developed and the interaction that occurred among the various elements of the program. In answering these questions, the book details the complex process of institution building within a revolutionary society and provides an in-depth look at the candid insights and criticisms revealed by the campaign's national staff. Such questions are used as a means of examining major issues related to literacy efforts, assessing their role and impact in a concrete situation, and, as a consequence, providing practical lessons for future literacy planning, especially in relation to campaign-type programs.

Readers no doubt wonder how information was gathered in order to respond to these questions. A variety of research methods were used. They included a survey of the pertinent literature, a complete review of crusade documents and central office files, a twelve-month period of working in the campaign as a participant/observer, and a series of interviews conducted with key actors in the program and experts in the fields of education and development (see Appendix A for a more detailed description of research methods and a list of the types of people interviewed and Appendix B for the general interview format).

The Nicaraguan experience is one response to the challenge of illiteracy and inequity. It is hoped that questions raised by the campaign's efforts can provide insights for others engaged in similar challenges. What do the organizers of the campaign have to say to their colleagues around the world—educational planners and politicians—who wrestle with these problems daily in their search for solutions? What do the teenage teacher and the grandfather student in a dusty Nicaraguan village have to say to the millions of people in the world who have not had the opportunity to learn basic literacy skills or to participate fully in their societies?

2

The Campaign: Context, Purpose, and Goals

Somoza never taught us to read. It really was ungrateful of him, wasn't it?
He knew that if he taught the peasants to read, we would claim our rights.
—Peasant in a literacy class
commenting on Anastasio Somoza García,
founder of the family dynasty that
ruled Nicaragua for over forty-five years

Country Overview

The country in which the Nicaraguan National Literacy Crusade took place is a small Central American nation of considerable economic potential, the approximate size of the state of Iowa. Some 57,000 square miles in area, Nicaragua is an agricultural nation of great diversity, producing coffee, cotton, lumber, cattle, and basic grains such as corn, rice, and beans. Part of the "chain of fire" that extends from South America to Alaska, Nicaragua is divided by an impressive range of active volcanoes, which, over time, have enriched the soil base and productivity of the western section of the country. For that reason, agronomists refer to the land as the future food basket of Central America, and geologists praise its geothermal potential for electricity, but these positive aspects have their negative side. Severe earthquakes are common to Nicaragua. Managua, the capital city, has been destroyed twice in the last century, the most recent quake occurring in 1972 and killing some 10,000 to 15,000 people.

The majority of the Nicaraguan people live in the productive western part of the nation and are relatively homogeneous racially and linguistically. Most share a mestizo heritage of both Caucasian and Indian ancestry and a common Hispanic culture. Principally Spanish speaking and Catholic, they number some 2.7 million. Of this total population, some 170,000 live in the isolated eastern section of the country, which until recently was only accessible by plane, boat, or mule. The majority of these people are members of the Moravian church, a small Protestant group that came to Nicaragua's Atlantic Coast during the 1800s when England controlled that part of the country. Approximately 50,000 East Coast inhabitants speak English as their first language, live in urban settlements, and are African in ancestry. In addition, an estimated 100,000 belong to a variety of indigenous cultures and live in remote hamlets. The vast majority of these people speak Miskito, and a minority of about 10,000 to 15,000 speak Sumo. Significant numbers of both groups are bilingual, and some are even trilingual.

For more than four decades, Nicaragua was ruled by a single family, which was brought to power by the United States in 1932 and supported by that country until the late 1970s. Power and wealth became highly concentrated, corruption and repression commonplace. In 1978 and 1979, a national insurrection led to the overthrow of the dictatorship and the establishment of a revolutionary government committed to a program of rapid social transformation.

Historical Foundation

> *You can fool everyone once, but you can't fool all the people forever.*
> —Augusto César Sandino
> Leader of peasant army 1927–1933

The Nicaragua literacy campaign emerged from a political struggle that began in the early part of the twentieth century. In the mid-1920s, a young general named Augusto César Sandino organized a rural army to fight against the foreign occupation of his country by U.S. Marines (Selser 1978). His decision to seek education for his peasant forces provided the inspiration for and established the initial commitment to universal literacy, which was taken up by the campaign some fifty years later (Cardenal, March 1980).

The conflict that served as the impetus for the struggle originated principally over territorial and financial disputes with the United States that had begun as far back as the mid-1800s (Pearce 1981). After independence from Spain, wealthy families from two Nicaraguan cities, León and Granada, became embroiled in a fight for control over the country and the spoils of power. The dispute intensified when gold was discovered in California in 1848 and Nicaragua became a point of transshipment, a shortcut for Americans eager to go west. Nicaragua's newly found importance resulted in both the United States and Britain eyeing the country as a potential site for a transocean waterway.

In 1855, as a consequence of the intensified domestic power struggle, a U.S. soldier-of-fortune, William Walker, was invited to Nicaragua by members of the León faction, the Liberals, to help them defeat the Conservatives of Granada. However, Walker surprised everyone by quickly proclaiming himself president of the republic. English was declared the official language, and slavery was legalized. Unwittingly, Walker succeeded in uniting the two feuding groups, along with all the other countries of Central America, against his foreign rule. He was executed soon afterward.

At the beginning of the twentieth century, the conflict over foreign domination resurfaced when the United States moved to strengthen its economic control over the region and to secure construction rights for an interocean canal through Nicaragua. These moves eventually led to a policy of direct intervention in the internal affairs of the country, with the United States backing one political party against the other.

In 1909, the Liberal government of José Santos Zelaya refused to authorize the long-coveted construction rights, so the United States threw its support to the Conservative party opposition in return for certain guarantees. The Conservative forces, upon seizing power in 1910, opened the path to U.S. domination of the country's economic system by granting the United States the means to control the national banking, railway, and customs operations. Open revolt resulted. In 1912, the tottering Conservative government of Adolfo Díaz called for U.S. military support to quell the growing rebellion against such policies, thus beginning an almost twenty-year period of occupation by U.S. Marines (Selser 1978).

Tensions between the two political parties and their respective armies increased throughout the next fifteen years, as did the economic and political power of the United States over the country—in 1914, Nicaragua signed a treaty granting exclusive rights in perpetuity to the United States for construction of an interocean canal. As the years passed, political frustration increased. By 1927, tensions had reached the explosion point, and Liberals took up arms in a widespread uprising that threatened the Conservative regime and U.S. control over the area. Employing a combination of political promises and military threats, the United States convinced the two forces to halt the conflict, an accord that was achieved with the assistance of sixteen U.S. naval vessels and the rapid deployment of 215 officers, 3,900 soldiers, and 865 marines (Selser 1978). To justify the intervention, the dangers of communism were invoked. Mexico had just recognized the Soviet Union, and the threat of encroaching "Bolshevik" revolutionaries was used by U.S. officials to quell congressional doubts and gain time for the administration's policy to show results. General elections were agreed to, and a National Guard was established to maintain public order. Marine commandants from the United States took charge of the guard's organization, operations, and training program (Millet 1977).

Augusto César Sandino: David Faces Goliath

However, one Liberal officer refused to accept the mediated settlement, and for seven years, General Augusto César Sandino and his peasant army fought against the occupation. Internationally, Sandino gained acclaim as a type of Central American Robin Hood, a cowboy David looking like a diminutive Gary Cooper (ten-gallon hat and all) fighting off Goliath, the blond giant of the North. Cecil B. DeMille even went to the U.S. State Department to get approval for a film about the romantic figure but was refused (Black 1981). Unable to defeat this increasingly popular leader, the marines were finally withdrawn in 1933 by the newly elected president of the United States, Franklin Delano Roosevelt, who demonstrated a certain sympathy for Sandino and his struggle. With the marines' withdrawal, Sandino signed a peace treaty with the Nicaraguan government, agreed to disarm his troops, and retired to organize peasant cooperatives in the northern part of the country.

The U.S. forces selected Anastasio Somoza García to replace the U.S. Marine Corps commandant as the head of the National Guard, an appointment that was rumored to be due, in part, to his affair with the influential young wife of the aging U.S. special diplomatic envoy to Nicaragua (Selser 1978). One year later, Somoza ordered Sandino assassinated, his cooperatives destroyed, and the members and families of those cooperatives exterminated. In 1939, President Roosevelt accorded Somoza a warm welcome to Washington, pleased with the allegiance the Nicaraguan leader had promised to the United States on the eve of World War II. Admiration for Sandino was replaced by a certain cynicism, however, as Roosevelt reportedly admitted that although Somoza was a son of a bitch, he was "our" son of a bitch (Waksman 1979). An American alliance was forged that would remain strong for over forty years.

During his relatively short life, Sandino had sought ways to assure the social and economic development of his people (Román 1979). He set up cooperatives for agricultural production and created a special department in his army for adult education. He encouraged his troops to learn to read and write and was especially proud of their achievements, but he was acutely aware of the inadequacy of any educational effort conducted during wartime.

> I can assure you that the number of our illiterate officers can now be counted on fewer than the fingers of one hand. Unfortunately, due to a

shortage of people who can teach, progress among the soldiers has been almost negligible.

When General Pedro Altamirano first joined us he did not know how to read or write, but . . . during the fighting, and only because I insisted on it, Altamirano learned, stumbling and mumbling as he went along. Despite his age, he has made great strides since then, and now, as amazing as it may seem, he actually knows how to type—even if it is only with one finger. [Román 1979, 135]

Illiteracy and Inequity

The roots of illiteracy and poverty were deeply embedded in the society's structure of power and wealth. The Somoza dynasty ran Nicaragua as a family plantation; disparities were great, and corruption was commonplace. During the period of Somozan rule, the government development strategy was narrowly focused on the economy's agricultural export sector. Under this economic system, national projects, often financed by international agencies such as the U.S. Agency for International Development (USAID) and the World Bank, were essentially used to enrich Somoza's personal fortunes and those of his close associates. Despite rhetoric about benefiting the poorest of the poor, Somoza's programs served to buttress the regime's power structure by enlarging the government bureaucracy and enabling his partners to engage in lucrative business ventures involving opportunities for massive graft. Although small, isolated sectors of the population benefited from the programs, the basic causes of economic and political disparity were never addressed. Ultimately, development projects led to further concentration of wealth and to the expansion of the government's patronage system. Programs designed by international experts to alleviate inequality ended up exacerbating overall disparities. Poverty increased, as did repression (Lafeber 1983).

Under the dictatorship, the wealth of the nation was poorly distributed. Statistics reveal the depth of the poverty the majority of Nicaraguans lived in. About half of the population survived on between $200 to $300 per person per year—in a country where prices for food and clothing were similar to those in the United States—while large sectors of the rural population subsisted on a yearly income of less than $120 (USAID 1975). In 1978, the USAID estimated that over half the rural dwellers lived on less than $39 per year (USAID 1978). Access to education, health care, and public services was poor, and most people lived in inadequate housing and survived on a meager diet. Life expectancy was low even for the region. In 1979, it was some ten years shorter than the area as a whole and eighteen years shorter than the leading nation in this regard, Cuba (Walker 1982).

The poverty and disparities were reflected in the educational system as well. The dictator's priorities were clear. "I don't want educated people. I want oxen" (quoted in Lernoux 1982, 85). Under the Somoza dynasty, the educational structure was stagnant and corrupt, and formal learning opportunities for the poor were restricted. The structure served to enforce an inequitable set of economic and political power relationships and depended upon a system of incentives, which promoted graft and incompetence. The educational disparities that the structure engendered were stark. Of the approximately 70 percent of the children who were of elementary-school age who actually entered the primary grades in 1976, over half dropped out within a year. Although approximately 50 percent of the population lived in rural areas, two-thirds of the students enrolled were from urban centers. Official statistics reveal that during the 1970s, only 5 percent of the students entering primary school in the countryside completed their studies; the figure was 44 percent in the cities (Nicaragua, Ministry of Education 1980b). During 1977, 17 percent of the total secondary-school-age population was enrolled in high school; 8.4 percent of the nineteen-to-twenty-four age group attended institutions of higher learning (Nicaragua, Ministry of Education 1980b). The curriculum, whether taught in city or village, had an urban focus and a heavy U.S. influence. Rural studies and traditional peasant culture were largely ignored.

Teaching standards were notoriously low, incentives for excellence nonexistent, and opportunities for professional development restricted. The system rewarded certain top-level functionaries with advancement, international scholarships, and opportunities for graft. Some officials, for example, received phantom teaching appointments that allowed them to collect double salaries. In rural areas, political favorites were assigned to teach in village schools and then allowed to play hooky for most of the year. Teachers who questioned the structure were often removed or reassigned to remote locations; activist student organizations were subject to surveillance and repression. For the majority of students and teachers alike, the social order and its corresponding educational system affirmed attitudes and values of both classroom passivity and competitive individualism. For the poor, they generally created feelings of inferiority; for the wealthy and middle class, attitudes of superiority.

Illiteracy was both a condition and a product of this overall system. In 1979, a special census conducted for the literacy crusade revealed that over 50 percent of the population was illiterate, a figure that soared above 90 percent in some rural areas. (During the campaign, it was discovered that the effective illiteracy rate was closer to 40 percent.) The problem of illiteracy was never seriously addressed during the dictatorship, because the promotion of universal literacy was neither politically advisable for the maintenance of the system nor economically necessary for its functioning. In economic terms, support for universal literacy went against the logic of the system. The development model of export agriculture depended upon a large pool of unskilled workers, and therefore, it neither required nor encouraged an educated labor force. Politically, it was clearly unwise for Somoza to undertake any type of genuine nationwide literacy program. Basic education might have provided the poor and the disenfranchised with the tools to analyze and question the unequal power relationship and economic conditions under which they lived.

Under Somoza's government, however, literacy teaching did exist. Church-sponsored groups organized small community programs, the leaders of which were often harassed by the regime. In the early sixties, the opposition newspaper, *La Prensa*, organized a national literacy program with the initial support of the minister of education, but when Somoza discovered the government's cooperation, he fired the minister and persecuted the teachers and organizers involved in the project. (The father of Daniel and Humberto Ortega, future leaders of the Nicaraguan revolution, was the author of the program's literacy primer.) The *Frente Sandinista de Liberación Nacional* (FSLN), an armed resistance movement that was organized in 1961 to overthrow the Somozas, also held clandestine literacy classes for peasants while training in the mountains and pledged that universal literacy would be among its first priorities after victory. Even the Somoza government conducted a literacy program, but it was used as a cover for counterinsurgency operations in the North. "Plan Waslala," according to the Ministry of Education's own report in 1978, provided for over 100 literacy teachers to act as spies in order to identify peasants who were sympathetic to the *Frente* (FSLN). People singled out by this operation later disappeared—even the program's title was threatening for it was the name of an infamous concentration camp where hundreds of peasants had been tortured and killed in the mid-seventies.

Over the long years of dictatorship, resistance to the system of inequities and repression increased. During the early 1960s, the *Frente Sandinista* took up General Sandino's military and educational challenge, and his struggle for literacy and liberation was given new life and meaning by the young FSLN leaders. The organizational efforts of the *Frente*, coupled with decades of military repression, corruption, inequity, and foreign domination, finally led to a massive civilian rebellion in 1978. Under the direction of the *Frente*, the dictator was toppled, and victory declared in July 1979. But as Carlos Fonseca, the founder of the FSLN, had predicted many years before (Meiselas 1981, 48), the price of victory was "both costly and sad"—some 40,000 to 50,000 dead, 100,000 wounded, 40,000 orphaned, and countless thousands homeless. Somoza left the nation with an international debt of $1.6 billion and escaped with all but $3.5 million of the national treasury.

Campaign Rationale: Development and Transformation

In August 1979, with the violence of the war less than two weeks behind them, the new leaders of Nicaragua took on what to many outsiders seemed an impossible task. Young revolutionaries, inexperienced in the practice of governance, undertook the challenge of designing, planning, organizing, and implementing a literacy campaign that would involve more than half a million people—and be completed within only twelve months. Prospects for success seemed bleak. Somoza had left the country destitute, war damage was heavy, food was in short supply, psychological trauma was widespread, health conditions were grim, and the leaders of the new government had no experience in public administration. How in that environment could a national program of such magnitude and scope be even contemplated, much less implemented?

There were several pragmatic reasons for the immediate consideration of such a program. First, the young government wanted to prove its commitment to the poor by initiating programs that would immediately benefit the most needy. Second, the leadership believed that effective national development depended upon an educated populace, and third, it also believed that opportunities for citizen participation needed to be created in order to lay the groundwork for the society's transformation. With no public money available, any national project of this type would by necessity have to depend on volunteer labor and the government's ability to capture the interest of the international community for financial support. A literacy campaign filled these needs and requirements.

Development would be difficult for the country as Nicaragua had been devastated by war and dictatorship and the majority of its people lived in poverty. Yet the country was rich in agricultural potential. Land was fertile and abundant. If international cooperation could be obtained to renegotiate the debt and to establish reasonable credit terms, Nicaragua possessed a natural resource base that was sufficient to build a healthy economy. If adequate energy sources could be found, the government planners felt that the nation would eventually be capable of overcoming its traditional pattern of underdevelopment. But the fulfillment of such an ambitious goal would also depend upon being able to mobilize the human energies of the country for national reconstruction and finding the means to establish the foundation for an enduring system of equitable development.

Motivated by this challenge, the new leaders oriented their policies and programs toward the poorest sectors of the population. They believed that such a development strategy largely depended upon the participation of an educated, committed, literate populace—people able to analyze, plan, think, and create; people motivated by a sense of social responsibility rather than by personal gain. It was believed that a literacy campaign, implemented through a volunteer teacher corps, would be a fundamental first step in achieving these aims. The campaign staff defined the situation this way: "Without literacy, it will not be possible to prepare our people to assume the responsibilities that the great challenge of national reconstruction demands" (Saenz et al. 1980, 11). Such a program would provide an opportunity for people to acquire the skills and attitudes necessary to meet the development challenge.

The development efforts were seen as being embedded in a larger process, a process of transformation encompassing the entire society. 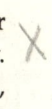 The old system was viewed on all levels—moral, political, social, economic, and cultural—as bankrupt and in need of radical change. Development activities in different areas such as health, agriculture, industry, education, and community organization were thought of as threads to be woven into an integrated plan for transformation, a plan that would facilitate the creation of a more equitable, more productive society. As such, the literacy crusade was considered an important beginning to this many-faceted national program. Participation in the campaign would help affirm and strengthen the values, attitudes, and structures that had been denigrated and suppressed by the dictatorship. By providing learning opportunities to the poor and the disenfranchised, the program would also serve as a crucible to forge new power relationships that would favor the majority sectors of society. The campaign was considered vital to these change processes because it would help provide citizens with the basic skills and an affirmation of values necessary for their active participation in the challenge of transformation and in the economic and political life of the nation.

Other reasons also added weight to the proposal for an immediate literacy program—reasons that were spiritual, psychological, and political. A campaign would give the many young people who had fought and suffered the traumas of war a constructive way to make the transition from the past to the present. It would provide them with a concrete means to channel their energies positively into building the new nation and into developing a commitment to the poor. For those people who had not been military combatants, the crusade would provide an opportunity to become educational combatants in a new war of liberation. The successful completion of such a program would also establish the credibility and capacity of the government to direct and manage national development.

Yet another reason prompted the new government to undertake such a venture—a reason that was echoed by families throughout the nation. Thousands of Nicaraguans had been killed in the war. Their sacrifice had led to the overthrow of Somoza and had given the country an opportunity to build anew. The government and the revolutionary leadership pledged to honor the memory of those killed by working to transform the system of inequities that had been inherited from the dictator. The crusade was to be a first step toward redressing those injustices and paying homage to the dead. It was considered "a moral commitment, a labor of justice" (Saenz et al. 1980, 11). Each person learning to read and write would become a living tribute to the sacrifice, commitment, and hope of those who had given their lives in battle. Through the achievements of the living, the memories of the fallen would be made immortal. The campaign was named in their honor— the National Literacy Crusade: Heroes and Martyrs of the Liberation of Nicaragua.

Military Metaphors

The metaphors and terminology of the campaign were purposefully military (although the term "crusade" also had a religious connotation)— "the war on ignorance," "the cultural insurrection," "the second war of liberation," and "the National Literacy Crusade: Heroes and Martyrs of the Liberation of Nicaragua." The "literacy warriors" of the "Popular Literacy Army" were divided into "brigades, columns, and squadrons" and were located along six "battlefronts," which were identical to the battlefronts of the war. The "brigadier teachers" (*brigadistas*) joined forces with the "peasant and workers' militias" and the "Urban Literacy Guerrillas." Each battle unit chose the name of a fallen combatant as a means of honoring his or her memory. The choice of names and terms conveyed many meanings—psychological, political, and spiritual. Military metaphors, however, were not intended to evoke the glorification of violence but rather to instill commitment and courage.

> In no way was the use of military terminology designed to glorify war or violence. Anyone who lived through the horror perpetuated by Somoza's guard was acutely aware that the pain and trauma of violence and repression were not worthy of glorification. On the contrary, the choice of military metaphors was designed to help young volunteers integrate the memories of the past, transforming terms related to the war into positive associations with teaching and sharing. Military terminology also helped the *brigadistas*

see the crusade as a vital part of the nation's continuing liberation struggle and to understand that, as such, it demanded the seriousness, dedication, and discipline of a military offensive. In essence, we wanted to make clear that peacetime battles demanded the same selfless, disciplined commitment as did the war effort; in fact, they demanded more.

The use of military terms and the naming of fallen heroes had a deeply spiritual significance. The crusade owed its very existence to the revolution and to the sacrifice of thousands of men and women who fought and died for liberation. By calling forth their names and memories, the young volunteers kept alive the courage and example of their fallen compatriots. A spiritual bond joined the living with the dead. [Cardenal, September 1980]

The crusade and its symbols were considered to be a living testimonial to the people who had died—to their sacrifice, dedication, and faith in the future.

Nature of the Crusade: Political and Pedagogical

The crusade was always considered a political project first and an educational one second. Father Fernando Cardenal, the Jesuit director of the program and former philosophy professor at the Catholic University in Managua liked to quote Paulo Freire when speaking about the difference between the two emphases: "As our fellow companion and very good friend has said: 'This type of National Literacy Crusade is not a pedagogical program with political implications, but rather, it is a political project with pedagogical implications'" (Saenz et al. 1980, 12). Father Cardenal's arguments and those of Freire were based on a deep philosophical understanding of the meaning of "political" and on a sociological analysis of the function of education in society. Without being aware of this thinking, it is difficult to understand the nature of the crusade as it was perceived by its leaders.

Father Cardenal traced the roots of the term "political" back to Aristotle, emphasizing its positive nature as a force for the common good. This conceptual framework helped contribute to the philosophical foundation of the campaign. The crusade was political according to this understanding because the aim of the program was to improve people's lives and the lives of their fellow human beings.

For the Greek philosopher Aristotle, the term "political" was derived from the word "polis," which meant city. Political or politics related to a concern or interest in the city, the science that studied the social relations, the way of living, of those who dwell in the city, which nowadays we would call the nation.

Therefore politics is the science that is concerned about all those people who live in our nation. In biblical language, it is the love I have toward all those who live with me in the same society, the love for my neighbor, for my fellow citizens. Politics in its true sense is a science completely opposed and antagonistic to the selfish, egocentric attitudes which give rise to exploitation. People who take advantage of or exploit others only see them as objects to be manipulated, as cheap labor to be used, while the true politician starts from a basic position of love and concern and sees people as fellow human beings living in the same nation, sharing and working together.

We believe that politics is the art of assuring that all people in this nation progress, that all of us conquer and win our freedom, our liberty, our independence, the peace and justice necessary so that love can be nourished, grow, and reign over all. This really is politics—the constant loving search and struggle to improve our lives and the lives of others.

We believe that our education is not only political but it is based on the political sense that emerges from love and the political sense that attempts to build a world of justice and community. . . . This love, of course, is not a purely sentimental emotion, but it is the kind of love that is concerned with transforming the degrading living conditions to which fellow human beings are subjected. Politics is the love by which people work together to transform inhuman and unjust conditions; it is part of the noble quest and struggle of humanity for dignity and justice. [Cardenal, November 1980]

The understanding that the crusade was first and foremost a political project also had its roots in the premise that no education can be neutral—that all education is political. Internationally, this premise is commonly held by educators who define programs of education as being essentially designed to maintain social realities or to transform them. Members of the 1975 International Symposium for Literacy in Persepolis, Iran, concluded that "literacy work, like education in general, is a political act. It is not neutral, for the act of revealing social reality in order to transform it, or of concealing it in order to preserve it, is political" (FAO 1975, 42).

According to this view, a nation's educational system supports certain power interests in society and upholds their particular vision of the world, thereby protecting and reinforcing their positions of authority over and, often, against the vast majority of the population. As an example, Father Cardenal explained how education functioned during the Somoza dynasty. He emphasized that under Somoza, the educational system had served to fill the dictatorship's labor needs while justifying the unequal power relationships between different social groups. It had made Nicaraguans believe that they deserved their place in society, whether high or low.

Public and most private education under the Somoza period, or for that matter, education under similar systems, doesn't only serve to prepare new professionals, technicians, or skilled labor but prepares and shapes people to accept the role they are occupying in the social system as normal and just, not questioning that there is a small elite who own the land and factories and control society to the exclusion of another group, the majority—the laborers who must sell their time and skills at a price determined by the landlords and owners—the majority who have no say over decisions that affect their lives, not politically, economically, culturally, or socially. They do not participate except as servants to the interests of a tiny group of lavishly wealthy people.

Such an education in that type of society justifies and supports this kind of unequal power relationship between people and groups, between social classes. For example, those from the higher classes leave the university believing that it is natural and fair that there are many other people, indeed the majority of the population, whose function in life is to serve them. They do not question that, it seems just fine. Education in such a situation serves to reproduce those kinds of relationships and to rationalize and justify inequity.

For the poor—the peasants, the laborers, the farmworkers—this type of education works to instill the same kind of acceptance, only from a different viewpoint. It affirms that there are some gentlemen who live very well in the world and that they, the poor, must serve these gentlemen, work for them, and that that is as it should be, normal and just. Furthermore, it affirms that social peace depends on each person maintaining their individual position in that power relationship. [Cardenal, November 1980]

This type of education preserved the status quo and reinforced the power bases of the controlling social classes. *also applies Sandinistes*

How is the educational system different in a transition society that is undergoing rapid change to overcome inequities and establish, in their place, relations of equality? One member of the national crusade staff explained how the educational system changes when a society undertakes a transformation process that is designed to benefit and involve the poor. Education in such a transition context, she argued, is neither static nor status quo oriented but, rather, serves a creative, generative purpose. The bases of power are expanded to include the vast majority of the population and to serve their needs and interests.

whose?

It is true, no matter in what nation, education serves the interests of those with power, those groups who dominate and control society.

The question, here in Nicaragua, is how the nature of education changes in a nation undergoing a profound structural transformation process—where power is being redistributed, where new economic and political power bases are being developed. Education in Nicaragua now is serving to create and support new forms of social organization. It is attempting to help construct a new type of society based on citizen participation, on power shared and exercised by the people—people long denied their rights. The concepts of power, government, and the state have radically changed. The national leadership is creating structures and organizations so that people can assume responsibility and real power over all dimensions of their lives—the political, economic, social, as well as the cultural. Education is part of that process to redistribute power, recast to serve the interests of the majority. [Suarez 1980]

On the international scene, a growing number of educators agree that to be effective, adult education should be part of a political process of social change and liberation. At the 1976 conference of the International Council for Adult Education in Tanzania, the council president and member of the Indian Parliament, Malcolm Adiseshiah, concluded that "adult education is not politically neutral . . . if it is effective, its crucial and decisive test is how far it is part of the processes of changing our political networks, the upsetting of our socio-economic decision-making centers . . . for the liberation of humanity, of people, by people and for people" (quoted in Hall and Kidd 1978, 11).

As Father Cardenal has emphasized, since all education is political, educators and politicians are confronted with a choice of what kind of political vision they will support in their educational programs: those of submission or those of liberation—no one can remain neutral. Nicaragua, he affirms, has made its choice.

All we can do as educators and politicians is decide which kind of political view we want to transmit or promote through education—one that maintains people alienated, submissive to a system of inequity and injustice, or one that serves to liberate them, to set free their creativity, their energies, and their intelligence in order to build a society based on participation and equity.

Sometimes people say that the education provided through the crusade was political and that affirmation is said as if it were an accusation.

We have never denied that our education was political. On the contrary, we affirm it. It was political because in the process, peasants began to conquer their own freedom and students began to win theirs—a freedom that begins with knowing and understanding your own reality and history and continues freely through a process of committing yourself to transforming that world, to choosing your future [Cardenal, November 1980]

The following anecdote, related by Father Cardenal, illustrates the political-educational choices made during the campaign and the discussions they provoked. He challenges the view that educators can remain neutral.

I remember one day an educator, a technical specialist from Asia, arrived at the office to discuss our work. He wanted to know why we had chosen the word "revolution" to begin our primer. Why was the content so political? He suggested that we start with something more universal or neutral like water, emphasizing its uses, its chemical composition. He said he preferred an apolitical approach, but indeed, what he was proposing, in actuality, was profoundly political.

Water is not a national problem; it is not a burning issue that brings all people together. The word does not touch them deeply nor emerge from their shared reality or history. The revolution, however, the struggle against the dictator, the building of a new society, is an intimate part of their past and their present. It is a beautiful word, it is part of the nation's history and heritage—a source of pride, of pain, of hope. It touches the soul and finds resonance with reality.

To use words like water in the way this man proposed denies people their history, their power, their pride. It contributes to keeping them passive and alienated. It inhibits their ability to understand and act upon their world. What could be more political?

He was supporting one kind of politics, and we were proposing another. But I must confess that besides our political reasons, on a purely pragmatic, technical level *"la revolución"* was the perfect way to begin the primer. We wanted to launch the learning process by presenting the basic building blocks of the language—the vowels. *"La revolución"* contains all five. What could be better? [Cardenal, November 1980]

The government leaders of the country believed that the campaign was political, not only because of its content, but, perhaps more important, because of the process selected and the skills it was supposed to develop. Through dialogue and discussion and participation in the many activities sponsored by the crusade, analytical and critical thinking skills were affirmed, and attitudes of empathy and service were reinforced. The FSLN delegate to the crusade, a respected member of that political organization's advisory assembly, described the revolutionary nature of the campaign in terms of the skills and concepts it developed. In discussing the methods used, Carlos Carrion insisted on the intrinsically political nature of the campaign.

It's not just that we speak of Sandino or of Carlos Fonseca or of the *Frente Sandinista*. The most political, the most revolutionary, aspect of this literacy approach is the fact that we are providing scientific knowledge and analytical skills to our brothers and sisters in the fields and factories who do not know how to read or write—the skills to reason, think, compare, discern, and the ability to form their own human and political criteria, their own critical framework. [Carrion 1980]

Society in Transformation

To understand the nature of the campaign and its goals in their full complexity, it is important to place the crusade in the context of a society engaged in a process of profound transformation. From the beginning of the liberation struggle, it had been clear to the revolutionary leadership that the institutions and structures of the old society had not met basic human needs or served the interests of the majority of the population. The leaders believed that the only way to respond to the nation's urgent development requirements and address the decades of injustice and inequity was to embark upon a course of rapid social transformation. The founder of the *Frente Sandinista*, Carlos Fonseca, described the purposes of the struggle: "In Nicaragua we are fighting for justice . . . for social transformation" (Fonseca 1970).

Concerned with more than simply equity with growth, the leaders of the *Frente Sandinista* shared a general development orientation that was socialist in character. Although interpretations of the precise meaning of this orientation were rich in variety and number, FSLN members did agree on certain common points. Development and transformation, they believed, depended in the short run on national reconstruction and in the long run on a transition to socialism—"the creation of a society based on both economic and political equality" (Cardenal, November 1980). According to their view, attainment of such a society required economic growth, extensive redistribution of power and wealth, and broad-based citizen participation. Some observers described the process as a nationalist revolution moving toward a class-based revolution, one with a clear redistributive goal favoring the poorer classes of society— the workers and peasants (Flora et al. 1982).

Such a course implied transforming not only the structures and systems inherited from the dictatorship but the interests that the dynasty represented and the human values and cultural traditions it had legitimized. Creating dynamic and equitable systems of distribution, participation, and production and affirming complementary values and attitudes were the means by which the changes could be facilitated.

New Vision: Logic of the Majority

Implicit in this process of transformation was the vision of a new society, and of an educational model that would help bring about its fulfillment. According to revolutionary thinking, that vision rested principally on the intelligent, creative involvement of a new kind of citizen working in new participatory forms of social organization. Essentially, it called for the formation of "the new man" and "the new woman," a revolutionary citizenry inspired by goals of community service rather than by individual gain, motivated by such values and attitudes as sacrifice, humility, love, discipline, cooperation, creativity, hard work, and a critical consciousness.

To form such a new social order meant starting from a new perspective—"the logic of the majority"—and creating a different set of institutions that would respond to the interests, aspirations, and needs of the majority—the nation's poor. As the top economic adviser to the minister of planning put it:

> A new logic, a new way of thinking needs to be created, a system based on the logic of the majorities, not on the logic of transnational companies or the rich, but a logic that responds to the interests and needs of the vast majority of the population. . . . The key point is not paternalism— the rich giving to the poor—but, rather, the development of a new protagonist to build this nation, . . . to put the power, the resources, the land, the health, and the education in the service of the poor, something that never before has been done here. [Gorostiaga 1980]

The system was to be built upon a network of economic enterprises and political structures managed and directed by workers and community members. These organizations, which were to be the foundation of a new participatory form of democracy, were to work closely with government in setting priorities, making decisions, and planning and coordinating national development.

The first year's development plan, which was designed to facilitate the transformation process, emphasized economic reactivation and national reconstruction. The plan set the standards, goals, and structures for the new nation, and education and literacy were among its top priorities. It attempted to encompass the national hopes and dreams for change and depended on a great deal of cooperation, sacrifice, luck, and hard work. In designing the program, the government leaders were painfully aware of the limitations and the obstacles confronting them. The economic crisis was of unknown dimensions, but available information made it clear that the emergency situation was grave and could continue for many years. How quickly the nation would recover depended on a combination of factors, some of which were outside the government's control, such as international market prices, weather conditions, and elections in the United States.

Domestically, the program was designed to reduce inequities and gave preferential development opportunities to the poor. First, it established a socioeconomic policy that was based on commitments to full employment, improved social services, universal literacy, land reform, self-sufficiency in basic foodstuffs, increased production for the common good, and a mixed public/private-sector economy. Second, the program encouraged popular participation through a network of citizen and labor associations; worker-managed enterprises; a representative legislative body, the Council of State; a series of community development projects in health and education; and a variety of public forums for open debate and dialogue between government and citizens. Third, the program called for the birth and affirmation of "the new Nicaraguan" and emphasized personal values of sharing and service. Finally, to accumulate the necessary capital for domestic investment, to pay the nation's staggering debt, and to begin redressing past economic injustices, the plan stressed both austerity and equity. Salary differences were drastically reduced; wages, rents, and the prices of basic goods were controlled. Luxury imports were also curtailed. In the government sector, salaries were cut in order to reduce the wage differential between the highest and the lowest paid state workers from ninety to one under Somoza to ten to one in the new government.

Internationally, the program was also directed at reducing economic and political disparities, and it called for a broadening of relations with the world community. The government leaders recognized the historic dependence of the nation's economic and political system on one country and believed that that inequitable dependency was unhealthy and a potential threat to Nicaragua's sovereignty (Nuñez 1980). Nicaragua depended on the United States for the majority of its trade and commerce, most of the nation's machinery was imported from the north, and most of its products were exported there. Nicaraguans were well aware that if the United States wished to do so, it could exercise an inordinate amount of economic pressure on Nicaragua simply by blockading exports, refusing imports, and closing down credit through its decisive influence over the international banking system—not to mention using the covert force of the Central Intelligence Agency (CIA), against which defense was difficult. Past events made the Nicaraguans fear the use of covert action. The United States had employed such tactics against the democratically elected governments of President Salvador Allende of Chile (1973) and Jacobo Arbenz of Guatemala (1954), and the young leaders reasoned that the U.S. administration would not hesitate to do the same in Nicaragua. They knew that Reagan's advisers had informed him as early as October 1980 that the situation in Central America required that the Sandinistas be removed from power as quickly as possible (Di Giovanni 1980). This knowledge increased their concern and sense of urgency about establishing new international relationships.

Their development plan therefore sought to alleviate the serious inequities and dangers inherent in this situation and to defend "national sovereignty by broadening the bases of the dependency" (Gorostiaga 1980). The Nicaraguan leaders were acutely conscious of their nation's economic and political position in the world. Realists and pragmatists, they accepted their country's dependency as an inevitable fact of life but wanted to reduce its inequitable, potentially destructive force by seeking a more balanced relationship with the world community. In explaining their position, they stressed their commitment to freedom— they did not want Nicaragua to be dominated by anyone, neither East nor West, North nor South. To meet this goal, the government leaders developed an international strategy by which relationships in trade, commerce, banking, and diplomacy would be expanded to encompass the globe. Dependency would be safer, they argued, if it were balanced on four relatively equal columns: (1) Western Europe, (2) the United States and Canada, (3) Latin America, and (4) the nonaligned nations and the socialist-bloc countries.

> We are building an economy which rests on four equal legs. We are seeking a new balance, an equilibrium unknown before. In the past, the economy and the health of this nation rested very precariously on two uneven legs—one very big one in the form of the U.S. and one much smaller one made up by the rest of the world. Such an unbalanced situation prevents a society from being really stable or free. . . . We must diversify our dependency. It is the only way a small nation can free itself from domination and protect its sovereignty. . . . After all these decades of subservience, Nicaragua has had enough subjugation. We want a chance to develop in a way that serves the needs of this people and maintains our integrity and freedom. [Gorostiaga 1980]

The leaders felt that this model, which attempted to equalize power relationships, would guarantee—as much as was politically and economically possible—Nicaragua's sovereignty and independence as a nation.

Education and Transformation

On the national level, education was considered an integral and important part of the overall transformation and development process. The First Proclamation of the new government emphasized this relationship.

> A thorough reform of the objectives and content of national education will be undertaken so that a critical and liberating process of education can be designed and become a key factor in the humanist transformation

of Nicaraguan society. . . . a national literacy campaign will be launched.
. . . programs of liberating adult education will begin in order to allow
full participation in the process of national reconstruction and development.
[Nicaragua, Government of National Reconstruction 1979, 2]

First, the educational system would have to undergo a transformation—
a review and revision of its purposes and programs in light of societal
goals and aims—in order to design and create a compatible, mutually
supportive system. The literacy crusade was to be one of the first steps
in both the transformation of the educational system and in the process
of overall social transformation.

These processes were mutually related. Education in such a context
was to serve as a catalyzing force to energize and propel the transformation and guarantee effective citizen participation in the design and
management of the emerging structures. The words of junta member
Sergio Ramirez underscore this position: "We are teaching the poor and
disenfranchised to read and write, not out of charity, but rather, so that
they will be prepared both politically and technically to become the
genuine authors of development and the only legitimate owners of the
revolution" (Sergio Ramirez 1980).

The fulfillment of this vision therefore depended upon the creative
and active involvement of precisely those sectors of society that Somoza
had marginalized. Education would have to provide the poor and the
disenfranchised with opportunities to acquire skills and knowledge so
that they could assume leadership responsibilities and fulfill more complex
technical roles. Only then could they fully become what Fernando
Cardenal, the national coordinator of the crusade, called the "architects
of their own destiny" and the "protagonists of history" rather than
"spectators."

Literacy is fundamental to achieving progress and it is essential to the
building of a democratic society where people can participate consciously
and critically in national decision making. You learn to read and write
so you can identify the reality in which you live so that you can become
a protagonist of history rather than a spectator. . . .

We believe that in order to create a new nation, we have to begin with
an education that liberates people. Only through knowing their past and
their present, only through understanding and analyzing their reality, can
people choose their future. Only in that process can people fulfill their
human destiny as makers of history and commit themselves to transforming
that reality. . . . A liberating education nurtures empathy, a commitment
to community, a sense of self-worth and dignity. It involves people acquiring
the knowledge, skills, and attitudes necessary for their new community
responsibilities. [Cardenal, March 1980]

yet They give Them a closed choice –

According to the top *Frente* leadership, education was an active force for change. As Bayardo Arce, member of the National Board of Directors of the *Frente Sandinista*, stated: "The function of knowledge is but one—to transform reality" (Arce 1979). As explained by Father Cardenal and Commander Arce, the basic purpose of education in the new Nicaragua was liberation. Its basic function was to transform reality—to help people critically understand their world in order to take an active, creative part in shaping and improving it. Education in this context involved a frontal attack on the inequities that had been inherited from the dictatorship and on the passivity and subservience the system had engendered. As such, revolutionary education needed to focus on helping people recover their sense of dignity and self-worth; take charge of their own lives, both as individuals and as community members; and learn to become knowledgeable decision makers and how to function as responsible citizens with rights as well as obligations. In this regard, the *Frente Sandinista* described literacy as "an apprenticeship in life because in the process, people learn their intrinsic value as human beings, as makers of history, as actors of important social roles, as individuals with rights to demand and duties to fulfill," (*Frente Sandinista* 1979, 1). Following the principles of the renowned Brazilian educator Paulo Freire, the process implied people working together in community to acquire an understanding of society's economic, political, and social forces in order to act upon them and transform them for the common good.

Adult education also required a heavy emphasis on the acquisition of technical skills and knowledge to maximize productivity and guarantee a solid economic foundation for development and transformation. In a speech on education and the revolution, Bayardo Arce pointed to these technical aspects as being fundamental in the assurance of greater social equity and justice. "We need men and women who are acquainted with, have mastered, and can effectively use technologies appropriate to the field of production so that we can generate the wealth and economic base for the revolutionary programs of social justice" (Arce 1979).

The specific educational standards the new government set for itself were high, and they provide a framework for an assessment of the achievements of the campaign. The director of the Educational Development and Planning Office in the Ministry of Education (Arrien 1980, 89–90) has described the characteristics of the new education in detail.

reality-based (centered in reality, born out of it and oriented toward its . transformation)

critical (analytical of all elements that make up reality, above all the social factors, dissecting them for study; analysis capable of judging those structures which alienate and disfigure humanity so that unjust situations may be denounced and adequate and viable solutions proposed for their transformation)

consciousness-raising (capable of helping people develop a commitment, an awareness of their personal and social responsibilities especially toward situations of institutionalized injustice)

active (energizing and propelling of human potential, not repetitive or receptive)

personalized (respectful of the value and right of the person to full, complete development—development that is only possible within a social relationship, in community)

creative (supportive of all originality, innovation, and initiative that opens new pathways and possibilities and produces results)

transforming (with the specific purpose of acting on reality in order to change and transform it when needed, a transformation always made to humanize the world, that is to say, to make reality the means of development and fulfillment for the human being)

participatory (facilitating of a dynamic mutual relationship, involving all the educational community in a process of true democracy in the solution of community problems and needs)

integration of theory and practice through work (making work the point where all the above characteristics effectively converge)

Revitalization and Socialization

In social science terms, the crusade and the national transformation that gave birth to it can probably best be understood as processes of revitalization and political socialization. However, these terms need to be expanded if they are to fully describe the purposes of the campaign and the process of change in Nicaragua.

According to Anthony Wallace (1956), revitalization is a social movement that involves a planned effort to change the culture and improve society. It is a conscious attempt by people who are discontented with their society to create a new, more satisfying system and pattern of social relationships. Wallace's analysis sheds light on the Nicaraguan situation. Under the system of dictatorship, the majority of the population was dissatisfied. The struggle against the dynasty was the first organized step by people in what could be called a revitalization movement, a movement designed to change and improve their lives and their society. Rather than being a superficial modification of programs, the new cultural system—which was being created and evolving as a result of the struggle to transform the old order—required profound changes in structures as well as new relationships and traits. The campaign was a means to affirm and reinforce those changes and develop those relationships.

The "making of new citizens," as described by Merriam (1931), and their political socialization—all deliberate learning of political information, values, and practices—were part of the transformation and revitalization process. However, in the Nicaraguan campaign, the process of socialization and inculcation was not as narrowly conceived nor as deliberately instilled by "instructional agents" as some theorists describe (Greenstein 1968). The learning process was one of mutuality and reciprocity, more open and creative. The "instructional agents" were both the literacy volunteer and the literacy student, each learning from the other in "an act of creation in which people offer each other their thoughts, words, and deeds. It is a cultural act of transformation and growth" (Cruzada Nacional de Alfabetización 1979a, 3).

The literacy process was an act of co-creation, and in that sense, the making of the new citizen was more cooperative and dynamic, allowing for increased originality and participation. It is likely that this emphasis on mutuality was probably the result of the fact that some of the values and information the new leaders hoped to instill were related to overcoming poverty and affirming compassion and respect. Who could be a better instructor than the peasant to teach city youngsters about rural culture and wisdom, about underdevelopment and malnutrition? What could be a better learning situation than the family experience of living together and sharing daily life?

Purposes and Goals

Overview

From the very beginning of the campaign there was a clarity of purpose among the educational planners. Certain shifts in emphasis regarding program priorities and goals occurred, but the overall focus on education for liberation and transformation remained constant. In essence, this focus involved teaching people the fundamentals of literacy and providing participants—both students and teachers—with opportunities to develop analytical learning skills, attitudes, and knowledge that would deepen their understanding of their world, their revolution, and their commitment to become engaged in the national process of social transformation. During the course of the campaign, increased emphasis was given to the sociopolitical dimensions of the educational effort. Volunteers worked with community members on development projects. They also worked together in the formation of citizen and labor associations to act as organizing vehicles for national development and as channels for participation in national decision making. In the final month of the campaign, the focus was redirected exclusively to the achievement of literacy.

although

The overall purpose of the crusade was to help people become more effective, productive, involved members of their nation—committed to social transformation and to participating as informed citizens in the political, economic, and cultural aspects of their society. On the practical level, the program was designed to help participants acquire elementary skills in reading, writing, mathematics, and analytical thinking—skills that would serve as the foundation for further technical preparation and citizen participation. In the process, people would gain a basic knowledge of history and civics, an understanding of the national development plan and the emerging political and economic structures, and an appreciation of themselves and their culture. The campaign was also intended to make the general public sensitive to the problems and rights of the poor, to promote empathy and social commitment, and to prepare citizens for their responsibilities in meeting the challenge of national development. The crusade had one other important function: It gave the young people who had undergone the traumas of battle a positive channel for their energies and enthusiasm. Their participation as volunteer teachers would help them make the transition between the violence of war and the challenge of transformation.

The first goal of the campaign was to eliminate illiteracy as a social phenomenon. Specifically, this task meant reducing the illiteracy rate to 10 to 15 percent, establishing a nationwide system of adult education, and expanding primary school coverage throughout the country. Other important goals were to encourage an integration of and understanding among Nicaraguans of different classes and backgrounds; to increase political awareness and the ability to make a critical analysis of underdevelopment; to prepare people to become active in the process of democratic participation; to nurture attitudes, values, and skills related to creativity, productivity, cooperation, empathy, discipline, humility, and analytical thinking; to forge a sense of national consensus and of social responsibility; to strengthen channels of economic and political participation; to acquaint people with national development programs; to record oral histories and recover popular forms of culture; to conduct research in health and agriculture for future development programming; and to develop the foundation of a new educational system from insights gained during the campaign (Cardenal and Miller 1981).

Dimensions of Goals

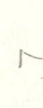

For the purpose of this analysis, the goals of the crusade are discussed along six different critical dimensions: political/civic, social, spiritual, cultural, economic, and pedagogical. These categories were not mutually exclusive or totally separate from one another. Goals overlapped and were often related to more than one dimension.

On one level, the crusade's goals and purposes were both political and civic—concerned with changing social power relationships in order to improve the living conditions of the citizens. The programs' goals were designed to provide the nation's poor and the disenfranchised with the skills and knowledge they needed in order to become active participants in the political process. As individuals were strengthened by this learning, so, too, would the organizations or institutions to which they belonged be strengthened because of the increase in group skills. Moreover, an effective campaign would earn legitimacy and credibility for the new government and instill a sense of national consensus and pride in citizens. The experience of helping to implement the campaign would give institutions—government agencies, citizens' associations, and labor federations—practice in planning, organization, and evaluation. As such, the strengthening of the citizen and labor groups would help lay the foundation for and reinforce the Nicaraguan concept of democracy. The individual and collective gains in understanding poverty and the increased political awareness would serve to guarantee the liberation goals of the revolution and the crusade. With the fulfillment of these interrelated objectives, a powerful new political force would be consolidated, and the power of the traditional elites could be challenged.

In regard to the social dimension, the campaign's goals supported activities that would benefit people in the areas of health and education—reading and writing skills, community development projects, surveys, inventories, evaluations—all of which would lay the groundwork for better education, health, and medical care and more relevant learning programs. The goals emphasized the creation of new relationships among previously separated social groups, such as between city people and rural dwellers and between students and teachers. Certain goals also reflected the desire to forge a new social contract between citizen and state, one that would be based on community service and on a clear understanding of the relationship between human rights and citizen responsibilities in a society at war with poverty. Certain attitudes, values, and behaviors were set as ideals, and a different kind of social being was called for—one who would act with humility, generosity, political awareness, compassion, commitment, and discipline while working unselfishly for the common good.

In the spiritual and psychological realm, goals were directed toward the affirmation of dignity; a sense of self-worth, confidence, and respect; and empathy for fellow human beings. The incorporation of excombatants and people who had been severely traumatized by the war into the positive, giving activities of the campaign would help them overcome the past and become active productive members of the present. By helping people see themselves as makers of history rather than as passive

a Transformation of human nature, without the willingness of human nature to transform itself.

recipients, the campaign participants might discover a greater sense of self-realization. Life could then take on a new meaning and purpose.

Culturally, the campaign's goals repudiated the culture of poverty and silence and supported a popular cultural renaissance—a recovery of history, folklore, traditions, legends, dances, stories, songs, and the poetry of the poor, both rural and urban. The goals were oriented toward affirming the innovative spirit of people so they could see themselves as actual creators of culture and take greater pride in the contribution their social group made to the nation's culture.

In regard to the economic dimension, the campaign acted principally as a labor training program. The goals emphasized skill development in reading and writing, mathematics, and analytical thinking—skills that would serve as the foundation for subsequent technical training. As a result of this basic preparation, increased numbers of people could participate in more sophisticated training programs, thus guaranteeing a more skilled labor force and, it was hoped, a growing productivity. Attitudes and knowledge gained during the campaign in regard to service and understanding the causes of underdevelopment would better motivate workers as well. Institution-building purposes would also be served. By increasing the skill level and commitment of labor, economic enterprises would be strengthened, and workers could take on greater responsibilities and leadership roles. Activities such as agricultural surveys and development projects also formed a part of the economically oriented goals.

From a pedagogical perspective, the campaign provided a theoretical and practical experience for teachers and students to learn new educational philosophies and to practice and experiment with methods that linked theory directly with reality. Working side by side outside the classroom on the crusade's challenging tasks would also give students and teachers the opportunity to form more supportive, cooperative relationships with each other.

3

Organization: From Foundation to Operation

You know, Carlos, we could be put in jail for this. Do you think this is what they call conspiracy?
—Father Fernando Cardenal, S.J. (March 1980)

The Beginning

Audacity and faith were needed in great abundance during the first months of organization and planning. With nothing more than promises of international donations, Father Fernando Cardenal, campaign director, asked Carlos Tunnermann, minister of education, for a loan of thousands of dollars from the ministry budget—a highly irregular, if not strictly illegal, request since all crusade funding was to come from nongovernment sources. The two men thus entered into a temporary "budgetary conspiracy," which caused them some initial qualms, resulted in moments of teasing, and provided the campaign with the necessary monetary impetus to begin. They laughed together, knowing that jail was not a serious possibility, but if they did not succeed in their joint venture, they knew too that they would forever bear the burden of not meeting the trust placed in them by the revolution—a punishment for them far more painful than imprisonment. Without their willingness to take such a risk, the crusade would have been paralyzed and would probably have had to be postponed until the following year.

Father Cardenal and the First Days

On August 2, 1979, the new government of Nicaragua announced the formation of the literacy crusade and named Fernando Cardenal, a Jesuit priest in his mid-forties, to the post of national campaign coordinator. For Father Cardenal, this assignment could not have been happier or more meaningful, for both the historic challenge and opportunity it offered to redress past injustices but also because it meant he could come out of hiding.

Previously, Father Cardenal had taught philosophy at Nicaragua's Catholic University, and for a short time, he had been vice-chancellor of that institution. However, his support for a proposal calling for increased student participation in decision making had resulted in his dismissal by the university rector. Although Father Cardenal had lost his position, he had gained vast respect from the student body and had continued teaching. He became an active member of the FSLN in the mid-1970s and a leading figure in the "group of twelve," a prominent citizens' group of professionals, academics, businessmen, and priests. During 1978 and 1979, the group was instrumental in forging national unity and building international solidarity for the struggle against Somoza. Over the years, Father Cardenal served as the spiritual and academic mentor for much of the top leadership of the *Frente*. In the final months of the insurrection against the dictatorship, Father Cardenal, because of his prominence, had to work and live underground, carefully hidden away from the guard by family and friends. It wasn't until the ceremony on July 19, 1979, celebrating the end of the war that he felt free.

However, almost immediately after the celebration, Miguel D'Escoto, a Maryknoll priest and a fellow member of the group of twelve, unintentionally forced Father Cardenal back underground, into a clandestine existence that was necessary if Father Cardenal were to avoid what for him would have been a terrible fate—a life of "exile."

Father D'Escoto, the newly named minister of foreign affairs, wanted to appoint Father Cardenal to the position of ambassador to the United States. Father Cardenal had gone to that country in 1976 to testify before the U.S. Congress, and he had made a lasting impression there and was still remembered and respected by some liberal members of Congress. Father D'Escoto believed that Father Cardenal would be an excellent statesman, able to deal with the challenge that Washington presented for Nicaragua.

However, when Father Cardenal first heard the rumor about the diplomatic appointment, he quickly made himself scarce. Skills learned in the underground served him well, albeit unexpectedly. Avoiding Father D'Escoto, he began a lobbying campaign to convince some of his former students, now members of the National Board of Directors of the *Frente*, that the diplomatic corps was not for him.

> Me, an ambassador? Tuxedos and ties? Formal dinners, fancy receptions? Having to be polite and dignified? Sipping tea and going to cocktail parties? I would die. I don't even speak English, and liquor gives me a headache.
>
> What I like to do is work with the community, with the people, to organize. . . . I am a priest; my only family is Nicaragua. To be separated

from this nation and this people, to be alone in the United States without my family near would have been the worst punishment I could ever endure. My love and strength as a person and an activist rested in working with students. Surely I could serve this revolution better, I thought, by returning in some way to that kind of work. Miguel kept on sending me messages through friends saying, "Fernando, it will be only one year", then he relented, "it will only be temporary duty, six months, as a transition." But I knew, once I got there, I would be stuck. So while he was sending me messages, I was talking to National Board members of the *Frente*. Before Miguel could find me, they had named me to the crusade. [Cardenal, April 1981]

Father Cardenal tells the story with a twinkle in his eye, chuckling, but underneath the humor it is clear that he was profoundly moved by the responsibility and honor bestowed upon him by his former students.

Immediately after his appointment as national coordinator, Father Cardenal chugged off in his canary yellow Volkswagen, repainted during the last days of the war to disguise it from the National Guard. His own disguise was finally losing its ability to hide his well-known features as his salt-and-pepper hair was slowly growing out from underneath a black dye job. So, with his two-tone hair and his little dented bug, Father Cardenal drove off to a newly renamed neighborhood, Sandino City, on the outskirts of Managua. He was looking for a Jesuit colleague who had done some work in literacy. For this campaign job, he knew he was going to need help.

He sought out Roberto Saenz, a young priest who had worked with the Center for Agricultural Development and Promotion (CEPA), a Jesuit-run institution organized in the early seventies to provide assistance to peasant groups. Saenz had been involved in a small community-education project as an administrator of a neighborhood volunteer literacy program. He accepted Father Cardenal's proposal to help in the crusade with enthusiasm. Since Saenz's experience had been more in the area of organization and coordination, he felt the crusade also needed someone with a pedagogical background so he recommended a young Nicaraguan woman who had recently completed graduate work in education as another team member. Fathers Cardenal and Saenz also remembered a young teacher both had worked with—Father Cardenal in the Christian Student Movement and Father Saenz in the literacy project—and they asked him to join them as well. A university colleague of Father Cardenal offered his volunteer assistance to the team, and the minister of education provided the services of a well-known national poet. Saenz's sister became Father Cardenal's administrative assistant and secretary. The organizational period had begun.

For Father Cardenal, the first weeks of August were filled with confrontations between the old system and the new. Although the top functionaries of the Somozan government had fled the country, most of the mid-level bureaucrats had remained. They returned to their offices after the fall of Somoza hoping that they would be retained, and the majority of them were. As Saenz and others on the staff liked to tell, in the very beginning Father Cardenal had to share an office with some of these functionaries. The minister had assigned him space and a desk in an office that had been known as Cultural Extension. The only hitch was that the desk belonged to a thirty-year veteran of the ministry, and he was not anxious to give up his territory, much less share his desk. His officemates did not look too kindly on the prospect either, whispering and complaining about the revolution behind Father Cardenal's back. Only when the man would leave the office was Father Cardenal able to occupy the desk in relative peace, still having to contend, of course, with the disgruntled looks and mumblings of the others. The rest of the literacy campaign staff worked at home and met during the evenings at Father Cardenal's house.

Soon the situation was remedied, however, at least somewhat. The small staff was given its own space—a dusty, dirty office that had been abandoned and sacked during the insurrection. When the staff members first opened the door, their initial impression was not altogether encouraging: one broken chair, one desk, one telephone perched on a stack of cement blocks, and several other telephones resting on the floor. Cobwebs completed the decor. Undaunted, the group immediately took up a collection, bought a broom and mop, got some rags and soap, and formed its own cleanup brigade.

The cement blocks were used as seats until more chairs could be found, and the desk was shared. The problem of furniture was finally relieved, at least temporarily, when the staff received a much appreciated donation from the government leadership—the junta gave the team the old desks and chairs that had been used in the provisional offices in Costa Rica during the months prior to Somoza's fall. As the size of the crusade staff increased, classroom desks were requisitioned from the university. The first task of new personnel was often to go to the campus in order to pick up furniture and transport it back to the office so they could have a place to sit and work.

A National Campaign

Beginning with the first official document concerning the crusade, a draft proposal developed in Costa Rica two weeks before Somoza's defeat, the campaign was conceived of as a national project to take place during the first year of the revolution. Written by two prominent

Nicaraguan educators, Dr. Carlos Tunnermann and Dr. Miguel de Castilla (who later would become minister and vice-minister of education, respectively), the proposal called for a short, intensive nationwide campaign. The top crusade leadership never considered a regional, selective, step-by-step approach, but other people in the government, especially those directly involved in national planning, had some serious reservations about a full-scale, immediate effort. They wondered if the administrative and professional capacities of the fledgling staff would be sufficient to launch such an endeavor so soon after the war, especially since no organizational experience or infrastructure existed to support the effort. They also expressed concern about the economic resources the campaign would require. Some of the international experts advising the crusade team also raised questions about the consequences of a national program of such magnitude, pointing out that hundreds of thousands of new literates at the end of the campaign would have high educational expectations. To respond effectively to their needs would make heavy demands on an increasingly overextended educational system.

The force of Father Cardenal's convictions, his private discussions with top government leaders, and the planning capacity that was demonstrated by the crusade's team finally convinced the doubters, but even Father Cardenal admitted he was not entirely sure that the program was going to go forward as planned until January 1980. In mid-January a lengthy meeting was held with members of the government junta and the National Board of Directors of the *Frente*. Until then, all such meetings had been canceled for lack of attendance; only in January did the necessary officials finally come together.

Father Cardenal's arguments at that encounter reflected many of the government leaders' own sentiments about the crusade. He argued that the campaign had to be national because only a massive, immediate program could engender the maximum amount of enthusiasm and participation necessary for such an endeavor, building on the spirit of sacrifice and commitment that had been generated during the war. More important, since no other national social program was being contemplated for the first year of the revolution, he felt that the campaign had to be conducted immediately to demonstrate to people the concern and commitment of the new government to programs of real benefit to the poor. He stressed that as a result of the crusade, the revolution would gain active, dedicated supporters to continue the national programs of reconstruction, defense, and development. All of these arguments were in accord with the sentiments of the decision makers.

Political advantages aside, financial considerations were uppermost in the minds of some top officials. When first appointed by the government, Father Cardenal was informed that he would have to finance the entire project from nongovernment sources. At the January meeting, the campaign team demonstrated to the satisfaction of officials that sufficient international donations had been secured to guarantee the operation, which meant that public funds would not have to be used.

The egalitarian spirit of the revolution added force to the proposal for a national model, but perhaps what won the argument most effectively was the demonstrated competence of the crusade's team members, their detailed planning and their ability to prove that the project was economically viable. At some point, the fact that Father Cardenal was a colleague and housemate of another Jesuit who served as the top adviser to the minister of planning proved helpful as well. It established an indirect channel of discussion and debate with one of the principal opponents of the campaign approach and made it possible for differences to be heard and accommodations reached.

The crusade was conceived of as a short five-month campaign. The five-month figure was chosen for basically two reasons, one linguistic and one economic. First, Spanish is a relatively phonetic language, which means that it is easier for illiterate people to learn how to read and write. A variety of educational experts had advised that because of this fact, basic literacy skills could be acquired by adults within approximately four months. One month was added to that calculation to allow for the problems of both slow learners and fledgling teachers. Second, economic reconstruction demanded skilled laborers, technicians, and professionals. The pace of development would in large part depend on the speed with which the educational system could produce well-qualified people. Because schools had been closed for an extended period during the war, the top government leadership felt that there was a special urgency to keep the system open as much as possible. They believed that shutting down for more than five months in order to allow students to teach in the literacy campaign for a longer time would be irresponsible in light of the economic needs of the nation.

Once the length of the crusade was decided, the only reasonable time for its launching was mid-March because of one immutable fact of nature—the harvests. The only time the majority of rural Nicaraguans are in their home communities is between March and September. The rest of the year a significant number of people migrate to the coffee plantations or the cotton fields where work is often exhausting and therefore not conducive to intense, systematic study.

Crusade Structure

The organizational structure of the crusade evolved over time as new needs and demands emerged. It underwent two major changes during the first eight months, moving from a centralized operating structure to a more decentralized network. From its inception, the crusade was organized as part of the Ministry of Education, because it was believed that with such a direct relationship, coordination would be more effective and the campaign staff could more easily draw upon the technical and administrative support services of the ministry. The campaign itself was managed by a single executive structure, the National Coordinating Committee, which was headed by Father Cardenal.

The first organizational structure was a simple one in which the entire professional staff, all six of them, performed two basic functions: research and planning. In addition, they also did some fund raising and personnel recruiting. The initial planning focus was essentially on educational matters, although basic organizational issues were also addressed. Father Cardenal dealt with intergovernmental matters, relationships with community organizations, and the requisitioning of furniture.

By mid-October, the number of personnel had increased to about thirty, activities had become more clearly defined, and two separate working units had been formed: first, the Technical Unit—in charge of (a) educational matters such as curriculum, training, volunteer recruitment, and research, (b) statistics and census, and (c) production of materials; second, the Administrative Unit—responsible for (a) publicity/ public relations, (b) financial promotion, (c) library and documentation, and (d) logistical support. No regional structure had yet been formed. Father Roberto Saenz was chosen to head the Technical Unit, and Catholic Brother Ernesto Vallecillos, a former high school mathematics teacher, was chosen to lead the Administrative Unit.

In practice, this first organizational arrangement did not work as originally structured. Because the Technical Unit's responsibilities for developing the pedagogical aspects of the campaign were so intense, Brother Vallecillos's unit took on the planning for and the implementation of the census. In the next months, it also became clear that the volunteer recruitment and organization function that had been delegated to the Training Section of the Technical Unit would also have to be picked up by the Administrative Unit. Developing and conducting the training program was too time-consuming and the staff too small to be able to handle volunteer recruitment and organization as well. In the rush of events, one major task was not specifically included in the organizational chart—that of establishing the crusade's regional network of provincial offices. Fernando Cardenal first took on the responsibility of coordinating the formation of the provincial-level organization, which included identifying, interviewing, and selecting staff members, establishing local literacy commissions, and putting them into operation. After the completion of the census, Brother Vallecillos continued these organizational tasks.

By January, a new structure had been designed that better reflected the growing complexity of the operation. The two units increased to six, and the organization was expanded to include provincial, municipal, and community structures. The revised system included necessary campaign support services, such as communications and transportation, and incorporated the organizations that would serve as the crusade's volunteer teacher force—the rural-based Popular Literacy Army (EPA), which was coordinated by the Sandinista Youth Movement, and the Urban Literacy Guerrillas (GUAS), which were organized by the citizen and labor associations. This organizational structure remained almost unchanged for the duration of the campaign. The only significant modification in the organization chart between January and the commencement of the crusade in March was the addition of three new sections: Health Care, Food Distribution, and the Internal Technical Secretariat. A part of the Organizational Division, the Internal Technical Secretariat was responsible for the campaign's personnel records and files. Under the Administrative Division, the Food Distribution Section was in charge of providing basic food supplies to the volunteers, and the Health Care Unit was in charge of coordinating medical services through the university health brigades.

On the national level, the final organizational structure of the crusade consisted of six divisions: Technical/Pedagogical; Production and Design; Technical/Organizational; Public Relations; Financial Promotion; and Administrative. A special subdivision was also established to design and implement a multilingual literacy program in English, Miskito, and Sumo for people living on the Atlantic Coast. The Technical/Pedagogical Division had four sections—Curriculum, Research, Training, and Library/Museum—and was designed to provide the educational expertise for the program. Production and Design was in charge of the graphic design and the publication of tests, other learning materials, and posters. The Technical/Organizational Division essentially served as an information collector for the campaign staff, a support-control structure for the literacy promoters, and as a liaison with the different sponsoring organizations. It had four sections: Statistics and Census; the Popular Literacy Army (EPA) and the Urban Literacy Guerrillas (GUAS); the Mass Citizen and Labor Organizations; and the Internal Technical Secretariat. Responsibility for community relations, publicity, and press relations belonged to the Public Relations Division, and the Financial Promotion Division handled all fund raising, both domestic and international.

The Administrative Division was separated into two departments: Logistical Support, which was made up of Supplies, Health Care, Food Distribution, Transportation, Communication and Maintenance, and Plant Maintenance, and the Department of Administration, which contained Control, Accounting, Personnel, and Budget. The provincial and municipal structures were each organized along lines similar to the national structure—Technical/Pedagogical, Statistics and Census, Logistical Support, and Publicity.

To coordinate the campaign structures, the crusade consulted with a National Literacy Commission, which provided initial assistance to the campaign in the form of resource mobilization, coordination, and distribution and was the formal structural vehicle for citizen participation. Presided over by the minister of education, Carlos Tunnermann, the commission was composed of delegates from twenty-five public and private institutions, government ministries, universities, workers' associations, and citizens' groups, including the following.

National Board of Directors of the FSLN
Association of Nicaraguan Women
Farmworkers' Association
July Nineteenth Sandinista Youth Association
Federation of Secondary Students
Armed forces
Confederation of Parents
Nicaraguan Educators' Association
Federation of Catholic Teachers
Sandinista Community Civil Defense Committees
Roman Catholic church
Union of Nicaraguan Journalists
School of Radio Broadcasters
Sandinista Workers' Confederation
Institute for Nicaraguan Development
Institute of Agrarian Reform
National University and Catholic University
Ministries of Education, Social Welfare, Health, Labor, Planning, Transportation, and Interior
Nicaraguan Development Institute (Member of the Superior Council of Private Enterprise)

The national commission functioned briefly but was not as effective as hoped, in part because of the divisiveness of certain groups like the representatives from the private enterprise organizations.

Parallel commissions were established on both the provincial and municipal levels with representatives from the same institutions and organizations as the national commission. Presiding officers were to be the provincial and municipal directors of education, but in practice, some commissions found that the literacy crusade coordinator was the more appropriate chairperson. Subcommissions were formed on the township and neighborhood levels. During the course of the campaign, the local commissions worked more effectively than the national because representatives of divisive groups often did not participate.

August to April: Planning and Organizing Activities

Settling into their newly cleaned office in August, the small team began its awesome task. Brooms and mops were replaced by books and pencils; stacks of papers on literacy programs stood on the one desk. Father Cardenal spelled out the challenge facing the team members and their feelings as they confronted the massive problems to be surmounted.

> Frankly, I think the challenge confronting the crusade staff would have discouraged most educational planners. At times we were overwhelmed. The lessons of the war, however, provided us with a special source of strength and inspiration. During the insurrection we had learned to take unimaginable risks. We learned about organizing and about trusting in people's extraordinary capacity for daring, creativity, and perseverance. We were confident that we could translate that spirit into the literacy crusade. But, initially, we weren't quite sure how to prepare, organize, and mobilize the large numbers of people necessary for the battle or how to finance it. The problems appeared formidable.
>
> Somoza had left the country destitute. We could not count on public financing. The massive effort would cost millions of dollars—how many we did not know. Since the war had affected much of the nation's transportation system, and years of government corruption had impeded the development of a rural infrastructure, new methods had to be devised to maintain communication with the isolated regions of the country, to transport the tens of thousands of *brigadistas* to the countryside, and to distribute massive amounts of equipment and teaching materials. [Cardenal, July 1980]

The problems did seem insurmountable. The long months of battle had destroyed industry so that supplying even the basic necessities of the crusade required a herculean effort. Machinery had to be imported, factories reorganized, cottage industries developed, and materials ordered from foreign markets to provide the necessary uniforms, lanterns, mosquito nets, boots, raincoats, malaria pills, water purification tablets, and study materials. Agricultural production had been interrupted, and scarcity in rural communities was commonplace. Basic foodstuffs first needed to be imported and then distributed to supply the *brigadistas.*

Because decades of repression had prevented the development of community groups and labor associations under the dictatorship, the campaign had to depend on organizations that were still in their infancy for the crucial tasks of mobilizing and supporting the crusade's volunteer personnel. Long years of neglect had deprived the poor of adequate health care and had resulted in high levels of parasitic and skin infections, malaria, and malnutrition. Conditions in rural areas were especially severe, so medical supplies and basic health information would have to be provided to the *brigadistas.* To mount a campaign of such magnitude, a network of offices needed to be established. Since the number of trained and experienced administrators was limited, the crusade would have to act as a learning laboratory and crucible to forge new educational managers.

The initial planning and research of the first months took place in an atmosphere of constant interruptions. Immediately after the announcement of the campaign's formation in August, community people began arriving at the office requesting information, materials, and teachers. They were ready and anxious for the program to begin. The flow of traffic seemed unending, from both near and far. During the war, the citizens of Nicaragua had gained much sympathy throughout the world, and the announcement of a national literacy campaign captured the imagination of many people and groups that had supported the struggle. People from Latin America, the United States, Canada, and Europe came to volunteer their services as educational experts and literacy teachers. International agencies, church groups, and foreign government representatives arrived to offer financing and technical assistance. The small office was inundated.

A reception area was created, and wooden partitions were constructed; Father Saenz attended the visitors. Community groups were informed of the crusade's schedule and asked to be patient and, in the interim, to organize fund-raising drives in their neighborhoods. International volunteers, unless they had exceptional credentials and recommendations, were thanked for their offer of help but told that the best means of assistance would be to return to their home country and raise funds for the campaign. Fathers Cardenal and Saenz usually dealt with the official international delegations that offered financial or technical assistance, but on occasion, the entire team participated in discussions and negotiations.

During August and September, the core team of six people began to work simultaneously on different planning, research, and programming tasks. These tasks included a detailed examination of the draft proposal for the crusade (written by Drs. Tunnermann and de Castilla); the clarification of program goals, scope, length, and starting date; an analysis of available resources and information needs; the establishment of program targets; preparation of the budget and a fund-raising program; investigation of previous literacy efforts in Nicaragua; the study of prominent educational philosophers and practitioners; and research on other countries' experiences with literacy campaigns. The principal programs examined were those that had been conducted in Brazil, Colombia, Cuba, Guinea-Bissau, Panama, Peru, and São Tomé. At different moments during this initial planning stage, the team was assisted by experts from UNESCO, the Organization of American States, the World Council of Churches, the Latin American Ecumenical Community Education Center (CELADEC), the United Nations–affiliated Latin American Center for Basic Education (CREFAL), and Cuba. Selected educators were hired directly by the crusade to provide technical support. They came from Argentina (2), Canada (1), Chile (1), Colombia (4), Costa Rica (1), El Salvador (1), France (1), Honduras (1), Mexico (2), Peru (1), Puerto Rico (1), Spain (4), the United States (3), and Uruguay (1). The Cuban government provided a team of four educational experts.

During the last week of September, the core team visited the island of Cuba, site of an internationally acclaimed 1961 literacy campaign. There the team members interviewed the former directors of the 1961 literacy program and spent four valuable days delving into the archives of the Literacy Museum. The team was especially interested in the organizational framework of Cuba's program and the system of mobilization that had been used to support and place the more than 200,000 Cuban literacy volunteers.

The team found the visit to the museum instructive and the discussions with the Cuban educational leaders inspiring, filled with poignant anecdotes about their campaign experiences, but some twenty years of time had dimmed memories. Father Cardenal felt the pressures of the crusade closing in on him, and he needed more than personal vignettes. He needed specifics about different kinds of organizational structures and literacy methods in order to plan effectively, assess program possibilities, and anticipate the problems that surely lay ahead. Yet he could find no detailed account of either the Cuban campaign or other national literacy campaigns that spelled out the process and problems of organizing and implementing such a program. Reports and evaluations existed, but they did not go into the detail or analysis he needed. For this reason, he was pleased when the Cuban government offered to send some of Cuba's experienced adult educators as advisers to the crusade. Even though they would not be able to arrive until late November, when most materials and training would have already been designed, he felt their long-tested experience would contribute to the further development of the campaign.

Immediately after the visit to Cuba, during the first week of October, an intensive five-day national planning seminar was held with a team of experts from Colombia, Costa Rica, Mexico, and the United States. It was sponsored by CELADEC (a Latin American ecumenical peasant education group), the Freiderich Ebert Foundation of West Germany, and the Federation of Central American Universities. After a detailed clarification and analysis of the crusade's proposed campaign plan, the participants began to develop some general operational guidelines. They specifically worked to determine the crusade's organizational structure, its functions and responsibilities, and to determine personnel allocations, a training model, curriculum design, research plans, and the time line for the entire crusade. March 24, 1980, was set as the target date for the initiation of the program. In mid-October and early November 1979, Paulo Freire and some World Council of Churches colleagues visited Nicaragua for two weeks, and they provided valuable input to the planning process.

To keep the staff informed about the progress and problems of the ever-expanding organization, Father Cardenal established a weekly bulletin so that "we can keep ourselves up-to-date on all that is happening and keep on track, learning the route so if we get detoured along the way, we can find the proper road again" (Cruzada Nacional de Alfabetización, December 1979, 11). The bulletin provided details about some of the bureaucratic detours and unexpected, sometimes humorous, curves the route took. It extolled virtues and pointed out problems.

> Last week Totin [head artist of the Design Department] urgently requested a curtain for the office window and if possible, an airconditioner or fan. The art staff has a serious problem. They are ruining their drawings, sweat constantly dripping off their hands and forehead. . . . When the government junta came to visit, *compañero* Daniel Ortega stuck his head in the door and asked, "What is this place?" and don Carlos a staff artist said, "The land of fire [Tierra del Fuego]. How about an airconditioner?" [Cruzada Nacional de Alfabetización, December 1979, 11]

Specific administrative advice was given to address other common problems. "A principle we should all follow: Avoid unnecessary interruptions of your coordinators. Establish daily meeting times to discuss and evaluate program activities and concerns" (Cruzada Nacional de Alfabetización, January 1980, 2). When concrete solutions were found to problems, they received praise.

Compañera Mayra Barrera, Statistics Department, requested three typewriters for her team . . . but since there weren't any more available at
the moment, they found another solution. The group decided to stay later
and use the office typewriters, normally occupied during the day, after
hours in the evenings. When you really love and are dedicated to something,
you can find a solution no matter what. The most important thing is to
serve our people . . . and continue moving forward. . . . Nothing will
stop this campaign! [Cruzada Nacional de Alfabetización, January 1980,
4]

The bulletin served to stimulate commitment and pride. In the process,
it sometimes revealed the special bond and sense of inspiration felt by
other Latin Americans toward the Nicaraguan revolution. One striking
account was chronicled over several issues. A December bulletin described
the enthusiastic visit of Salvador Ricardo Samayoa, minister of education
in El Salvador, and his hopes for implementing a literacy campaign in
his country. A later issue reported he had sent a personal telegram to
the crusade staff announcing his resignation from office and expressing
his gratitude for the kindness and friendship shown him by the campaign
staff. After much frustration, Samayoa and the majority of the other
civilian cabinet ministers and junta members resigned their government
positions in protest over the continued brutality of the military and
inability to implement needed social programs. Later, he and many other
former public officials joined the FDR/FMLN, the political and armed
opposition movement of El Salvador fighting against the government.

Establishing Records: Census and Statistics

One of the most important planning-related activities undertaken
during the first months of organization was the completion of a national
census of all Nicaraguans over ten years of age. Because of the magnitude
of the task, in many ways it served as a dress rehearsal for the crusade.
The census was not just a gathering of data but a miniature campaign
in itself. Besides providing valuable statistics, it helped inform people
about the literacy crusade, overcome cultural barriers between city and
country, develop personal relationships among participants and communities, measure the organizational capacity of each region, and identify
the massive problems such as transportation and health that the crusade
staff would later have to confront. The census process also instilled in
many of its participants an enthusiasm and a commitment to the campaign
and the revolution.

In terms of concrete statistics, the census determined the level of
illiteracy and the precise location of those people in the country who

did not know how to read and write. The census also gathered information about those people who were willing to offer their services as volunteer teachers. The availability of teaching locations was also recorded. The census was quickly and inexpensively organized and completed with the assistance of a UNESCO expert and the cooperation of the Nicaraguan Institute of Statistics and Census. The newly formed citizen and labor associations were also crucial in fulfilling the tasks of organization and implementation. Enthusiasm for the undertaking was high as it was the first activity of the campaign to be organized on a national scale. Students were especially excited and volunteered in large numbers through their schools under the sponsorship of the Sandinista Youth Association. After a short, intensive training period, the volunteer census takers were sent throughout the country, and within two weeks, the majority of the nation had been canvassed.

Each province had a census coordinator who worked in conjunction with a special support commission made up of government institutions, citizens' associations, labor organizations, and church and student groups. Along with the commissions, the provincial coordinators oversaw the organization, management, and training of the census brigades, which were composed of students, parents, teachers, labor union and citizens' association members, army personnel, and peasants. The brigades were divided according to municipalities and then split according to urban and rural areas. They were provided with survey forms, an instruction manual, a list of the approximate population in a given municipality or township, and when available, a census map done either by the census office or the Malaria Control Agency.

The census was carried out on a minimal budget. Provincial offices were in charge of raising their own funds. Radio marathons were held locally, money was donated, dances were held, and in one case a Brahman calf was raffled. On October 20, volunteers were mobilized throughout the country. Since this was the first experience with mass mobilization, the effort was not without its problems. Because the volunteer response in Managua was much greater than anticipated, not enough public vehicles had been secured for the operation, and because it was Sunday, all offices were closed. Not wanting to dismiss needed recruits, the crusade's administrative coordinator, Brother Vallecillos, borrowed money from his mother to rent private transport—he did not want any volunteer to be turned down. Once off the beaten track, however, most census takers ended up paying their own way, or being very stubborn and creative about avoiding costs. A report from one of the brigades recounts the story of one group that tried to cross a river with no bridge and no money.

When we arrived at Quilalí, we separated. Our brigade headed off to our assigned territory—Wiwilí County. On the way, we encountered our first big problem—the big Quilalí River. We explained to the owner of the passenger canoe that we were from the crusade's census brigade. We showed him our official letter and asked him for his cooperation so we could continue on our way and allow the campaign to proceed on schedule. The answer we received was firm. If we didn't pay the two pesos per person, we didn't cross the river.

But remembering our challenge—that no matter what happened, come hell or high water, the campaign would go on—we decided to cross the river by whatever means possible.

So part of the brigade hitched a ride with a passing tractor, and the others went in the jeep that the tractor was pulling. We had crossed part of the way when suddenly the current was too much and the jeep turned over. There were nine of us in the vehicle—us and the entire supply of census forms. We all fell into the water. Everyone rushed to save the forms, worrying first about the crusade and not messing up our work. The fact that we might have drowned didn't enter our minds. We were too concerned about rescuing the questionnaires and not botching up the first task the revolution had entrusted us with. [Cruzada Nacional de Alfabetización, November 1979d, 1]

All surveyors were given a letter of identification, which helped them in obtaining free transportation from cooperative bus and taxi drivers. Canoe owners seemed the least helpful. The Institute of Agrarian Reform provided a fumigation helicopter to airlift some brigades into inaccessible areas, but at road's end, most rural brigade members had long hikes into the mountains and jungles. They usually conducted their census taking in pairs. Sometimes they got lost, but usually before too long, helpful peasants offered to be their impromptu guides. In villages and small towns, many of the brigades held community meetings to explain the purpose of the census and to introduce the literacy campaign. In the process, they gained an increased sensitivity and commitment to the peasants and their plight. The stories of two brigades in northern Nicaragua, named after brothers killed in the war, give an idea of the experience and insights gained through the encounters.

Our brigade was in charge of the census in and around Mozonte. The experience made us realize the commitment that we should have toward our peasant brothers and sisters; we, who have had the fortune of schooling and education, our commitment should be ever deeper and greater to those who have not . . . that commitment will mean that medicine, education, politics, and culture will be part of their lives too, part of the development of the entire national community. [Cruzada Nacional de Alfabetización, November 1979a, 1]

A teacher tells the story of his students:

> The road to Portrerillo is rather difficult. The rains have turned it into deep muddy ruts. Today we finished census taking at 6:30 P.M. because it got dark. Our work consisted of talking with families, instilling confidence in them, and conveying the importance of the Crusade and the reasons why we are here doing what we are doing. As we visited each house, we invited people to Ramon Morales's place for an evening get-together. When we were finally finished with our surveying, it took us almost an hour and a half to get there. The rain had been hard, and the shallow streams we crossed earlier had become deep rushing rivers in a matter of hours. About fifteen members of the community managed to make it. We spent the evening in dialogue, discussing and explaining many things.
>
> We held the meeting in a family setting. What was noteworthy was the participation of my high school students who had accompanied us as part of the brigade—how they spoke about the true meaning of politics and education as being the progress of the whole community, everyone working together. [Cruzada Nacional de Alfabetización, November 1979b, 1–2]

On the whole, community people were cooperative, but fears and doubts interfered in some cases. Women did not want to let surveyors into their homes until their husbands could be present. Rumors that were spread by groups opposed to the revolution increased doubts. Stories were circulated that peasants had been blinded with pencils stuck through their eyes—assailants unknown. Brigades were accused of being Communists. Some families were reluctant to give information because they feared their land or children might be taken away from them as a result. In a small number of cases, rumors led people to believe that churches were going to be closed and religion prohibited.

The census uncovered unexpected revelations and administrative difficulties. In their journeys, brigades often discovered new communities that were unrecorded on any of the previous census maps. Some villages claimed to be part of other municipalities. Administrative problems internal to the census process were also revealed. Disorganization was general; census forms were not provided in sufficient quantities and had to be reordered. As a result, record keeping according to the planned consecutive-number system did not work. Census maps were inaccurate, and consequently, some brigades overlapped in area assignments. Transportation was difficult, and remote areas were not completely covered. But most problems centered around the poverty and misery encountered by the brigades in the countryside. Many census volunteers became ill, and almost all registered shock at the health conditions they encountered—serious malnutrition, tuberculosis, whooping cough, malaria, eye infections, and measles epidemics that practically decimated the infant populations of villages. One brigade's report indicates the extent of the problem. "In Walakistan, thirty-seven children died in thirteen days, three in the same family. They buried them all in the same box because there was not enough money to make three coffins and not enough nails to close them shut" (Montenegro 1979, 3).

The national census was completed in most areas in less than three weeks. A two-day wrap-up meeting was held with the provincial coordinators on the tenth and eleventh of November in Managua to evaluate the accomplishments of and problems encountered during the undertaking.

The original plan called for then processing the data on computers. However, given the amount of information collected, this task would have required the use of every computer and data processor in the country for two weeks. Because this requirement was economically unacceptable, the decision was made to process the data by hand. About 2,500 especially trained volunteer tabulators completed the task in less than ten days, processing the information on auditorium and gymnasium floors.

The results indicated that 722,431 Nicaraguans were illiterate, over 50 percent of the population—approximately 30 percent in urban centers, and approximately 75 percent in rural areas. Children between ten and fourteen years of age accounted for 21 percent of the illiterate group. According to the census findings, for every three illiterates, one literate person was available to teach. This ratio, of course, varied according to region, with a surplus of available volunteers in the cities and a deficit in the countryside.

Testing Procedures and Effective Illiteracy Rate

The census provided a more complete picture of the nation's illiteracy levels and their geographic distribution. As the crusade began, however, it became clear that people's notions of illiteracy varied. Some who classified themselves as totally illiterate could recognize the alphabet and read simple words but could not write. Exact skills were not known until *brigadistas* actually went out to teach and gave program applicants a qualifying test. This brief exam was the first in a series of three given during the campaign. The initial test was designed to determine the actual skill level of each participant, beginning with a simple exercise— drawing a straight line. This step was included so that people who were unable to continue beyond the first question would have some sense of accomplishment and understand that they, too, possessed the potential to master the alphabet. The next level of skill tested was the ability to write one's name, which was followed by reading and writing exercises—single words first, then short sentences. The test concluded with a comprehension exercise. People who completed all sections successfully were considered literate, and those who could read and write a few words were classified as semiliterates. Illiterates included people who could not read or write more than their own name.

After completing the first half of the primer, an intermediate test was given to assess a learner's progress and diagnose individual study needs. The ability to read and write different syllabic families was determined so that specialized review could be oriented toward practicing those syllabic groups that had not yet been fully mastered. The final exam was administered by the literacy volunteer under the guidance of a technical adviser. It consisted of five parts and tested reading, writing, and comprehension skills. To be considered literate, participants had to be able to write their name, read aloud a short text, answer three questions based on the reading, write a sentence dictated to them, and write a short composition. They were expected to be able to read with comprehension, pronouncing words as a whole and not as a series of isolated syllables. They were to write legibly, leaving appropriate spaces between words, and to spell phonetically. With such skills, participants could, within their vocabulary range, read newspapers, application forms, technical information pamphlets, and books.

Records kept on each student during the campaign included such general information as name, age, sex, date of enrollment, residence, occupation, and past school attendance. A monthly progress chart indicated the lessons and exercises completed in both the primer and the math workbook, as well as the total number of sessions attended. Test results for each of the three exams were recorded, as were observations about individual learning difficulties, health problems, and areas of personal interest for future study.

These reports revealed the history and the progress of the crusade. They also indicated the poor conditions under which the majority of Nicaraguans lived and the tragic human costs of underdevelopment. They revealed one other important fact: Although the initial illiteracy rate had been calculated at 50 percent, the effective rate was closer to 40 percent. Poor health was the principal cause of this difference as many Nicaraguans were handicapped by excessive malnutrition, which impaired sight and hearing, limited memory, and often caused early senility. Health statistics indicated that 25 percent of all newborns in Nicaragua fell into the high-risk category. Many did not reach five years of age, and those who did often suffered serious mental and physical disorders.

As much as the staff did not want to accept the fact, some people simply did not have the ability to master reading and writing skills in the campaign. Reports from volunteers and technical advisers indicated widespread learning difficulties and cases of disability. In all, about 9 percent of the population was found to have severe learning disabilities that prevented their acquiring basic literacy skills.

Development of Literacy Offices and Commissions

In early November, the formation of regional crusade offices and literacy commissions began in earnest. Father Cardenal, Brother Vallecillos, and an international adviser spent almost three months organizing the nationwide network. First, they sought out provincial coordinators to direct the regional crusade offices by consulting closely with representatives from the FSLN and the Nicaraguan Educators' Association (ANDEN). The process was slow and difficult as many candidates were already carrying out other important reconstruction activities. But by January, after an exhaustive search, all eighteen provincial-level coordinators had been selected.

The first major task of these officials was to set up the infrastructure for the crusade's training program. Local workshops were to be held to prepare the campaign's regional educational teams, which meant that each coordinator had to arrange for a training site, food, lodging, and support staff. The provincial coordinators also assisted the national staff in the continuing search for 144 municipal coordinators. By February, the local staffs were almost totally in place, and further support was on the way. That same month, a specially selected group of teachers, called the Red and Black Brigade, named in honor of the FSLN colors, was sent to assist the municipal coordinators. Each provincial staff consisted of one coordinator, an assistant, two educational advisers, one statistics specialist, two supply officers, and a radio operator. Each municipal staff was composed of one coordinator, an assistant, one educational adviser, one statistics specialist, and one supply officer.

As crusade staffs were being selected, provincial literacy commissions were also being formed. The original plan called for each of the participating organizations in the National Literacy Commission to instruct their provincial offices to appoint representatives to the local commissions. Although this plan worked in some instances, encouragement and explanation from the National Literacy Office was also needed in each province. The first recorded meetings of the provincial commissions occurred in mid-February 1980. At such gatherings, problems of initial organization on the provincial and municipal levels were discussed. Many municipal commissions could not be completely constituted because in certain areas, the citizen and labor organizations were still in the development stage. For more effective communication and access, provinces had to be mapped accurately, and some municipalities had to be divided because of their large geographic extension and difficult terrain. Before the crusade started, the commissions helped locate lodging for the *brigadistas*, prepared the infrastructure for various levels of training, and launched publicity campaigns to convince parents that their children should be allowed to participate in the crusade as volunteer teachers.

Crusade Financing and Costs

To determine crusade costs and to formulate a program budget, two financial specialists from the Ministry of Planning were temporarily allocated to the campaign. After they were provided with program details such as the crusade's proposed scope, duration, and personnel and material needs, they developed a tentative budget that called for approximately $20 million (200 million cordobas). A finance office was immediately established to coordinate the effort.

Fund raising for the campaign depended heavily on international support. Requests for assistance were mailed to governments, institutions, and solidarity groups around the world. Crusade staff members met with representatives from all embassies located in Managua, and then official delegations were sent to Europe, the United States, Canada, and Mexico. Visits to Nicaragua by international representatives were also encouraged. The fund-raising effort often served as governments' and organizations' first contact with the new Nicaragua and provided a positive introduction to the programs and purposes of the revolution. For example, the director of UNESCO, Amadou-Mahtar M'Bow, was so impressed by his visit to Nicaragua and conversations with the campaign staff that he put out an international call to support the crusade. During a speech in Paris before UNESCO's entire staff, he was moved to tears as he described the enthusiastic efforts of the Nicaraguans to rebuild their country.

In Nicaragua, the crusade staff established a program of patriotic literacy bonds and encouraged community fund-raising endeavors. Employees from all sectors, public and private, tithed one day's salary each month to the campaign. Marketwomen from Managua and peasants from distant mountain villages came to the national office in order to make their contributions personally. For example, three representatives of the newly formed Revolutionary Sports Committee of Chontales, two peasants and one young student traveled six hours on a crowded bus to contribute the 1,000 cordobas that had been collected in their village through community raffles. Enthusiastic high school students filled the city streets carrying tin cans. Following some of the same tactics that had been used during the insurrection, they set up roadblocks to collect "pennies for pencils" and called on radio stations to read official declarations of war against ignorance and to make appeals for financial help. Dances, song fests, concerts, and poetry readings all added to the fund-raising effort.

Including cash and materials, some 120 million cordobas ($12 million) were raised overall. Since the program had been carefully streamlined to cut out all excess expenses, these funds covered the costs. Catholic and Protestant organizations were the first to contribute. The countries that were the most generous in their donations were, in order of contribution, the Federal Republic of Germany, Switzerland, Sweden, Holland, and Great Britain, although support was given from countries all over the world. In this way, Nicaraguans felt that people everywhere formed part of the crusade and shared in its achievements.

In the financial reports, specific examples of donations were sometimes related in order to give an idea of the scope of support that the campaign was receiving. "A beautiful thing occurred on Sunday February 17 in New York—the wedding of Beverly Keene and Victor Alderete. Their wedding invitation requested that no gifts be sent but, rather, that donations should be made to the National Literacy Crusade and two other institutions for which they work. All of Nicaragua wishes to thank them for such a noble gesture" (Crusada Nacional de Alfabetización, March 1980, 14).

Supplies and Logistics

Obtaining the massive quantities of equipment necessary for the campaign was a challenge that staggered almost everyone's imagination. For example, denim and cotton had to be ordered from abroad for crusade uniforms and knapsacks, then given to local sewing cooperatives for assembly, and finally distributed to *brigadistas* according to some approximation of individual size. It soon became apparent that equipment ordered from overseas required special attention if it were to arrive on time. Nicaragua needed an international expediter who could hustle and talk fast.

The crusade staff chose John McFadden, a six-foot-four-inch training adviser from California, and sent him to Florida where he located the necessary equipment, ordering some of it from as far away as Europe via Africa, and organized an airlift from Miami to Managua. He cornered and exhausted the U.S. rubber-boot market and had to look to Spain and Guatemala for more boots. Some *brigadistas* would get fancy blue-and-yellow yachting boots from Neiman Marcus, and others would receive ill-fitting, ill-made boots manufactured elsewhere. Mosquito nets that had originally been intended for the Portuguese army in Angola were found in a British warehouse and purchased from the speculator who had bought them after Portugal left its African colonies. The Coleman lanterns that had been ordered from the United States could not be delivered on time because of factory delays, so old-fashioned kerosene railway lanterns had to be located quickly and purchased. After the equipment arrived, a national control and distribution system had to be instituted. Commercial school students were found to manage the operation, and the Transportation Ministry helped with the distribution.

The National Teaching Corps

In rural areas, the teaching corps consisted of the Popular Literacy Army (EPA), the Peasant Literacy Militia (MAC), and the Workers' Literacy Militia (MOA). Their efforts were complemented by the work of the cultural and health brigades. In urban locations, teaching was carried out by the Urban Literacy Guerrillas (GUAS) and MOA.

Rural Organization

The main rural teaching force was the EPA. Separate from the crusade structure, the EPA was an autonomous body created to oversee the administration, morale, and discipline of the rural volunteer corps. The challenges of forming and leading the EPA were given to the national youth organization—the Juventud Sandinista Diecinueve de Julio (Juventud), which selected its name, the Nineteenth of July Sandinista Youth, in honor of the day victory was proclaimed over the dictatorship. The young people's association had emerged from the Federation of Secondary and University Students, which was organized under the auspices of the FSLN during the long years of struggle against Somoza. The federation and its members had played an important role during that time, organizing students, leading study groups, coordinating strikes, working with the poor, as well as publishing and distributing clandestine literature and information. The Juventud leaders began their organizing activities for the EPA in November on an experimental basis with several high schools in Managua. During December, working in conjunction with the crusade staff, they designed the teacher corps' field structure and chain of command. From this design, they developed a manual for the *brigadistas* on the literacy army's organization and duties.

During January, the top Juventud and EPA leadership, some forty people in all, took part in a workshop on popular community education conducted by CELADEC, a Christian peasant education group based in Peru. In February, the workshop participants organized a similar seminar for other representatives of the literacy army in order to prepare the teacher corps leadership in general education theories, development issues, political concepts, and cultural questions and to alert them to potential problems of personal adjustment to life in the countryside. Workshops were held weekly until March, with some 120 young people attending each session. The major weakness of this training was its lack of contact with the crusade's educational staff. The EPA workshops were designed and implemented independently, without the direct input or supervision of the campaign's training team. This initial separation was dysfunctional because it contributed to a division between the EPA and crusade staff and inhibited the development of a mutually reinforcing educational approach.

For the young EPA staff members, February was a month of intense organizing. They sponsored educational and promotional activities in honor of the crusade; organized seminars in first aid for teachers and volunteers, in cooperation with the Ministry of Health and the Red Cross; and coordinated school vaccination programs for the *brigadistas*. Convincing parents to give permission for their children to participate was sometimes difficult and became a major challenge for the EPA. Fear of pregnancy and retaliation by former guardsmen were common worries. As one girl explained, "My mother thinks I'm going to come back from the mountains with my knapsack on my front instead of my back." To promote membership in the corps and allay fears, EPA staff members organized parents' meetings, discussions with church people and prominent citizens, parades, films, sports contests, student assemblies, concerts, dances, and panel discussions. They set up seminars for new recruits to acquaint them with the organizational structure of the literacy army and to discuss development questions, political issues, and current events. An Outward Bound type of physical training program was designed, rigorous daily exercises were held, and long hikes in the country were taken.

The EPA literacy corps was first structured into teaching battlefronts, then into brigades, columns, and squadrons, and was separated according to sex. Each structure of the corps was named after a fallen martyr of the revolution. On the national level, the EPA was organized along the same six battlefronts as the war of liberation as follows:

Battlefront	*Name*	*Provinces and Areas Covered*
Western	Rigoberto López Pérez	Chinandega, León
Eastern	Roberto Huembes	Chontales, Boaco, Rama
Northeastern	Pablo Ubeda	Mountainous areas of Matagalpa and Jinotega and Zelaya (Siuna, Bonanza, Rosita)

Central	Camilo Ortega Saavedra	Masaya, Carazo, Managua, Granada
Northern	Carlos Fonseca Amador	Nonmountainous areas of Jinotega and Matagalpa and Estelí, Nueva Segovia, Madriz
Southern	Benjamín Zeladón	Rivas, Río San Juan

The battlefront organization had no actual operational functions but served as a term of identification and as a means to instill in the literacy volunteers a sense of national purpose and a proud association with the wartime struggle.

The next level of organization was the brigade, which was composed of all the *brigadistas* working in one municipality. The brigade structure was designed to coordinate the activities of the EPA and to provide support to the crusade's municipal offices. Each brigade was coordinated by a command staff consisting of a brigade leader, an assistant, and the heads of all the columns located in the municipality. All EPA leaders, whether on the brigade, column, or squadron level, were called *responsables*, a term that was selected to instill a different view of leadership and authority. The title was chosen to emphasize a leader's responsibility to the group and the program. The duties of the top brigade *responsables* including meeting regularly with the command staff, sending status reports to the municipal offices of the crusade, and making regular visits to the column and squadron *responsables* and *brigadistas*. These visits were made to provide orientation, discuss problems, inspire enthusiasm, keep track of the statistical progress of the literacy teaching, and distribute materials.

The next level following the brigade was the column. It was organized to coincide with township boundaries, although sometimes the geography of an area made such distribution impossible. Each column consisted of several squadrons—the ideal number was four for every column. Column leaders were selected from among the most outstanding squadron leaders. The column command staff was made up of the column *responsable*, an assistant, and the squadron *responsables*. The column structure served to coordinate corps activities on the local level and to support the work of the crusade office in the township. Similar in scope to the responsibilities of the brigade leaders, the duties of the column *responsables* and their assistants consisted of informing and meeting with the brigade *responsables*, holding regular meetings with their command staff, and making periodic visits to the squadron leaders and volunteers under their jurisdiction. Site visits were conducted to provide information on policy orientations, to motivate and supervise the *bri-*

gadistas, to check on the progress of the literacy effort, and to distribute supplies.

The foundation of the EPA rested on the squadrons, the smallest organizational unit of the literacy corps' structure. Ideally, each squadron was to contain thirty members plus one squadron *responsable,* one assistant, and at least one professional teacher serving as the unit's educational supervisor. The command staff included the squadron leader, an assistant, and the educational advisers. The squadron *responsables* were in charge of informing their column leaders as to the geographical placement and relocation of each volunteer and providing them with timely reports on the problems and progress of their unit. Their responsibilities also included the following: visiting their *brigadistas* regularly, distributing materials to them, discussing problems with them, keeping a registry of all corps members under their supervision, organizing a speedy mail system, overseeing squadron health needs, and checking to make sure that the *brigadistas* performed their literacy duties and wrote their parents.

By April, after several weeks of operation, certain weaknesses in this original organization network had been detected in the field, and new structures were designed. One major oversight discovered was that although the crusade had an important operational structure functioning on the provincial level, no parallel body existed for the EPA. The literacy corps was too decentralized for effective coordination, either with its own national office or with the provincial structures of the crusade. To improve coordination, therefore, provincial-level EPA offices were established. Each of these offices functioned as a liaison with the crusade staff and between the EPA national office and municipal brigade structures.

The overall municipal organization remained almost the same with one important addition: A special coordinating body was established. This new municipal-level structure included the EPA brigade *responsables,* the municipal coordinator of the crusade, the municipal educational advisers, the teachers' association delegate, and the Ministry of Education representative to the crusade. Scheduled to meet on a weekly basis, this body was designed to address municipal issues and problems. Its purpose was to adapt national policy to local needs, specifically on educational, political, union policy, and disciplinary matters. The group also handled staff requests for permission for temporary leave from duty. On the township level, a similar working team was organized to improve coordination and address local matters. It was made up of crusade staff members, squadron educational advisers, and *responsables* from the EPA.

One other major organizational problem discovered was that geography and population distribution on the micro level made it difficult for the

EPA to fit into neat, preconceived organizational structures. Sometimes problems of terrain and uneven population distribution meant that the volunteers had to be divided into smaller units than the squadron. A nucleus cell unit was established in such circumstances; its number depended upon the number of people in and the geography of the area.

The EPA formed the bulk of the rural educational corps. However, its numbers were reinforced by other teaching units. Working alongside the EPA members, but under the auspices and structure of their own organizations, were two additional groups of volunteer teachers. The Farmworkers' Association (ATC) organized a small but effective team called the Peasant Literacy Militia, whose members contributed to the effort in their own communities during their free time. The Sandinista Labor Federation formed the Workers' Literacy Militia, which sent out a specially selected number of volunteers to participate in the rural areas. These people received their full wages while in the field. In order not to affect production, their fellow workers pledged to cover the normal duties of the volunteers during their absence.

Assisting the rural corps were the cultural brigades numbering some 450 students in all. Organized by the National University and the Ministry of Culture, these brigades collected oral histories and promoted popular culture in the rural communities through theater, puppetry, song, poetry, sociodrama, and dance. Armed with tape recorders and detailed questionnaires, these teams conducted different types of research studies and collected information in the areas of anthropology, biology, botany, and geography. They had no literacy teaching duties and were divided according to municipalities.

Completing the rural forces was a special medical corps, but these health brigades were not formed until after the crusade had begun and the medical problems in the countryside had become fully known. Some 750 medical and nursing students attended a week-long preparation seminar conducted by the National University. A group of Boy Scouts with special first-aid training reinforced their numbers. The crusade staff provided them with uniforms and basic equipment, and the Ministry of Health gave them medical kits and supplies. Organized under the auspices of the university, the health brigades had a central coordinator and an assistant who worked as liaisons with the campaign staff in the crusade's national office. The four-to-five-person brigades were divided according to municipalities. Each maintained a central office in the municipal center and traveled to the volunteer sites in order to provide basic medical treatment to the other brigades. Their services were primarily intended for the *brigadistas*, but they also attended community people when possible and gave health education presentations both to volunteers and to their students.

The public sector National Basic Grains Distribution Program (ENABAS) also provided valuable assistance in basic health care to the rural literacy corps. Originally, planners had assumed that peasant families would be able to feed their volunteer teachers, but economic conditions were much worse than anticipated. In order to respond to the emergency, ENABAS provided volunteers with double rations of basic foodstuffs (rice, beans, corn, cooking oil, sugar, and salt), both to feed themselves and to assist their host families. Soap was also provided. The system was plagued by problems of transport and distribution, with some *brigadistas'* receiving large quantities of sugar, rice, and beans but no oil or salt. Weekend visits by parents and care packages from home helped improve their diet as well as that of the community since most food packages were shared.

Urban Organization

The urban literacy effort had a looser structure and received less attention and concern than the more dramatic and romantic rural work. The urban effort suffered as a consequence and was the weaker of the two. Work in the cities was coordinated under two structures. The principal citizens' organizations—the women's association and the neighborhood groups called Sandinista defense committees—were responsible for recruiting one force, the Popular Literacy Volunteers. The coordination and structure of this teaching corps, however, was under the direction of the crusade staff and the responsibility of the local director of education from the ministry. The group was made up of housewives, working students, professionals, international volunteers, and interested private citizens. This group had less of a sense of belonging and a more limited commitment than the members of the EPA. In order to help increase enthusiasm and spirit for the effort, the Popular Literacy Volunteers were given increased administrative attention and provided with a new name midway through the campaign. They became known as the Urban Literacy Guerrillas, and some of the more dynamic groups raised funds to purchase their own uniforms, choosing brightly colored peasant shirts to complement the gray ones worn by the rural volunteers.

The second urban force was the Workers' Literacy Militia, which was coordinated by the Sandinista Labor Federation. This group was composed of factory workers, office personnel, market vendors, and government employees. This militia had a tighter structure than the other urban force and possessed a greater identification with its teaching units and with the crusade. As a group, its performance was considered more effective than that of the GUAS. T-shirts with the brightly colored letters MOA served to distinguish members of this militia.

Teaching Support Staff

The Nicaraguan Educators' Association (ANDEN) was in charge of recruiting and overseeing the teachers who served as the professional support staff for the EPA brigades, the militias, and the urban guerrillas. Like the Sandinista Youth Movement, ANDEN had also been formed during the liberation struggle, but it had generally been considered a fairly weak group, and its members had been less committed to the revolution than those of the citizen, labor, peasant, and professional organizations.

Most of ANDEN's more experienced and dedicated staff had been recruited directly for the campaign, which left a depleted and weakened leadership in charge of the massive support effort. In some cases, perhaps because of their dual tasks—union organizing and crusade support— members of the regional ANDEN staffs seemed to spend more time institution building than attending to their direct crusade responsibilities of supervision and support. To complicate matters, ANDEN functions overlapped with functions of the campaign's educational team, and confusion and bickering sometimes resulted. ANDEN leaders often felt that the crusade professional staff, because it included a mixture of university students and teachers, was not always the most experienced or academically qualified. Therefore, some ANDEN members tended to balk at receiving pedagogical instruction and orientation from college students.

Besides direct crusade functions, ANDEN was also responsible for two of the campaign's auxiliary activities: the Retaguardia, a summer day-care program for primary school children, and the Quincho Barrilete project, a literacy and basic education program for child street vendors. ANDEN supervision was also provided for a special literacy program for the blind. The crusade primer had been written in Braille, and classes were conducted in urban centers for blind children and adults.

Summary

From the very inception of the crusade, Nicaraguan educational planners saw it as a short, intense national campaign. Their ability to raise nongovernment funds for the program and to plan effectively won over the public officials who had questioned the viability of such a massive effort. Some of the major overall planning activities undertaken by the crusade staff between August and March involved the establishment of records. The national census was conducted, revealing an overall illiteracy rate of some 50 percent, and a series of record-keeping documents and tests were also devised to determine the progress of literacy students during the campaign.

The management and organization of the program were characterized by a single national coordinating structure, a decentralization of responsibilities through a regional network of provincial and municipal campaign offices, and the participation of citizens' groups and public institutions on all program levels through the nationwide system of literacy commissions. For organizational and mobilization purposes, the country was divided into two main areas—rural and urban—and each had its own separate corps of literacy promoters and support organizations.

4
Materials and Methods

At our first meeting, Fernando gave us this mountain of materials about literacy programs—primers, instruction sheets, books, evaluations, pamphlets, texts, heaps of paper. He pushed them over the desk to us and said, "Here, they're all yours. Check them out and see what makes sense!" They were from everywhere: Costa Rica, Peru, Brazil, Cuba, Guatemala, Mexico, Colombia, Tanzania, Guinea-Bissau, and São Tomé. Some places we had never heard of before.

—Roberto Saenz (1980)
Pedagogical Division Coordinator

The materials and methods of the campaign emerged from an intense, creative process of debate and discussion, a process that did not end with the publication of the literacy primer but continued throughout the crusade, enriching and strengthening the program. The basic learning materials consisted of a primer, a math text, and a teacher's guide. A ten-step teaching methodology was used with the primer. Two methods— a field diary and a process of community research—were used to facilitate the learning of the volunteer teachers, which was considered equal in importance to the learning of the literacy students. The daily living experience the rural volunteers shared with peasant families created a special bond that ultimately proved to be the most effective ingredient in the learning methodology.

As the campaign proceeded, weaknesses in the materials and difficulties in the method were identified. *Brigadistas* uncovered some; supervisors discovered others. Municipal and provincial staffs then compiled the findings of the two groups. The problems were reviewed and strategies were devised to solve the problems in a collective way, drawing upon the strengths and experiences of the different levels of the campaign structure. Sometimes this work was carried out in small groups of the national pedagogical staff, sometimes in shared discussion with provincial and municipal personnel, and sometimes in national meetings that included representatives from all levels of the crusade.

The design of the campaign's materials and methods presupposed the capacity of these people to learn and to grow together. They tackled problems, overcame difficulties, recognized some mistakes, ignored others, confronted contradictions, and proposed solutions, which sometimes worked as intended and sometimes did not. The development of the educational program was the result of the creative force of people who were given the opportunity to think, analyze, and learn from their experience in order to apply that learning directly to their work and life.

Initial Staffing, Planning, and Organization

Beginning with the announcement of the crusade in August 1979, the campaign's top leaders felt that the design of a literacy text and its accompanying teaching methods was the first important educational task facing the program staff. The challenge demanded inspiration and hard work. Roberto Saenz, the coordinator of the Pedagogical Division, remembers the first time he and the curriculum team leader, Katarina (Kitty) Grisby, arrived at Father Cardenal's temporary office:

> Fernando always knew how to challenge us even from the beginning. He said, "Well, we may have no chairs or tables or typewriters, but there are countries in the world that have Ministry of Education buildings twenty-three stories high that have never done literacy campaigns before." We felt like David facing Goliath, confident that even without tables and chairs, Nicaragua was going to be successful. After all, we had confronted the dictator with stones and homemade bombs and won. So when Fernando gave us this huge pile of literacy materials from countries all over the place, we were excited and eager. The only thing that worried us a little was whether we could read it all fast enough. [Saenz 1980]

Thus began the long, arduous task of reviewing and analyzing documentation from all over the world.

Grisby had recently received her master's degree in education from Canada's McGill University where she had studied for some six years. Her specialization had been curriculum development for primary school children, but she had no background in adult education or community organizing. In her early twenties, she was a tall woman of commanding presence, poised, convincingly articulate, and authoritative in both Spanish and English. Serious and hardworking, she attacked all tasks with zeal.

By the end of August, the efforts of Saenz and Grisby were reinforced by the addition of two more Nicaraguans—Guillermo Rothschuh and

Cesar Campos. Rothschuh was a well-known bushy-haired poet, flamboyant in word and verse, who had studied in Paris during the forties. He had been an early teacher of Carlos Fonseca, the founder of the *Frente*, and was a member of the Nicaraguan equivalent of the Royal Academy of the Spanish Language. Campos, a wiry, curly-haired twenty-eight-year old, was a former rural school director and had worked with Saenz in a small church-sponsored literacy program during the mid-seventies. Quiet and unassuming, he walked painfully with a limp from a wound sustained during the war. Campos had previously worked with Father Cardenal as a member of the Christian Student Movement. In fact, on the night of the 1972 earthquake that destroyed much of Managua, he and Father Cardenal had been together in the national cathedral participating in a hunger strike against Somoza. They were both fortunate to have survived the quake as the damage done to the church and nearby buildings was severe—just across the square more than fifty people in a nightclub were killed when the roof collapsed.

During the initial planning stage that took place in August and September, Grisby, Rothschuh, and Campos concentrated their efforts on reading, discussing, and writing position papers on different approaches to literacy including both national and community-based strategies as well as revolutionary and traditional ones. Saenz was already inundated with administrative duties and unable to participate with them in this work. They first examined the small Nicaraguan church projects and *Frente* efforts that had been conducted during the struggle against the dictatorship. They went on to study a range of programs from the more traditional Alfalit type (words studied in isolation with no teaching of problem solving or analytical skills) to those inspired by Freire and finally programs of national scope with the goal of social transformation. They carefully analyzed efforts from Cuba, Panama, Peru, Colombia, Costa Rica, Guatemala, Brazil, and São Tomé. They read *Letters from Guinea-Bissau* by Freire, Richard Fagan's classic book on the Cuban campaign, *The Transformation of Political Culture in Cuba*, as well as the UNESCO evaluation of that campaign's accomplishments.

One book by a private Colombian educational institution helped the group clarify the different programs under examination. *Lucharemos* contained a thoughtful, detailed analysis of the many different literacy programs of Latin America and was an attempt to demystify and provide a careful critique of the much-lauded efforts of both Freire and Cuba. The team thought so highly of the work that they wrote to Colombia inquiring about the possible participation of the authors as advisers to the Nicaraguan campaign. The Colombians, four in all, accepted and became part of the staff in October.

The campaign staff also followed the progress of a provincial literacy program in Estelí that had been organized by local teachers after the insurrection and approved by the new city government. Estelí had been a center of revolutionary organization and heavy fighting during the war. The experimental effort sought to prepare people in basic literacy so they could assume the new responsibilities that the revolution would require of them. The curriculum and teaching method were based on Paulo Freire's approach. Through dialogue with learners, literacy teachers chose study themes and words that were of individual interest to the students. The national team recognized the importance of the experiment as the first literacy effort under the revolution and as a means to predict the kinds of problems that the campaign would have to confront— problems of poor eyesight, resources, and transportation. The national team members concluded that the Estelí approach, while effective on the community level, could not be applied on a national level because of its specialized local characteristics, its individualized approach, and its demand for highly trained teachers. They reasoned that a national program that was to be carried out by nonprofessional volunteers and based on issues common to the entire country needed greater standardization.

Toward the end of September, just prior to the team's visit to Cuba, the group began to clarify certain general aspects regarding methods. Rothschuh submitted a first draft of the primer, and although the draft was considered too poetic and too linguistically complex for the campaign, it did serve as the impetus for later designs. The flavor of the proposed primer can be summarized by quoting part of its first lesson: "The long and terrible night is over, the black nightmare dead. In each home will shine the Nicaraguan sun of flaming gold" (Rothschuh 1980, 2). Another draft outline was submitted, but it, too, was rejected for being excessively political and rhetorical.

Immediately after the Cuban trip, the team attended the October planning seminar sponsored jointly by CELADEC of Peru and the Ebert Foundation of West Germany. Out of this meeting emerged the idea for the two organizational units that would be in charge of the development of the campaign's learning materials—the Curriculum Section, headed by Grisby, and the Research Section, directed by Campos. The Curriculum Section was assigned the specific task of designing the primer, the text on mathematics, and the teaching guide for the volunteers. The Research Section was to assist in this process by conducting the necessary research and by proposing lesson themes for the primer and content for the teaching manual. The tasks before them were enormous, their time line was all too short, and their problems were considerable. At that point, the two section directors had practically no staff; no chairs, desks, or typewriters; and less than three weeks in which to design the initial primer lessons and the accompanying teaching methodology. November 1 had been designated as the beginning of a national pilot project to test the materials, and January 1, the date for publication.

Personnel were urgently requested. The Ministry of Education provided two full-time staff members for the curriculum team, each of whom had had long years of experience in the educational system writing children's textbooks. The Colombian group contributed a curriculum expert in adult education. The specific task of developing the math text was given to a team of experts from an institute that had conducted radio programs to teach mathematics under the auspices of a U.S. Agency for International Development–funded project. For the Research Section, the *Frente* recommended a Puerto Rican sociology professor with experience in literacy programs, the Colombians offered part-time assistance, and the United Nations–affiliated Latin American Center for Basic Education (CREFAL) provided the services of two consultants in research design for six weeks. With their tasks assigned, the different teams divided up and began to work.

Primer: The Dawn of the People

Literacy Themes

The first challenge facing the teams in charge of the literacy primer was the selection of the lesson themes, themes that would serve as the basic organizing content of the book. In order to develop these literacy themes, the newly formed curriculum and research teams reviewed the work that had been done by the original planning group in August and September. A certain overlap of functions occurred. Each team discussed the pros and cons of the different approaches that had been studied and began to formulate a tentative list of themes. At the same time, the curriculum team began examining possible teaching methodologies. In mid-October, both groups presented their separate outlines of lesson themes to the Pedagogical Division coordinator. They turned out to be quite similar. The two groups felt that the themes should be national in scope, both because of the massive nature of the campaign and because of its importance in establishing a common knowledge base about the government's reconstruction and development plan. The research team proposed three broad theme areas with accompanying lesson topics focused on the revolution. These areas were history, current affairs of the nation, and international relations. The curriculum group also suggested three theme areas, concentrating on the defense of the revolution, its consolidation, and the socioeconomic development programs of the government.

A group composed of members from both teams drew up a consensus proposal that combined elements from each of the proposals and specified individual lesson topics. The final thematic structure of the primer included three major areas: (1) the history and development of the revolution, (2) aspects involving the defense and consolidation of the revolution, and (3) the socioeconomic programs of the Government of National Reconstruction. After the individual lesson themes were chosen, the Pedagogical Division coordinator assigned specific topics to different experts within the government. They developed one-to-two-page briefing papers on each topic, which included basic background information. It was felt that this material would be useful to the young volunteer teachers in promoting discussion and dialogue. When completed, the background papers were reviewed and revised by Father Cardenal and the *Frente* representative to the crusade, and finally they were approved for incorporation into the volunteers' teaching guide.

After the crucial decision on lesson topics had been made and the individual themes had been selected for the teaching manual, the curriculum group returned to its other urgent tasks—defining the teaching methodology, refining the structure of the primer; and choosing the actual topic sentences, key study words, syllable families, and photographs for each of the first lessons. The following is the list of theme sentences developed for each lesson.

Lesson	Theme Sentence
1	Sandino, leader of the revolution.
2	Carlos Fonseca said, "Sandino lives."
3	The FSLN led the people to liberation.
4	The guerrillas overcame the genocidal National Guard.
5	The masses rose up in an insurrection made by the people.
6	The Sandinista defense committees defend the revolution.
7	To spend little, save much, and produce a lot—that is making the revolution.
8	The revolutionary workers' associations propel production forward and keep vigil over the process.
9	People, army, unity: They are the guarantee of victory.
10	The agrarian reform guarantees that the harvest goes to the people.

11	With organization, work, and discipline, we will be able to rebuild the land of Sandino.
12	1980, the year of the war against illiteracy.
13	The pillage of imperialism is over: Nicaragua's natural resources are ours.
14	The nationalization of Somoza's businesses helps us recover our wealth and strengthen our economy.
15	Work is a right and a responsibility of every person in the land.
16	The revolutionary government expands and creates health centers for the people.
17	With the participation of everyone, we will have healthy recreation for our children.
18	We are forming work brigades to construct and improve our housing.
19	Women have always been exploited. The revolution makes possible their liberation.
20	The revolution opens up a road system to the Atlantic Coast. The Kurinwás is a navigable river.
21	Our democracy is the power of people belonging to organizations and participating.
22	There is freedom of religion for all those churches that support and defend the interests of the people.
23	The Sandinista revolution extends the bond of friendship to all peoples.

While the curriculum team was busy developing the primer, the research group was studying additional content areas for the teacher's manual—information for the *brigadistas* on first aid and on the different regions of the country, such as specifics on the kinds of food and illnesses prevalent in an area. This group also explored different approaches to research design and their applicability to the literacy campaign. At the same time, the team began meeting with a group from the National University to plan a linguistic study to be used in the design of the primer. This study, however, was never conducted, becoming a victim of time constraints.

During the later part of October, Paulo Freire spent two weeks visiting campaign personnel and working with the groups developing the methodology. In November, a member of Freire's Guinea-Bissau team spent almost three weeks with the national staff. Toward the end of November, during the revision of the primer's first draft, two Cuban experts in adult education arrived to work with the team as well.

Structure

The basic organizational structure of the primer changed significantly over the course of its development with respect to the sequential placement of syllables, but the lesson topics, sentences, and key words remained almost unchanged. The final structure of the primer consisted of twenty-three lessons and included the study of forty-two different syllable families. The text began with some reading-readiness exercises and a photograph showing a group of people reading. The photograph was selected to stimulate discussion about why people were interested in learning to read and write. To motivate participants and to give them a sense of accomplishment, the prelesson work concluded with a section on how to write one's own name. The following is a lesson-by-lesson list of key words and syllable families studied.

Lesson	Key Words	Simple Syllable Families	Inverse and Compound
1	la revolución	a-e-i-o-u	as, sas
2	Fonseca	sa-se-si-so-su	as, sas
	vive	va-ve-vi-vo-vu	vas
3	liberación	la-le-li-lo-lu	al, las
4	genocida	na-ne-ni-no-nu	an, nas, nal
5	masas	ma-me-mi-mo-mu	mas, mal, man
	popular	pa-pe-pi-po-pu	pas, pal, pan
6	defensa	da-de-di-do-du	ad, das, dal, dan
	Sandinista	ta-te-ti-to-tu	tas, tal, tan
7	poco	ca-co-cu	can, cal, cas
	mucho	cha-che-chi-cho-chu	chan, chas, chal
	hacer	ha-he-hi-ho-hu	has, han, hal
8	trabajadores	ba-be-bi-bo-bu	bas, ban, bal
	trabajadores	ja-je-ji-jo-ju	jas, jan, jal
	vigilan	ge-gi	gen, gel, ges
9	ejército	ci-ce	cen, ces, cel
10	recupera	ra-re-ri-ro-ru	ras, ran, ral
	recupera	ra-re-ri-ro-ru	ar, ran, ras, ral, rer
	tierra	rra-rre-rri-rro-rru	rres, rran, rril, rrer
11	llegaremos	lla-lle-lli-llo-llu	llas, llen, llar
	llegaremos	ga-go-gu	gas, gon, gal

12	año	ña-ñe-ñi-ño-ñu	ñas, ñan, ñal, ñar
	guerra	gue-gui	gues, guin, guel, guir
		gue-gui	guen, guis
	analfabetismo	fa-fe-fi-fo-fu	fas, fal, far
13	ya	ya-ye-yi-yo-yu	yas, yan, yal, yar
	saqueo	que-qui	quis, quin, quel
14	nacionalización	za-ze-zi-zo-zu	az, zas, zon, zul, zur
15	trabajo	tra-tre-tri-tro-tru	tras, tran, tral, trar
16	amplía	pla-ple-pli-plo-plu	plen, plar, plas
	pueblo	bla-ble-bli-blo-blu	blas, blen, blor
17	tendremos	dra-dre-dri-dro-dru	dras, dran, dril, drar
18	brigadas	bra-bre-bri-bro-bru	bras, bren, brol, brir
19	siempre	pra-pre-pri-pro-pru	pros, pren, prar
	explotada	ex-xi-xo	max, tex, exa, exis
20	integración	gra-gre-gri-gro-gru	gran, gres, grar, gral
	Atlántica	tlan-tlen-tlin-tlon-tlun	tlas, tlen
	Kurinwás	ka-ke-ki-ko-ku	
	Kurinwás	wa-wi	was, wen, wal
21	democracia	cra-cre-cri-cro-cru	cris, cran, cla, clan, clar
22	iglesias	gla-gle-gli-glo-glu	glan, glas
23	fraternales	fra-fre-fri-fro-fru	fras, fron, frac, fla, fle, fli, flo, flu, flan, flor, flic

First Draft and Pilot Project

The first draft of the primer was put together in October and included five lessons. It was written for the pilot project that was scheduled to begin in November and was designed to test the basic effectiveness of the approach. Less complex in structure than the later versions, the first draft was more innovative in some ways. After beginning with the practice of reading-readiness skills and the study of vowels, the pilot primer focused on simple direct syllable families (syllables beginning with consonants and ending with a vowel), five in all—*v, l, n, m,* and *p*. It introduced the concept of inverse syllables (those beginning with a vowel and ending with a consonant) in lesson three with the *l* family— al, el, il, ol, and ul—but returned to presenting only the direct families in lessons four and five. In the later versions, inverse and compound syllables (those beginning with a consonant and ending with a consonant) were introduced in the second lesson and presented in every subsequent lesson. The first primer, unlike the others, used drawings as well as photographs to stimulate discussion and highlighted each lesson's syllable family in red. The red highlighting, despite its effectiveness, had to be dropped from the final primer because it was too expensive to print.

The pilot project to assess the effectiveness of the primer draft began in November. Organized by the curriculum team and conducted in ten different rural and urban locations around the country, it began with a brief three-day workshop. Some thirty-three teachers and students selected from ANDEN and Juventud were trained as literacy promoters and supervisors for the project.

The training workshop for the pilot project participants began on schedule, November 1. As described by some of the pedagogical staff, it was a rather last-minute affair, and there was considerable improvisation. In the end, however, the workshop provided the organizers with many important insights. The training team was responsible for conducting the workshop, but its work was frustrated by organizational difficulties because there had not been prior coordination of the three pedagogical teams—research, curriculum, and training. Time pressures and different work priorities were the attributed causes of this lack of coordination. In the future, such coordination problems would surface frequently. Despite unanimous agreement after the workshop about the importance of joint coordinating meetings, they were not held. Requests were made for more participation by the Pedagogical Division coordinator, but he was busy with overall administrative tasks and could never find time.

About a day and a half of the pilot project workshop was devoted to curriculum activities. The primer and the teaching method to be used were presented, and one simulation conducted to practice their application. Time was allocated to mastering the evaluation instruments designed to assess the materials, to reviewing the organizational structure of the pilot project, and to defining responsibilities and tasks. Another day was dedicated to general research activities, learning how to take field notes and how to study community life from a sensitive, committed perspective rather than from the traditional elitist, academic neutral one. The remaining time was used for introductory speeches, presentation exercises, and final evaluations.

The three-day workshop revealed several weaknesses in the materials and method, some of which were later overcome. In certain cases, new materials were created on the spot, such as several record-keeping documents. The "Pilot Project Workshop Evaluation" (Cruzada Nacional de Alfabetización 1979b, 1–2) points out specifically that the guidelines for the decodification of the lesson photographs were too general and that the language was too academic. A similar criticism was made of the community research materials, and there was concern that their use might detract from other activities. The importance of including simulations in order to practice skills and apply knowledge that had been presented in an expository form was verified by the evaluation. Despite the problems of coordination, the workshop participants left with great enthusiasm and, as the project reports would later reveal, with sufficient skills to carry out the task.

The pilot project that was implemented in the subsequent months demonstrated that the primer and its method were effective in helping people learn to read and write. Despite certain problems, the materials and method could also on occasion help volunteers generate an animated, if somewhat superficial, discussion among participants. There were several fairly immediate insights gained from the pilot project: some related to the primer graphics, others to linguistic context. Drawings proved inferior to photographs in stimulating dialogue. People identified more readily with the photographs. The line drawings seemed to be too stylized and removed from reality to involve participants actively. However, the quality of the photographs used was too poor for them to be completely and consistently effective. Certain members of the project staff also noted that some photographs were not conducive to generating a critical dialogue and that clearer criteria needed to be established for photograph selection. In terms of linguistic problems, there was a confusion between the symbols for uppercase *i* and lowercase *l* because they were indistinguishable. This problem was solved by writing the capital *i* like this— *I*. In the final primer, attempts were made to incorporate most of these insights into the text. (A separate primer was developed for immediate use with the armed forces.)

Final Drafts and Inconsistencies

The next draft of the primer, also only five lessons in length, was put together in November for the first real training group, eighty teachers and university students who would become the educational foundation of the entire program. After an initial fifteen-day workshop, this group of eighty spent a month in the field using the primer and testing the actual effectiveness of the training approach in preparing future volunteers. The primer they were given turned out to be significantly more complex and difficult to use than the first draft that had been used in the pilot project.

The curriculum team had decided to make, what seemed to many of its members, only minor revisions in the sequencing of the syllables studied. This decision, however, provoked an animated debate among some of the team members. Concern was registered that the changes being proposed might be more problematic than anticipated and should be tested first. Other team members argued that based on their teaching experience, the proposed modifications should cause little difficulty and promote a quicker rate of mastery. The changes were made, but what had seemed minor turned out to be major. Two revisions proved especially troublesome. One new syllable family was added—the *s* group—and the study of both compound and inverse syllables was introduced with the first syllable family. The study of these more complex syllable groups was continued in each of the following lessons as well. The *s* family was placed second in order of presentation, after the *v* group, and was added because its use enriched the number of words that could be formed.

Certain inconsistencies in the syllable sequencing were noticed immediately in the second primer draft; others, more fundamental, went undiscovered until the third and final draft had already gone to press. An obvious problem with the syllable sequence occurred in lesson two and involved a simple oversight: A compound syllable was introduced that had not yet been learned. To be specific, the first group studied was the direct syllable family—va, ve, vi, vo, vu—but immediately after its presentation, the compound syllable group was introduced—vas, ves, vis, vos, vus. The problem was that the *s* family had not yet been taught, so learners could not be expected to decipher the compound syllables being presented to them.

The final draft of the primer went to print with this inconsistency supposedly solved: The order of the syllables studied was simply reversed. The *s* group became the first family studied, and the *v* the second. This seemingly simple solution created serious, unanticipated learning difficulties for people, difficulties that might have been avoided if there had been time to do a linguistic study. As has been mentioned, there had not been such a study, even though one had been proposed.

Many members of the first training group identified the same linguistic problem in their practice teaching experience. Almost unanimously, they complained that the students got stuck on the *s* group. By the time the full extent of the problem was discovered, however, the primer had gone to press, and the *s* family remained. The basic difficulty was a linguistic one, complicated by the fact that compound syllables—sas, ses, sis, sos, sus—and the inverse ones—as, es, is, os, us—were being taught at the same time. Most Nicaraguans tend not to pronounce a final *s*, so it was difficult for the volunteers to determine whether a person had really mastered these syllables or not. It created confusion and frustration for everyone, and usually slowed down learning. During the actual campaign, in offices around the country, this problem jumped out from the graphs tacked to the walls that charted learners' progress. Large numbers of people remained stuck on lesson two, the *s* family, for long periods of time. Time pressures had curtailed the linguistic study that had originally been planned, and in the rush of deadlines, this important aspect had been overlooked.

Method

The teaching method and step-by-step procedures used to facilitate the use of the literacy primer underwent two significant changes. One was made after the pilot project and discussions with Paulo Freire, and the other was based on the experience of the crusade itself. Some minor procedures were simplified, others were expanded. The final method consisted of a dialogue discussion around each lesson's photograph and then a ten-step process to present and practice each syllable family studied.

Dialogue

The dialogue process underwent several revisions. Its evolution reflected a maturation in thinking on the part of the team regarding the special significance and contribution this part of the method provided to the learner. An understanding of the dialogue as an analytic, critical, and transforming process that was fundamental to literacy grew and deepened over the course of the campaign. The development of this process, however, was not an easy or a smooth one, and a workable, methodological approach was not put into practice until at least one month after the volunteers had gone into the field.

The documents for the pilot project training included the first concrete attempt at presenting the dialogue process on paper. The explanation and description provided were general and contained four steps: (1) description and analysis of the photograph, (2) relation of the photograph to the learners' personal lives, (3) relation of key sentence to the photograph, and (4) examination and planning of future tasks that were implied in the photograph's theme. Although a general question guide to direct the discussion was provided, the process was not clearly described. The essential purpose of the dialogue was seen as a means to transform reality. "We should describe and analyze reality so we can know it, but more important, so we can transform it" (Perezón et al. 1979, 3).

During training, the pilot project group found that the language describing the method was too academic and the orientations provided for the dialogue were too general. To compound the problem, the dialogue explanation presented to the group was poorly typed, the steps ran together with not enough space between paragraphs, and the pages were not in the proper order. Realizing these difficulties, the curriculum group attempted to respond on the spot by designing specific questions for each theme, but the questions developed were rather traditional, abstract information-seeking questions as opposed to personal problem-solving ones (except for the first photograph, which did not have an accompanying information backup sheet). The following (from Cruzada Nacional de Alfabetización November 1979c, 1–2) is an example of the questions that were developed.

Leading questions

I. 1. Describe what appears in the photo.
    2. Why are they meeting?
    3. Why could they not meet before?
    4. What is happening now in Nicaragua?
    5. How can we achieve better results from our meetings?
    6. What can our revolution gain from these meetings that are happening all over Nicaragua?

II. 1. Who is Augusto César Sandino?
     2. What role did he play in the Nicaraguan revolution?
     3. What importance does he have in history beyond Nicaragua?
     4. How does Sandino guide us today in the revolution? . . .

V. 1. What resources did the guerrillas fight with against the generals?
    2. What allowed our people to conquer the generals?
    3. What do the people obtain with the Sandinista revolution?
    4. What is our task in the actual struggle now?

VI. 1. What popular organizations participated in the insurrection?
     2. Who led our people in the insurrection?
     3. Why did the people participate in an organized way?
     4. What importance did people's participation have in the insurrection and what does it have now in the revolution?

Another fundamental problem that the pilot project participants identified during their training, although initially it was not clearly understood, was they had difficulty in generating an active discussion about the images in lessons two and three, a photograph of Sandino's face and a drawing of Carlos Fonseca, respectively. In the practice teaching during December and January, the first training group of eighty identified the root of the problem: Many people were not able to recognize the figures, much less have a personal identification with them, because Somoza's educational system had relegated the men to the category of bandit and terrorist. As a result, discussion was often limited, and the literacy teacher had to rely on a lecture and a question-and-answer method of discussion.

Taking into consideration the vagueness and confusion of the original explanation of how the dialogue was to be conducted and the fact that no specific discussion guidelines had been provided, the curriculum team, in a last-minute overnight rush to correct the problem, developed a series of concrete questions for each lesson theme. They basically believed that the dialogue was a "means to reflect over the past, speak about the present, and discuss the participation of everyone in the building of a new Nicaragua" (Alemán et al. 1979, 7). The study questions were intended only as a guide to facilitate a deeper understanding and analysis of issues, but because they were included as a suggested part of the dialogue process in the final teacher's manual, they were taken and used by many volunteers faithfully, word for word. The questions tended to be written in a formal academic style, based directly on the guide's information background sheet provided for each lesson rather than on a process of life-related dialogue based on a problemization or an analysis of the photograph. For example (Saenz et al. 1980, 45, 48, 60, 80):

I. 1. What are the reasons why more than half of the Nicaraguan population over ten years of age does not know how to read and write?
2. What effects will be felt by the literacy promoters as a result of their participation in the crusade?
3. Why is it essential to the revolution that peasants and workers learn to read and write?
4. Why will the crusade increase national unity? . . .

II. 1. Against whom did Sandino fight and whom did he defend?
2. At what time and why did the figure of Sandino emerge in Nicaragua's history?
3. Why and until what point does Sandino propose a political-military tactic of flexibility and alliance?
4. What kind of interests cannot be given up in this tactic and why?
5. What were the achievements of Sandino's struggle for Nicaragua and for the peoples of Latin America?
6. What was the experience and political-military lessons learned by the FSLN from Sandino?
7. Why is it said that Sandino was the guide of our revolution?
. . .

VI. 1. What support did the civil defense committees (CDC) provide to the insurrection?
2. On behalf of whose interests do the Sandinista defense committees (CDS) function?
3. What is the principal task of the CDS?
4. Why should all neighborhoods organize into CDS?
5. What work has the CDS carried out in your neighborhood?
6. What are the principal difficulties of your CDS and how can they be resolved? . . .

X.   1. What natural resources does the country have?
2. Who benefited from the exploitation before?
3. Why did the Somoza system permit the sacking of our natural resources?
4. Who is going to benefit now from our natural resources? Why?
5. Why is it important to care for the forests even though we need land to cultivate?
6. What is necessary in your region to protect the area's natural resources?

Time pressures caused by the campaign's fixed and immutable starting date made adequate planning difficult and affected this aspect of the method considerably. As the program evolved, severe weaknesses became apparent. In the first weeks of the crusade's operation, many of the young volunteers, despite cautions against such a practice, followed the background questions as if they were rigid, unbreakable rules and not as reference points as intended. Participant response to such an approach was limited, of course. Many volunteers got discouraged with trying to generate discussion, and some quit trying altogether, rejecting the questions because of what they considered to be their biased political overtones.

With these problems weighing on their minds, the month of April was a hectic one for members of the curriculum team. During Pedagogical Division staff visits to the field and in discussions with local personnel and observations of volunteers, it became clear to everyone that the difficulties people were having in generating a critical analytical discussion were widespread and serious. In a meeting of the national and provincial pedagogical staffs in mid-April, the problem was discussed, and different solutions were proposed. The provincial group, swamped with other duties, looked to the members of the national curriculum team to investigate and propose a better approach. The purpose of the dialogue was reevaluated, and once more, its transforming nature and problem-posing aspects were affirmed. "The dialogue is not only intended to examine reality but should contribute to transforming it" (Saenz et al. 1980, 35). In reflecting on the problem, the coordinator of the curriculum team emphasized that the team had come to realize that the process did not just involve acquiring information but depended upon people becoming active in changing and improving their community.

> As the crusade progressed, we realized the need for people not just to remain at a level of pure awareness or knowledge about what the revolution proposed but as going beyond that to become engaged in a process of transformation, actually transforming the world in which they lived by combining what the revolution's development programs offered with the concrete reality and experience of their existence. [Grisby 1980]

The research team shared this view and described the purpose of the dialogical method this way: "Literacy, a process to discover your world and transform it, to be able to read reality and write history" (Campos et al., October 1979, 3).

After much discussion and consultation, a concrete set of step-by-step guidelines was elaborated based on the actual photographs and not on the information sheets. The five-step process consisted of a series of suggested questions that were designed to help participants develop analytical skills, a sense of social responsibility, and a critical understanding of the commitment to the revolution. The questions proceeded from simple to difficult and encouraged the students to describe the contents of a photograph; analyze the situation portrayed; relate the particular situation to their lives, to their community, and to the problems facing them; solve problems identified by the group; and engage participants in transforming reality by committing themselves to solving the problem and becoming active in the national programs of social change.

The question format was, of course, not the same kind of approach advocated by Freire for a literacy program under a political system in which the poor are unrepresented and oppressed. The Nicaraguan approach took as a given the viability and legitimacy of the government's programs for reordering the society to benefit the poor. The process was designed for a nation undergoing a profound structural transformation in which power relationships among people, groups, and governments were changing radically. Through the creation of organized channels of civil participation, power was shifting from the wealthy elite toward the poor majority. The dialogue process was clearly intended to engage the poor in the challenge of the country's reconstruction on all levels—political, cultural, social, and economic.

The sample question guide, which was designed to address the method's weaknesses and was provided to the volunteers, was based on lesson six—dealing with community civil defense committees organized by the

FSLN. These local neighborhood groups had flourished in the cities during the war and had been used with great effectiveness to organize resistance and defense activities, such as food distribution channels, escape tunnels, bomb shelters, street barricades, and clandestine hospitals. Once the revolution had been won, these groups took the name Sandinista defense committees (CDS) and launched into new activities that combined both defense and development: organizing neighborhood cleanup and reconstruction projects, registering children for vaccination campaigns, conducting surveys for the literacy crusade to discover who in the community wanted to learn and who was willing to teach, watching for possible counterrevolutionary activity, and checking that store owners abided by the government price controls for basic commodities.

The five-part question guide, designed to promote a critical but committed dialogue, contained the following elements (Marino et al. 1980, 3):

Activities	*Example*
1. Description of photograph	*Who* appears in the photo? *What* are they doing? *Where* are they meeting?
2. Analysis of photograph	*Why* are they meeting? *For what* concrete purpose are they meeting?
3. Relationship of situation portrayed in photo to real life of the literacy student	*At this moment* is there a CDS in your community? *Since when* has it existed? *Before,* why did it not function? *What objectives* does the CDS fulfill in the Sandinista Revolution? *What activities* has the CDS conducted in your community? *What* are the problems that our CDS has? What are the *causes* of these problems?
4. Search for solutions	How can we *solve* the problems?
5. Group commitment to transformation	What can we *do as a group* in order to solve the problems? What do we *promise* and commit ourselves to doing?

One of the limitations of this revised process, however, was that the photographs in the primer had not been selected according to clear criteria for promoting a problematizing critical dialogue. Inexperience with the method, a limited selection of photographs, and a poor choice of the photographs that were available were the reasons for this situation. As a result, even with an appropriate question format, the dialogue process was difficult. For example, the photograph for lesson six, on community civil defense committees, showed a group of men, women, and children sitting and standing on what looked like a porch. A man with glasses stood in front of them reading from a tablet of paper. There was no indication in the picture that the group was a defense committee, the activity depicted was limited, and the relationships between people were sterile and uninteresting. The important community work that the committees were conducting was not depicted in the photograph, nor was the sense of participation. The people looked stilted, like they were posing for their first photograph, which they very well may have been. Instead, the photographs should have showed objects or scenes that could have provided the means for learners to personally project their comparisons, and they should have showed relationships between people in order to provoke thought and analysis.

Another related difficulty in generating an effective dialogue was the fact that although great emphasis was given to relating the situation portrayed in the photograph to the life of the learner, a certain fundamental element was missing—an intimate, direct, personal relationship of the individual with the problem situation presented by the photograph. Questions were oriented toward the person as a member of a social group, not as an individual. Questions like, How does this problem affect your own life? How are you individually helping to resolve it? and What has your personal experience been in this situation? were lacking. This omission was probably due in part to the concern that values and attitudes of cooperation and community responsibility should be stressed instead of those of selfish, self-seeking individualism. However, direct personal questions could have helped to engage participants in the development and education processes more effectively by stimulating their maximum interest in the study theme and more directly activating their sense of personal responsibility for transforming the problem situation.

In political and development terms, this omission was potentially costly and resulted in a debate at the campaign's conclusion when the time existed for a more thoughtful analysis. Some planners were worried that such wide-ranging discussions could have led participants to express opinions that were not in accord with the common good, thus disrupting the possibilities for developing a revolutionary commitment. Others believed that only through open discussion and confrontation could attitudes be challenged and eventually changed. Stressing the psycho-logical elements of such a process, these people believed that the personal aspects of the dialogue provided one of the most effective structured ways of overcoming selfishness and developing a community-oriented consciousness. More significantly, proponents of this approach argued that without reflection over personal issues, revolutionary consciousness would be superficial and tend not to endure over time.

Although the dialogue process had serious weaknesses, in comparison to education methods used previously in Nicaragua it was a great step forward, a first attempt to overcome the authoritarian practices of the past. The problems and achievements of the approach were put into perspective by one member of the training team.

> The initial part of every lesson was the dialogue, which during the training had been practiced in simulation form. In the pilot project, we detected problems in the application of the method, and as the crusade grew, it became obvious that we needed to deepen the dialogue process. As a result, we designed an instruction sheet to help the young volunteers.
>
> But the most diffiicult part for the kids was to pass from the superficial discussion of the photo to an in-depth analysis based on people's lives which would lead to action. Given the reality of the situation, we have to say that the dialogue in the context of concrete lessons was one of the weakest areas of the approach, but if you look at all the accumulation of these dialogues and compare the method to the kind of teaching that went on before, then we accomplished our mandate, but it was far from perfect. [Cendales 1980]

During the crusade, the team came to realize the obvious—that dialogue occurred during the literacy teaching process itself as well as in the daily living experience and that the latter was perhaps the richer and more profound exchange. A greater appreciation was also gained in regard to how difficult it was to generate dialogue as a pure educational method in the isolation of a study session. Effective discussion and analysis were best promoted when dialogue emerged naturally from concrete activities surrounding the organization and implementation of a community project. In such situations, dialogue was the result of an immediate problem-solving process in which theory and practice came together in a common praxis. People analyzed their environment, planned ways to improve it, and learned from their experience (McFadden 1983).

Ten-Step Process

A ten-step process followed the dialogue discussion and was used to present and practice each syllable family studied. The steps included:

1. The reading and relating of the lesson sentence to the dialogue—for example, "Carlos Fonseca dijo: Sandino vive."
2. The reading and explanation of the underlined key word: vive.
3. The separation of the word into syllables and the identification of the syllable family to be studied: vi ve.
4. The reading of the syllable family in its direct form, both in lowercase letters and beginning with a capital:

vi, ve, va, vo, vu

Vi, Ve, Va, Vo, Vu

5. Reading aloud, tracing in the primer, and writing on the blackboard the syllables in step four.
6. The creation and writing of words by participants combining all the possible syllables studied (both printing them in the primer and on the blackboard).
7. The reading of the inverse and/or compound syllable groups, beginning first with a review of the direct group:

vi, ve, va, vo, vu

vis, ves, vas, vos, vus

8. The reading and writing of words and sentences by participants:

vive vivo ave Eva

Visa vasos aviso suave

Eva vive.

Usa ese vaso.

Vi esas aves.

9. The writing of a dictation containing several separate words and at least one sentence.
10. The careful writing of a sentence for legibility:

Eva vio ese aviso.

This ten-step method evolved over time, undergoing important changes. During the initial planning stage in October, Freire made a valuable contribution to the process. After discussing the general idea of the method with the team, his principal criticism concerned the fact that at that time, no step allowed the learners to create their own words or sentences. He pointed out this oversight to the team and emphasized the vital importance of personal word creation to any literacy program but especially to a liberating one. The satisfaction and excitement of creating words increased a learner's sense of individual worth. The group immediately incorporated his suggestion into the method by adding step number six.

In the first draft of the primer, the process consisted of more steps than in the final draft. The number varied from ten to fifteen. It was felt that the original process was somewhat cumbersome and should be standardized, so four of the original steps were collapsed and condensed into two. The tracing of syllables in the primer was combined with writing them on the blackboard, and the oral and written formation of words and sentences were joined into one step as well. Three steps were eliminated because they seemed nonessential. One involved drawing the syllable family in the air, and the other two were simple identification exercises—drawing lines between like syllables and underlining the lesson syllables in unknown words. An early final step, involving word comprehension and creation, was eliminated because of its apparent redundancy. An incomplete phrase or sentence was given with an empty space left for the missing word. The learners had to read the phrase and think of a word they could write that would make sense in the context of the sentence. In the final primer another step was added— that of copying an entire sentence—to practice and test printing skills for legibility.

Although the streamlining of the method helped to make the process easier for the literacy teachers to master, it also had its drawbacks. For new learners, especially unsure, hesitant adults, the two syllable identification steps were relatively simple and helped to build their confidence and prepare them for later, more difficult steps. These steps were brief and required little time to complete. Their elimination shortened the number of procedural steps but probably did not result in a smoother learning process, especially at the beginning of study when the learners needed more reinforcement and practice. The emphasis on a common number of steps for the entire primer made this graduated approach impossible.

The experience of the campaign proved that eliminating one of the word comprehension and creation steps was a mistake. Probably one of the most valuable lessons learned from the crusade regarding the primer's ten-step method had to do with the fact that the learners needed more practice in both comprehension and word and sentence formation. In order to correct this weakness when it was discovered during the course of the campaign, educational planners developed an additional list of eight comprehension exercises for the learners.

To respond to difficulties that arose in completing step six (the word creation process that did survive the streamlining), some learning games were developed that were similar to Scrabble® and dominoes. The direct syllable families that had already been studied were written on small squares of paper, and these could then be moved around by the players in order to test out syllable combinations more directly. A simple Scrabble board was also distributed to be used with specially printed squares containing individual letters. Sitting in small groups for the domino type of game, participants were each given an opportunity to form words from the syllable squares for a certain time period. The group, in consultation with the teacher, would decide on the validity of each word, and then a partner would copy each accepted word down for comparison with other students' attempts. The Scrabble type of game was almost identical to the English version and was played after the domino game had been mastered.

This approach of direct manipulation and friendly competition proved far superior to the original teaching aid used in this step—a chart of syllables tacked on the wall from which learners were supposed to devise new words. The chart proved a failure. People encountered great difficulty in joining the syllables mentally to form written words on a page. The students needed to experiment directly with the individual syllables by moving them around, combining and recombining the syllable squares until they actually discovered and created a word.

During the pilot project and the continuation of the training program, it was discovered that the pace of learning accelerated significantly around lesson nine. As one teaching supervisor described it:

> A big change had occurred around Lesson 8 or 9, a kind of click. At that stage—sometimes several lessons earlier or later, depending on the individual—the logical pattern of the alphabet became evident. No longer was the learner performing an arbitrary act of memorization with each separate word and syllable. Instead, there was recognition of the actual relationship between letters and sounds, a relationship that in Spanish is utterly constant. Suddenly the pattern of the primer was falling into place. Each exercise brought a new consonant sound that combined with the familiar vowels to form new syllables . . . and new words. The exercises began to take on new meaning and the whole process was infused with the excitement of discovery. Although almost half of the consonants and blends still remained to be studied, the foundation was finished. . . . as we hit Lesson 10, the "clicks" could be heard like gunshot echoing through the valley. [Hirshon 1983, 162]

Community-Action Research: Learning for Transformation

In addition to the primer and its teaching method, another learning process was designed. Community-action research was created to stimulate a broader community involvement in the crusade and the national efforts of transformation. This unique research process was an attempt to incorporate the different methodological aspects of the campaign—both the political and the pedagogical—into one coherent whole. It was designed to involve not only the literacy students but the entire community in the process of learning and transformation. Essentially, the purpose of the research was to develop a means by which a community could study itself—its history; its culture; its social, political, and economic conditions—and examine its problems. In this way, it was felt that people could acquire the skills and personal commitment that were needed if they were to become involved in effectively addressing community problems and assuring equitable forms of development.

Philosophical Foundation

In developing the idea, the research team began with the premise that literacy was a process of discovering reality, interpreting it, and transforming it. Within this framework, the team members asked themselves what the role of research should be to complement such a literacy process. "What sectors of society should research support? What should research stand for? Who should carry it out? We reached the conclusion that if literacy is a process of inquiry, of revealing reality undertaken in a joint dialectical relationship between the learner who also teaches and the teacher who also learns, then we felt that research should be that same kind of reciprocal process" (Suarez 1980).

The foundation of community-action research rested on a certain understanding of human knowledge. The research team began its examination of the concept by stressing the fundamental nature of practice and of concrete experience in the formation of theory and the creation of knowledge.

> In order to know something, in order to comprehend history it is necessary to participate in the actual struggle to transform it. Human knowledge emerges from practice, practice being the basis of theory. . . . If we emphasize theory in our work it is because theoretical understanding can and should guide our actions. . . . Knowledge begins through practice—through concrete experience. All theoretical knowledge acquired in this continual process of learning needs to be rechanneled back to serve, nurture and improve our future action. . . .
>
> This process of knowledge we are describing leads us to a new understanding of truth. . . . the problem of knowing whether a theory is true or not . . . is solved only when we apply that theoretical knowledge to social practice, to concrete action within society and then examine whether it has achieved the intended results and met our objectives. . . . this is not determined on the basis of a subjective appreciation of a theory, but rather on its objective results when applied to a given social reality,

practice, or action, in other words it depends on its historic effectiveness, whether it's proven true by history. . . .

The truth, therefore, is a truth in process, a truth that is revealed in the doing. Each moment of knowledge is a relative truth on the road to reaching a fuller and deeper understanding of the complete truth. Dogmatism which considers the truth as something definitive, ahistoric and absolute is completely disqualified, therefore. Affirming the historic nature of truth, however, does not imply a support for relativism in which nothing is true or everything is true. [Campos et al., October 1979, 2–3]

The position of a researcher or educational planner in such a context should not be one of an elitist, omnipotent academic who comes with fixed theories to study and instruct the ignorant masses or to present them with preconceived frameworks into which all reality must fit. According to this view, the educational planner has to first learn from the people, from practice, from working together with the community.

Research for transformation is research based on dialogue, developed with the participation of the community, and taken up by its members to nurture and energize their development and the revolutionary process— the praxis of creation. . . . The role of the researcher who studies the reality lived by a human group cannot be one that is doctrinaire, which attempts to impose a science . . . but rather one which attempts to innovate, to make "critical" an already existing human activity. The task of the researcher cannot be a paternalistic one of popularizing a science elaborated by university scholars in ivory towers for the unschooled masses. Their task, rather, is to clarify and bring to light the knowledge already present in the life and practice of the people. . . . the community experience being their fountain of inspiration and point of reference. [Campos et al., October 1979, 5]

The team stressed the importance of this research process because it offered people permanent, enduring learning tools that would allow them to participate in society creatively and critically, committed to the process of social change. Team members emphasized that the changing dynamic nature of both experience and theory demanded this kind of approach. Knowledge is continually expanding, and life is forever evolving in new and different ways. Today's information and content, they stressed, become obsolete quickly. Moreover, living in a revolutionary society that is undergoing rapid transformation requires that people respond and learn in situations of accelerated change. Static, memorized information loses its usefulness quickly in such situations. People need to acquire learning skills, to become explorers, creators, and researchers in the constant building and pursuit of knowledge and social transformation.

> The deepening of our Revolution requires a scientific rigor. Reality is not static; we make and shape it by our actions. It is historic. Perceiving and understanding reality in relation to its changing nature is the only way to comprehend and know it in its full and complete dimension. . . . Revolutionary transformation requires that the people become permanent researchers. [Campos et al., November 1979, 1]

Specifically, community-action research was seen as a reciprocal, cooperative process. On the one hand, it was viewed as a means for the volunteers to learn about the living conditions of their literacy students so that they could be more effective, sensitive, and critical in their own work. Simultaneously, it was conceived of as a structured way for the students to teach the teachers and, in turn, to discover more about their own lives and history. By gaining a broader, increasingly critical perspective on their world and their role in its development, community members could become effective, thoughtful, committed participants in the social transformation process. The research process was also considered to be a way for community members to recover local history and culture and to discuss why these aspects of their lives had been so long repressed and denigrated by the dictatorship—stories about the origins of their villages from the times of Indian civilization through the Spanish conquest to the war of liberation, legends, folktales, family histories, poems, and songs. The process was created to help people take pride in their heritage and their rural culture and to understand the historic roots of their poverty, the nation's underdevelopment, and the revolutionary struggle itself. Through community-action research, it was felt that people could acquire the learning tools to continue studying their experience, analyzing and processing information and using that research to improve their own lives long after the volunteers had left.

Community Learning

The community research process was designed to occur in two stages, beginning with the particular—in the literacy groups—and proceeding to the general—in town meetings. The first phase included the development of a diagnostic study conducted by each literacy group in the community. This stage was aimed at examining the many different social, political, economic, and cultural aspects of the surrounding area, beginning with a study of the region's history and its relationship to the system of injustice under which the community had been living. The emphasis was always on searching out the reasons behind a given situation and not in just providing a simple description. A research framework was provided to assist the volunteers and participants that included categories to help focus the study and guide questions to facilitate the process of data collection. For example, one category dealt with the history of the area, and some of its study questions included

Who were some of the first people in the area?
What did they do for a living?
Why did they come to settle there?
What was the participation of the people in the struggle against the dictatorship? Why? [Campos et al., November 1979, 7]

Some other categories dealt with the production system, population, food, health, culture, and social organization of community.

The group was, first, to generate a list of specific categories and questions they wished to focus on and, then, to consult the framework for other possible areas of study that might have been overlooked and for concrete questions to guide their investigation. Finally, the group was to decide on how it wanted to gather the information—basically, either through observation or dialogue or a combination of the two.

The group's analysis of the information could be done after data collection had been completed and also midway through the investigation. The object of this step was to order the information according to areas, check its reliability as much as possible, and begin to sort out conclusions for each category studied so that final conclusions could then be reached. All the literacy promoters in one community were to meet as many times as was necessary in order to consolidate and cross-check the information. Each group was to write up a collective document describing the results of its work. The presentation of the final study, however, was not to be an academic report but was to be a presentation devised by the group itself, using such forms of expression as drawings, diagrams, maps, charts, folk art, poems, songs, and sociodramas.

The presentation would form part of the second stage of the process, which would involve the entire community in study, analysis, and planning. In a town meeting held in conjunction with citizen and labor organizations, the literacy groups would present their research effort to the community for discussion. In this way, understandings would be deepened and conclusions enriched. Out of this community assembly, or series of meetings, would come concrete action plans to address some of the priority problems that had been identified.

Volunteer Learning

Another part of the community research program focused solely on the volunteers—the writing of a field diary. These field notes were to be an integral component of the research process as they would help the volunteers draw conclusions from their practical experience. *Brigadistas* thus could begin to develop and test theory based on their own practice. The battlefield diary of the respected peasant commandant, Germán Pomares, was chosen as an example of this kind of learning tool in which the synthesis of experience became the basis for knowing—in this case, knowing what worked on the field of battle and what did not. As revealed in his diary, lessons were learned through concrete experience. Theories were developed and then confirmed or discarded depending on the results of action. Through the writing and sharing of the field diary with other squadron members, it was felt that the volunteers would gain practice in knowledge building, in learning how to learn and how to know.

Application

The concept of community-action research as developed by the Nicaraguan team, with its emphasis on people's participation and development, was similar in purpose to the ideas of the Colombian social scientist Octavio Fals Borda (1980) and the work done by the Participatory Research Group of the International Council for Adult Education (1981). The concept proved very effective in the first phase of training when workshop participants went out into the countryside for a month of teaching experience. The newly trained literacy promoters took inspiration from the basic research outline presented to them during training, expanded upon it, adapted it, and became articulate, enthusiastic advocates of the process. Their work with communities demonstrated the concept's creative power to motivate people, expand their awareness and understanding of the problems facing the community and the country, and engage them in the process of national reconstruction on the local level. In some villages after group discussions, the people created songs and skits about their local problems—town rivalries, personal inadequacies, fears about learning, or the need for a bridge. After performing before an audience of family and friends, further discussion and analysis were generated. In one or two instances, this process led to concrete collective actions to overcome the problem.

Before the results of the method could be evaluated, however, some members of the national pedagogical team registered serious concerns about the viability of the approach in a national campaign. They doubted that young people could coordinate such activities and were concerned that the approach might distract the people's energies from learning how to read and write. However, when the first training group returned from the field, its members convinced the top crusade leadership that the approach was effective in mobilizing communities and that it enriched the literacy learning and dialogue as well. Their committed enthusiasm was powerful and contagious, and the decision to include the approach as part of the program was made. However, because of a strict page limitation for the teaching manual and last-minute editing by people who were not familiar with the process, the original scope of the research was reduced to a field study to be conducted principally by the volunteers themselves.

The elimination of many elements of the community-action research is one more example of how trying to undertake a national campaign in a short time brought various pressures to bear on the program. Among these pressures were conflicting demands on staff, publishers' deadlines, financial considerations, technical errors, a staff that was spread too thin, logistic difficulties in bringing people in from the field for collective decision making, and differences in pedagogical orientation.

In the final version, the strong community participation component and the town meetings were not specified, so the cohesiveness of the concept was lost. Despite these serious oversights, however, the daily living and working experience with community members led some of the literacy brigades, often in cooperation with traveling cultural brigades, to promote some of the same activities that were involved in the community research approach. In such situations, town meetings and sociodramas were held and presented in order to generate discussion on local issues. These activities, of course, did not have the same coherence or emerge from the clear process that the original model proposed, but they did offer people an opportunity to develop some problem-solving skills and a greater political and social awareness of the development challenges confronting the community and the nation.

As originally conceived, the community-action research method overcame some of the inherent contradictions present in a massive campaign model. It addressed the problem of maintaining a dynamic balance between community issues and national priorities as well as making literacy study applicable to real life situations. The method added local community interests and concerns to the study of national issues in an active, coherent, and planned fashion, and it emphasized the direct application of literacy to life by involving the community in development planning and action.

In the context of a national campaign, the idea of community-action research was an ambitious and original one that underwent many revisions. The level of language and explanations was overly academic at the beginning, and the final documents for the teaching guide still needed some work in order to be comprehensible to the vast numbers of young *brigadistas*, although the materials had been tested effectively with older volunteers. If revisions could have been made in time, a common understanding gained by the national team as to the relevance of the program, and an extra day or two added to all levels of training, this method could probably have been very effective, especially when used by senior high– and university-level volunteers. However, the planning and training time line was too short to be able to implement the program as effectively as was intended. It is an approach that should be examined by other countries that wish to mount this type of national effort, for its possible benefits to the community and society are considerable.

Mathematics Text

To complement the study of reading and writing, the campaign included the learning of basic arithmetic as well. The math text was given the name *Calculation and Reactivation: One Single Operation*, a title chosen to indicate that the economic reactivation of the nation and the learning of mathematics by the new literates were interrelated elements of a single process, both vital to national development. The text went through several reviews and revisions, and for a time its actual publication was in doubt. Freire raised questions about its use during the crusade, because, as he pointed out, its printing would increase costs and its study would divert attention from the literacy effort (McFadden 1980). But in the end, it was decided that the study of mathematics would enrich the learning process, and the idea of the text was approved. The research team was assigned the task of writing the study themes on the economic reactivation; the curriculum team, the mechanics of mathematics. The overall delay and specific delays related to developing the book's study themes in coordination with other institutions slowed down the design and production schedule. Beginning chapters were tested in the continuing pilot project during January and February, and the book was finally sent to the printers in mid-March. The Cuban education experts were helpful in developing the technical aspects of the final draft, and a Nicaraguan economist from the Ministry of Planning reviewed the economic content of the text. The text received very high marks in its treatment of economics, but a certain weakness was noted in the integration of math and the study themes.

The book was organized around economic themes that were important to the reactivation program, and it was divided into six chapters. It contained 102 pages of math exercises. Each chapter began with a dialogue discussion that was generated by a drawing and the reading of a topic sentence summarizing the essence of the chapter's theme. Incorporated into the text in special type were teaching instructions that were designed specifically for the volunteers to facilitate the effective use of the material. Chapter 1 focused on ENABAS, the National Basic Grains Distribution Program, and the problem of food speculation.

Counting, weights and measures, and simple one-digit addition and subtraction were also presented in the first chapter. General economic concepts such as wages, unemployment, income distribution, the consequences of low production, inflation, and consumption patterns were the focus of discussion in Chapter 2. This chapter also included a further study of weights and measures and word problems involving the addition and subtraction of two-digit numbers.

Chapter 3 presented three-digit word problems through a discussion of the Agrarian Reform Institute and the Farmworkers' Association. Chapter 4 concentrated on the need for cooperation between rural and urban labor associations in order to increase production. The fourth chapter also included the multiplication and division of two-digit numbers and the study of geometric figures. In Chapter 5, more word problems were presented, and multiplication and division increased in difficulty to three-digit numbers. The discussion theme focused on the public sector of the economy administered by the government. Chapter 6 began with a discussion of the purpose and procedures of the National Development Bank and included the study of fractions, time, and the calendar.

The math text was introduced to learners after they had completed lesson seven of the primer and had mastered basic literacy skills. Since the math book had simple reading passages included in each chapter, the text served as a stimulus to the development of reading skills as well. One-half hour daily was the time scheduled for using the math text. In practice, the study of mathematics was greeted with great enthusiasm. People were intensely interested in learning how to use fundamental math skills and solve word problems. Sometimes the interest was such that once begun, students did not want to stop, but when the study of mathematics began to seriously interfere with mastering literacy skills, it was either limited to three half-hour sessions weekly or postponed until the follow-up stage of the campaign in September.

Teaching Guide

To facilitate effective teaching, the curriculum team developed an instruction manual for the volunteers. *The Handbook on Sandinista Education: Orientations for the Literacy Promoter* was a 101-page document filled with teaching hints and background information for the volunteers. Sixteen pages were devoted to a step-by-step explanation of the primer's teaching method; 6 pages to community-action research; 5 to the field diary; 1 page dealt with filling out student progress reports. Several pages were devoted to introductory information as well as a biography of Sandino, a glossary, the literacy crusade anthem, and student attendance sheets. The bulk of the book, some 60 pages, was dedicated to detailed background readings and study questions on each of the twenty-three lesson themes. The handbook was the main resource of the volunteers and their supervisors once they were in the field, and as such, it played an important support role. Weak in some sections, it was strengthened during the course of the crusade through the development and distribution of supplementary materials.

The guide was limited by financial constraints. Valuable material, such as background information on adult education and explanations of the community-action research method, had to be cut because of a strict budgetary limit on the number of pages. The language and format of the guide were rather pedantic and formal. An earlier version had been written in a more engaging personal style, more appropriate for teenagers, but that version had been discarded because some sections were considered too complex and academic. Later, during the campaign, a livelier approach was used in developing additional materials to supplement the manual. A cartoon series, for example, was designed to help volunteers understand the principles of dialogue and to demonstrate the use of the learning games. The wording and style were improved upon as well. The language became simpler and more precise, and the design became more sophisticated. A clear set of question guidelines was created to assist the *brigadistas* in promoting effective discussions. The design layout and different kinds of typeface used in the printing helped make the guidelines more comprehensible, thus making them more effective.

Summary

Working under the constraints of an unusually short time line and the chaos of reconstruction, the small educational staff succeeded in designing and pilot testing the program's curriculum and in meeting the campaign's crucial deadlines. However, time pressures and a certain tendency to work on tasks in isolated groups affected the overall quality and ultimate use of the learning materials and teaching methods. An openness to criticism, a commitment to excellence, and an honest, frank relationship with regional personnel allowed the national staff to address many of the program's weaknesses and respond to them effectively during the course of the campaign.

The primer provided specific information that was relevant to the developing society but was weak in some areas of linguistic sequencing, a weakness that resulted in learner and teacher frustration. The pilot test was conducted on one of the first primer drafts, but subsequent revisions were not tested. Therefore, the weaknesses of the final version remained undiscovered until after publication.

The ten-step dialogue method that was used with the primer was not only a means to teach the ABCs but also an attempt to engage the learners in active discussions of issues of community and national concern and to encourage collective action in response to these shared problems. In comparison to previous authoritarian teaching methods, the plan was clearly a step toward a more participatory, reciprocal learning process— however, the method was not as successful as it was hoped it would be. Supporting materials were inadequate, and the photographs were ineffective in provoking discussion. The individual-lesson question guides provided were too precise and tended to lead to formalized exchanges. As soon as these weaknesses became evident, a new question format was developed and distributed, which helped overcome some of the methodological deficiencies. Although dialogue was difficult in the context of the primer lessons, active discussions did take place outside the formal learning structure in the course of sharing everyday life.

The most noteworthy innovation in methodology was the development of a process of community-action research that was used in the first stage of training. It was based on the involvement of the entire community in research to identify, understand, and solve commonly shared problems.

The math text that was used in conjunction with the literacy book was greeted with considerable enthusiasm by the learners, sometimes surpassing that accorded the primer. Finally, a teaching guide was developed for the *brigadistas* to help provide additional information and specific advice on each lesson. The field staff and volunteers found the teaching manual to be inadequate and written in a rather stilted style, so early in the campaign, the national staff supplemented the material in the guide with several pamphlets and information sheets presented in a more engaging, often humorous way.

5
Training

We knew that the training program offered the greatest challenge and was going to be the most difficult. In Cuba, the process had been centralized and the trainers carefully selected. Our particular situation called for something very different, something new and untried. Our concern was whether people could actually learn the skills to conduct the training workshops. Could they become effective workshop leaders? Could they prepare the tens of thousands of literacy volunteers we needed?

—César Campos (1980)
Research Team Coordinator

The National Training Team and Its Challenge

One of the most challenging questions confronting the national team was how to prepare the program personnel and the volunteer teaching brigades for their educational responsibilities during the campaign. A small training staff of seven, charged with the immense task, slowly took form in October 1979. By the end of that month, the training team was complete, and the members began their work in earnest. Their responsibilities were focused on preparing the educational personnel of the crusade for their work.

The national team of Nicaraguans, Colombians, one Mexican, and one North American brought different experiences to bear on the design of the training program. Four came from religious backgrounds: one priest, one former priest, one former nun, and one active Protestant lay person employed by CELADEC, a Latin American ecumenical community education organization. Until his appointment to the crusade, the coordinator of the team, thirty-year-old Luis Alemán, a former schoolteacher and student activist, had been serving as an organizer for the Nicaraguan Educators' Association (ANDEN) and had had no experience in adult education or literacy. The youngest team member, active in *Frente* support work, had just finished her university studies in education at the University of Mexico. The international members of the team had had extensive practical experience in adult education, literacy projects, and community organizing among the poor. They had all worked with programs that had been influenced by Paulo Freire but felt that no approach could be a rote copy of another. Firm in this belief, they saw their role as learning from the Nicaraguans in order to work with them to create a program that was appropriate to the nation's particular needs and that reflected the unique character of the country's people.

The team came together with a rather stumbling start. Luis Alemán, the short, rail thin, self-effacing Nicaraguan director, tells the story of how he joined the crusade and of his first encounter with the pedagogical team.

The head of the Pedagogical Division offered me the post of training coordinator. Training? I said to myself, training? I don't even know what literacy teaching implies. What in the world does training mean? Frankly I thought the position was too much for me. I was really kind of worried so I went to the crusade's administrative director, a friend of mine, and confided my doubts to him. What he said helped convince me that I should accept it. "Look, my brother," he said, "we're all in this together. There's no one here who really knows about literacy or even exactly what this project will mean. We've got to learn together. We chose you because we felt that you could respond to the challenge and if you don't take it, someone else will who may not have your commitment and concern." How else could I respond—I took it. . . .

The first day I walk into the office. There, I find myself confronted with this huge hulk of a man, a Yankee professor—and me, his boss. Imagine me, a primary school teacher—my entire life ignored, oppressed, stuck in a place where there were no opportunities for development, me expected now to become a director of a section with a secretary, a desk, a staff. I felt like I'd gotten myself into an awful mess. I felt like a fish out of water—as we say in Nicaragua, like a "bought chicken," signed, sealed, and delivered for the chopping block.

I sat down and looked around. There was another man in the corner—a university professor, José Miguel Paz, very serious—writing away. He was chief of something, chief of what I wondered. Then, there was this other man with a commanding, imposing presence, the famous Nicaraguan poet Guillermo Rothschuh working in the Research Section. I said to myself, what in the world am I doing here? And then my eyes went back to the first member of the training team, this great big gringo sitting at what was supposed to be my desk, the only desk around. My shyness was such that, well, there he was. He had completely taken over the place. I approached him hesitantly, so timid that I couldn't even say, excuse me, but I think that's my desk. I didn't know how to begin or where. So I sat down, and he began to tell me about training and the ideas that the team had been discussing up until then. The more he talked, the more desperate I felt. This was going to be much more complicated than I had thought. [Alemán 1980]

Alemán's story is probably representative of the feelings and problems many new officials faced as they undertook the enormous responsibilities of the crusade. Despite the hesitant, awkward beginning, the training team coalesced quickly. Probably because of the nature of the task, the personalities of the team members, and their experience, they formed one of the more integrated working groups of the crusade's national staff. By December, the gringo, John McFadden, had earned the title "friend of humanity" instead of "enemy" (the phrase used in the FSLN anthem to categorize Yankee intervention in Nicaragua), and Luis had won the respect of the team through his enthusiastic commitment to the task and his passionate belief in people and their potential.

The team worked under extraordinary time pressure. In an October planning meeting, a December 1 target had been set as the starting date for the first phase of training. This target date meant that the group had fewer than six weeks to put together a training program that was eventually to prepare the educational supervisory staff of the crusade and the entire volunteer corps in the skills of literacy teaching and social analysis and action.

FOUNDATION: A PEDAGOGY OF SHARED RESPONSIBILITY

Training Design

A general training design was proposed in the October planning meeting that called for a series of short, intensive workshops to be conducted throughout the nation in four separate stages. The training team, in its first weeks of planning, proceeded to work out the details of the proposal, increasing the number of stages by one. In its final form, therefore, the program consisted of five phases and was decentralized in nature.

The major elements and stages of the design model are briefly described in this paragraph and in Figure 1 and will be discussed in detail later in the chapter. The program's success depended on both its multiplier effect and its decentralization. Beginning with the seven national trainers, it was expected that within fewer than four months more than 100,000 people would be prepared for their work. From December to March, workshops were to be held across the country, from mountain top to jungle valley. The driving force behind the training would be a "group of 80," 40 university students and 40 teachers, that would be selected for an intensive two-week preparation program, Workshop 1, and one

Figure 1
TRAINING MULTIPLIER MODEL

PHASE 1	ACTIVITIES	PARTICIPANTS	WORKSHOP FACILITATORS
11/30/79 to 12/14/79	Workshop 1	*80*	National Training Team
12/18/79 to 1/17/80	Laboratory, Stage 1	Teachers	
1/19/80 to 1/23/80	Evaluation-Planning	and university	
1/28/80 to 1/29/80	Planning	students	
		"Group of 80"	
PHASE 2			
2/2/80 to 2/15/80	Workshop 2	*630*	Workshop 1 participants (Group of 80) with
		Teachers and university students	national pedagogical staff serving as supervisors
2/2/80 to 3/24/80	Laboratory, Stage 2	Workshop 1 participants not selected to be facilitators	National Research Team serving as laboratory supervisors
2/17/80	Evaluation-Planning	All Workshop 1 participants	National Training Team
PHASE 3			
2/25/80 to 3/08/80	Workshop 3	*11,000*	Workshop 2 participants with Workshop 1
		Teachers	participants serving as supervisors
3/08/80 to 3/10/80	Workshop 3	*1,000*	Workshop 1 and 2 participants and
		University students	National Training Team
Phase 4			
3/14/80 to 3/21/80	Workshop 4	*125,000*	Workshop 3 participants with Workshop 1
		All primary, secondary, and university students from age twelve up, whether volunteers or not; adult volunteers	and 2 participants serving as supervisors
PHASE 5			
4/80 to 5/80	Workshop 5	All	Selected Workshop 3 participants
	(one week each)	volunteers who could not participate in Workshop 4	
5/80 to 8/80	Saturday Workshops	*80,000*	Literacy Squadron Teaching Supervisors
	Daily Radio Program	Rural and urban	(Workshop 3 participants)
		literacy volunteers	National Training Team

month's field experience. Forty of this group would be chosen to train approximately 600 students and teachers in the next phase, Workshop 2 (the remaining 40 would continue the field experience in order to further test the materials and methods). During late February, in Workshop 3, these 600 people would prepare more than 12,000 people, most of whom would be teachers. They, in turn, would conduct the eight-day intensive Workshop 4 for the thousands of literacy volunteers. Phase 5 of training contained three aspects: Workshop 5 (to prepare all those volunteers who had been unable to participate in Workshop 4); a radio program for volunteers in the field; and in-service workshops held on Saturdays for *brigadistas* to improve their teaching skills.

Rationale

The rationale for the design was based on pragmatic as well as on educational concerns. The process designed by the group became known as the Training Multiplier Model and was created to multiply skills and to overcome the limitations of both geography and poor infrastructure. By utilizing such a decentralized process, thousands of students and teachers could be prepared in the new educational methods and have actual experience in applying these approaches as workshop trainers. The decentralization, it was felt, would also allow the training to reflect the conditions of the various regions and to become more grounded in local reality. This approach would also acquaint the national staff with the regional situations. On a pragmatic level, the model was designed specifically to respond to the country's lack of adequate training facilities for such massive numbers of people. The multiphased approach also allowed schools to remain open as scheduled, causing only minor interruptions. As a measure of its effectiveness, the Training Multiplier Model was adopted the following year by many other ministries to train their personnel.

Philosophy

The philosophy and learning principles underlying the training program probably can be best summarized by the following statement, which is taken from the first training materials that described to the *brigadistas* their new revolutionary educational role. This description applied to the relationship between trainer and workshop participant as well.

You will be a catalyst of the teaching-learning process. Your literacy students will be people who think, create, and express their ideas. Together, you will form a team of mutual learning and human development. . . . The literacy process is an act of creation in which people offer each other their thoughts, words and deeds. It is a cultural action of transformation and growth. [Cruzada Nacional de Alfabetización 1979a, 3]

The training workshops were to be specifically based on what was called a "pedagogy of shared responsibility." Instead of the separate roles of student and teacher, this educational approach was founded on a group concept of learning that stressed cooperation, participation, creativity, discovery, confidence building, learning by doing, and collective problem solving. As Luis Alemán explained: "In training, we stressed popular communication, cooperative relationships, discussion, and analysis. Our aim was to help people understand that their words had value, that their ideas made sense. It wasn't us saying to them, do this or that. It was let us do this, let us build together. We wanted them to feel like artists creating a master work of great beauty" (Alemán 1980).

The teaching-learning relationship was to be collegial in approach. The traditional model of the active, all-wise professor and passive, ignorant pupil was specifically rejected and replaced by a situation in which the traditional teacher became a type of learning coordinator. In training, the role of the workshop director was one of facilitator, a role that involved motivating, inspiring, challenging, and working with the participants who were encouraged to become active problem solvers. Participants were considered the foundation and wellspring of the process. Their responsibilities were to explore, research, and create. Small group study, team teaching, and problem solving affirmed this new relationship. Under the coordination of two facilitators, workshop members were given a variety of educational tasks to accomplish. During the training, they reflected upon the group process and their progress, integrating both theory and practice.

The educational approach and reciprocal relationship between "student" and "teacher" that was defined specifically for the workshops was described in the trainer's manual, which was designed for the thousands of actual workshop trainers.

what they wanted, (dualism)!!

This new relationship takes place within a context of teamwork. There is no longer the "professor" who knows and teaches and "students" who don't know and who learn. But, instead, a group undertakes an activity together and reflects over and evaluates their action and process, thus attempting to integrate both theory and practice.

What is most important is to replace the knowledge-dispensing professor and the listening-absorbing student with learning coordinators who stimulate and workshop participants who investigate and research.

The aim is not to develop the capacity to repeat information but to solve problems. [Alemán et al. 1979, 83]

The trainer's manual outlined several concepts that the team considered fundamental to the educational process. They were (1) learning by doing, (2) learning how to learn, (3) development of creativity, (4) beginning with the knowledge and experience of participants, and (5) the unity between theory and practice. The team abided by the learning principle that people acquire knowledge and learn much more effectively by acting and doing rather than by only the verbal communication of ideas. Experiential learning was a key concept for the program designers.

One of the most important elements of the proposed educational process, described under the heading "Learning How to Learn," called for a complete reformulation of the traditional teaching methods practiced in Nicaragua. It stressed, not the acquisition of static knowledge or of memorized information, but the development of learning skills—the ability to acquire and apply knowledge on one's own. It therefore called for the group to make its own discoveries and in the process, to "learn how to know." The idea was not to give the participants already digested and established theories and information but, rather, to stimulate them "to produce and re-create their own knowledge so the group could develop its own theories and apply them" (Alemán et al. 1979, 81). Part of this process has already been discussed in regard to the use of field diaries and community research, but the process will be elaborated further in this chapter.

Related to this element was an emphasis on creativity and the development of intelligence through problem solving.

> The most appropriate environment for developing creativity is one in which people search for answers to problems they encounter while carrying out concrete tasks. Thinking and reflection emerge from a situation which is posed as a problem. . . . Memorization blocks intelligence, problem situations activate it.
>
> What characterizes education within a workshop is fundamentally an inductive pedagogy. Beginning with an activity and experience, problems arise in an inductive manner. In the workshop meetings these are transformed into themes for reflection. . . .
>
> From this, the search begins for the necessary concepts, categories, theories, etc., in order to better understand the experience and to better orient program activities.
>
> Problems aren't posed by the coordinator's or speaker's concept of what theories and principles should be transmitted but, rather, from the concrete questions which arise from the actual experience or practice itself. [Alemán et al. 1979, 81–82]

The national training team also stressed that the personal knowledge and experience of the program participants should serve as a basis for learning, for it was through this knowledge and experience that a group process of self-education could be generated and perpetuated. In this way, learning skills could be developed and reinforced.

Concerned that their focus on "learning by doing" might be over-emphasized, the planners also stressed the integration of action with reflection. "Theory is fundamental in order to shed light on practice, to understand experience. . . . It serves to interpret completed actions and orient new ones. Theory and practice are two poles in a permanent relation, one to another, and are meaningless in isolation" (Alemán et al. 1979, 82). In this regard, the team felt that it was essential to establish an educational approach that would begin "to overcome the separation between theory and practice, knowledge and work, education and life" (Alemán et al. 1979, 82).

Objectives and Aims

The main objective of the first three phases of training was to prepare the trainers of the literacy volunteers. Specifically, this goal meant acquainting future workshop coordinators—the schoolteachers, university students, and representatives from citizen and labor organizations—with the program's content, training materials, methods, and techniques. It also implied preparing the coordinators to conduct and administer the workshops.

It was assumed, though never clearly articulated, that in the process, a secondary objective would be met—the trainers would develop the skills that would enable them to take on technical support responsibilities as *brigadista* supervisors after the crusade began. This objective, however, was not met. The campaign planners realized during the course of the program's operation that it was one thing to prepare trainers of literacy volunteers and quite another to prepare an educational and administrative support staff. The duties and skills that were needed were very different. The support staff required more concrete preparation in supervisory skills such as critique and feedback, human relations training, cross-cultural sensitivity, statistics, and record keeping.

In Phase 4 of the training program, the principal objective was to prepare the actual literacy volunteers in the use of the program's learning materials and methods and to help them acquire the necessary skills, knowledge, and attitudes to become sensitive, creative, and committed participants in the social transformation process. The team felt that besides teaching literacy skills, the *brigadistas* needed to work in promoting community organizations and development projects.

The final stage of training, Phase 5, was aimed at two different groups and had two separate purposes: (1) to prepare all those people who were interested in becoming literacy volunteers but who had been unable to participate in Workshop 4 and (2) to provide continual in-service training to the volunteers already in the field.

Structure

The organizational structure used throughout the training process, from Phase 1 through Phase 5, for both study and management purposes promoted maximum participation. It was composed of a Workshop General Assembly, a series of small groups called squadrons and nucleus study cells, and several special groups such as the Feedback, Housekeeping, and Coordinating Committees and the Support Team.

The Workshop General Assembly included all participants, usually around thirty, and was used to discuss, synthesize, and evaluate workshop activities on an overall level. Each squadron ideally contained fifteen workshop members and served as the training "engine," a place in which all program activities could be channeled and processed and daily evaluations of each session conducted. Each squadron elected several people for special responsibilities: (1) a *responsable* who represented the squadron before the coordinating body of the workshop and who was also responsible for facilitating the activities and distributing and coordinating the tasks of the group, (2) a secretary to record discussions and two other people to assist in questions of writing style and accuracy, and (3) one or two members each for the special committees. In order to share the duties as well as the experience and learning gained from these leadership positions, the posts were rotated every three days.

The nucleus study cells were a smaller unit of the squadron, consisting of four to five members, and served as the central means to discuss and study issues on a deeper level. Their size guaranteed maximum involvement by all members. Each nucleus elected a rotating coordinator and a secretary. The structure of committees and rotating leadership embodied the educational principles underlying the campaign—the belief that everyone could contribute to the program and that people learn by doing and participating actively in concrete activities.

The overall coordination and management of each workshop was handled by two training coordinators who worked in daily cooperation with elected representatives on a joint Coordinating Committee. These delegates formed the workshop Support Team, which included one representative from each squadron, one of the two workshop secretaries (appointed by the training coordinators and responsible for minutes and the gathering of all materials produced by the workshop), and members of the special committees. The Support Team made recommendations to the coordinators on the overall functioning of the training and on the particular concerns of the participants.

The Feedback Committee served as a vehicle to discuss concerns and unanswered questions that the squadrons had regarding the daily activities. Its duty was to bring such issues to the attention of the Coordinating Committee so that they could be addressed. The Feedback Committee was also responsible for collecting items of general interest and the daily squadron evaluations, both of which were posted on the workshop's special information board known as the "newspaper mural." It also gathered the recommendations placed in the workshop's suggestion box. The Housekeeping Committee was in charge of supplies and maintenance—making sure that materials were on hand when needed and that the training locale was clean and in order.

Evaluation was considered to be fundamental to all activities. In addition to the daily evaluations conducted by the squadrons, an overall progress evaluation was held at the workshop midpoint. First, squadrons submitted reports, then, in the General Assembly, all the workshop participants discussed the results and proposed responses to the problems that had been identified. Finally, the Coordinating Committee incorporated the responses into a revised training plan. At the end of each workshop, a similar procedure was followed, and the information from these sessions was used to improve and plan the next phase of training.

Content and Methods

The actual content and methods used in the first four phases of training and in Workshop 5 did not vary significantly, even though Workshops 1 through 3 were designed to prepare trainers and 4 and 5 to prepare volunteer teachers. There were, however, two major differences and several minor ones. Workshop 1 included a month of field experience, the participants in Workshops 1 and 2 received preparation in a more complex application of the process called community-action research. Three minor differences should also be mentioned briefly. In Workship 1, and in some cases in Workshop 2, the principles and practice of critical feedback (criticism/self-criticism) were discussed and applied. Participants in Workshops 1, 2, and 3 received several hours of preparation in workshop management and facilitation; those in 2 and 4 received training in malaria control.

Although the contents and methods remained generally the same throughout the training until Phase 5, the length of the workshops, the time allocated to activities, and the quality of training changed over

TABLE 1
CONTENT AND TIME ALLOCATIONS FOR WORKSHOPS 1-5

PHASE	1	2	3	3	4/5	4/5
PARTICIPANTS	university students and teachers	university students and teachers	teachers	university students, members of citizen/ labor organizations	rural volunteers	urban volunteers
LENGTH	14 days, full-time in residence & lab	14 days in residence	10 days, half-time 2 days, full-time	9 days, full-time	8 days, full-time	10 days, part-time
Content (in hours)						
Introduction/organization of workshop	5	4	4	4	3.5	4.5
Development issues: economic, political, social, educational, organization of crusade	30	28.5	21	24	14	12
Study	(10)	(10)	(6.5)	(9)	(5.5)	(4.5)
Discussion/analysis	(20)	(18.5)	(14.5)	(15)	(8.5)	(7.5)
Literacy Materials/methods	65	50	24	34	25.5	24
Study/discussion	(30)	(28)	(12)	(15.75)	(15.5)	(14)
Practice	(35)	(22)	(12)	(18.25)	(10)	(10)
Artistic expression	8	2.5	0	4	3	2.5
Planning/management/facilitation of workshops	6	4	2	2	0	0
Health care/malaria control	0	16	2	2	8	0
Evaluation	10	5.5	3	3	2	1.5
Total Scheduled Hours	124	110.5	56	73	56	44.5

the course of the program (Table 1). Workshops 1 and 2, for example, had more experienced training coordinators. The first two workshops were also longer, and the participants actually lived at the training sites so more time could be given to learning activities. Since most of the participants were sleeping at the training centers, more hours could be devoted to study and application of lessons learned. Late-night sessions were common. Workshop 1 had a scheduled program of activities calling for 124 hours of training; Workshop 2, some 110; and Workshop 3, 56 hours on a part-time basis for teachers and 73 hours on a full-time basis for the other participants. (The 73-hour course was rarely given because the majority of the participants were teachers.) Workshop 4 and 5 ran about 56 hours for the *brigadistas* and almost 45 for the urban volunteers. As the training progressed to levels 3 and 4, the number of participants reached into the thousands and tens of thousands, and the effectiveness of the training—the presentation of the program's content and the practice of the methods, materials, and techniques—was diluted. It should also be noted that because of production and design delays, the math materials were not studied in any of the workshops; they introduced later in the field.

While planning the content and the methods of the workshops, the training team raised questions and identified weak points. The team realized that the design of a manual for the future workshop coordinators was fundamental in order to enhance the effective implementation of such a massive program. Such a manual had not been originally considered since the Pedagogical Division had first thought that the literacy materials themselves—the primer and the teaching handbook—would be sufficient. However, the training team insisted that the task of coordinating a workshop required a specific manual to provide support to the inexperienced trainers. Despite the questions raised by some members of the Pedagogical Division, the training team also insisted on the importance of integrating art and cultural expression into the methodology of the workshop and into the work of the campaign itself. The team pointed out that different forms of expression were necessary to affirm the sense of worth and potential in people who did not know how to read and write. Mere dialogue and discussion, it was felt, were not enough to develop people's rich and diverse talents or their sense of personal confidence. There were other more political arguments as well, based on the need to put into practice the goal of popular participation through cultural and artistic expression.

The specific content of and methods used in the different workshops included, first, an introductory exercise that was designed to acquaint people with one another and to establish a congenial, dynamic learning environment. The participants were divided into groups of five or six

Socialization of volunteers

in which they each introduced themselves by name, profession or area of work or study, membership in a citizen or labor organization, and political concerns and activities. They also discussed the meaning of the crusade and why they had decided to become volunteers, listing their responses on large sheets of paper and tacking them on the wall. In Workshop 1, the exercise also included a discussion of the participants' expectations and questions regarding training.

At the end of the introductory exercise, the participants were asked to create some two-line, rhymed slogans that summarized the group's discussion. This technique had its roots both in the traditional culture of Nicaragua, where couplets are a popular literary expression, and in the war. During the long years of struggle, short chants that synthesized and captured the spirit of popular demands and aspirations had been used to animate demonstrations and harass the National Guard. During the workshop, rhymes took on a life of their own as groups used their spare time to try to create new and more imaginative ones. A group would practice a new rhyme in a corner and, in a moment of relative silence between activities, shout out the new creation with great pride and enthusiasm. The members of the group would then prepare a carefully written copy of their work so others could join them in shouting their couplet. The effort generated a spirit of lively rivalry and boosted energy when long hours of work became heavy and fatiguing. It also served as a positive way to gauge involvement and comprehension levels. If, for example, a group did not understand an exercise or a reading, a humorous couplet would invariably indicate the confusion, and the group's frustration would surface. This technique proved to be a comfortable, nonthreatening way in which participants could give critical feedback and have input into program changes.

Following the introductory exercise, participants were presented with an outline of the workshop structure and divided into squadrons and nucleus cells; they then elected their internal representatives and their delegates to the different committees. Each group then chose the name of a fallen combatant for its squadron's name and guiding symbol, writing up his or her biography to hang on the wall for others to read. They would develop several couplets around the name and then copy the couplets onto poster paper and tape them to the wall. Finally, each squadron presented the results of its work to the General Assembly.

In the workshop, participants were provided with background information on general development issues and on details about the new education and the crusade itself. This information included specifics on the 1980 Economic Reconstruction Plan, background on the network of citizen and labor organizations, the concept of "revolutionary education," and the objectives and organization of the crusade. All information presented was read, analyzed, and discussed in small groups and finally synthesized in the General Assembly. This part of the training was designed to stimulate the participants to develop their own analytical framework in order to better understand the nation's development challenge of reconstruction and transformation.

In Workshop 1, ten hours were dedicated to studying these different issues and twenty hours to analyzing them and to presenting a synthesis of each squadron's conclusions to the entire assembly. In the *brigadista* Workshop 4, five and a half hours were used for study and eight and a half for analysis and presentation. Study was usually carried out in pairs, and analysis was usually done in the nucleus structure of four or five in the squadrons. The presentation of group conclusions took several forms—panel discussions, debates, couplets, the design of posters or sociodramas (skits based on real life situations)—and critical forums then followed in which the presentation was discussed. Artistic/cultural expression was emphasized and included in all levels of training, but it was also singled out in four of the five preparatory workshops for special study and application. Workshop 1 devoted eight hours to this area; Workshops 2 and 5, two and a half hours each; and Workshop 4, three hours each. Drawing, poetry, drama, and song writing were some of the artistic forms used in the workshops. The fact that cultural expression was not emphasized in Workshop 3 limited the trainers' understanding of its importance and their ability to generate it as a creative process.

Certain methods were used at all levels of training to spark enthusiasm, communication, and involvement. The newspaper mural was designed by the participants to record workshop events and display the creative efforts produced during training. The suggestion box was set up to give trainers feedback from the workshop members. The most popular activity, however, was the "secret friend." At the beginning of a training group, each participant was given a name of someone in the workshop. This person became their secret object of attention and special friendship. Poetry was written in that person's honor, drawings were made, jokes were shared. Notes and gifts were placed where they could be found without revealing the giver's identity. The training coordinators often served as cupids by pairing boys and girls in order to increase the possibility of a romance.

The major portion of the training was devoted to the study and practice of the literacy materials and methods. In Workshop 1, thirty hours were assigned to their study and discussion, and some thirty-five hours were devoted to preparing, presenting, and critiquing simulations of the actual use of the materials and methods. In Workshop 2, twenty-eight hours were scheduled for study and twenty-two for practice. In the teachers' workshop, Workshop 3, twelve hours were programmed for each, while the *brigadista* workshop, Workshop 4, dedicated fifteen and a half hours to study and about ten to simulations.

It is important to note the emphasis that was placed on practice rather than mere review, on analysis and criticism instead of only reading and receiving information. The time allotments reflect the crusade's educational philosophy that people learn the most when they can actively apply what they are learning, collectively synthesize it, critique it openly, and act upon it to improve it. However, the fact that the balance between study and practice shifted in Workshop 4 indicates some of the limitations of having only a week's training program for novices. A certain amount of time was needed for presenting and studying basic information and materials before they could be practiced or critiqued, and since the training time was brief, the practice had to be shortened.

In the first three phases—Workshops 1, 2, and 3—study of the planning, management, and facilitation of workshops took six, four, and two hours, respectively. About ten hours of specific evaluation activities were programmed for Workshop 1; five and a half for 2; three, for 3; and two, for *brigadista* Workshops 4 and 5, although evaluation was also to be carried out on a daily basis as a part of each squadron's overall tasks.

Some sixteen hours of basic health care and malaria diagnosis, treatment, and prevention were scheduled for Workshop 2; about two hours, for Workshop 3; and eight hours, for *brigadistas* in Workshops 4 and 5. Information on malaria control was presented by employees of the national malaria control agency.

In Phase 5, the in-service training program consisted of a daily radio presentation and Saturday workshops, the content of which soon became the actual problems encountered during the campaign. Discussions, simulations, and sociodramas were conducted to practice and improve on the solutions that were developed for the problems that arose.

FIVE-PHASE IMPLEMENTATION

Since each phase of training had its own special characteristics and provides unique and valuable lessons, each level will be discussed separately. First, however, it should be noted that while the workshops were being conducted, other parallel training activities were also occurring. Starting in January 1980, a weekly column appeared in both national newspapers under the title, "Degree in Literacy." It included background information on adult education and literacy teaching and was designed to encourage interest in the crusade and inform the general public about the basic educational philosophies and approaches. From

January to March, the EPA sponsored different educational activities for the volunteers to help prepare them for the rigors of their work, and for the students of the country at large to encourage new recruits. An Outward Bound type of program was implemented; first-aid courses were given; and seminars in development, economics, politics, and government planning were held.

Phase 1

The first phase of training took place in December and January and involved a two-week workshop and one month of supervised field experience, similar to a teaching practicum. During this time, the national training staff prepared the core group of eighty people—the group upon which the entire training program was to depend. Originally, this group was going to consist of only forty people, but after due consideration, it was decided that a team-teaching approach for the subsequent levels of training would be more effective so the number was doubled. This change meant that those selected to be trainers would then be able to share their facilitator role and not have to conduct the next tier of workshops alone and those group members chosen to continue the field-testing experience would do so in pairs. The core group was composed of about half university students and half primary school teachers—many of whom would later serve as the provincial technical advisers during the campaign. There were also a few participants from the citizen and labor associations, ministries, the army, and the *Frente*.

As originally planned, the participants were to be a specially selected group, carefully chosen by their respective organizations, ANDEN and Juventud. However, in reality, despite the constant insistence of and badgering by the training team, the associations did not develop special selection processes. The participants were in large part a self-selected group, volunteering for the task when their association first announced the need for delegates to the crusade. However, because these organizations were still in an initial stage of formation, their memberships were selective—composed principally of people with a demonstrated commitment to the struggle against Somoza.

This initial self-selection process, although unplanned and unintended, turned out to be essential in obtaining the most interested, enthusiastic, and committed members of the groups. Luis Alemán, the coordinator of the national training team, has emphasized the importance of this process and of the resulting personal motivating spirit the participants brought to the program, a spirit that characterized many of the people working in the crusade.

The nonselection turned out to be fundamental. Quite frankly, the people were not specially chosen. They came because they wanted to, because they wanted to be there. We managed to obtain people who entered the work with a sense of the *mística*, of the spirit of what the campaign was all about. . . . What happened to me, happened to them I think. I came to understand that for me, the crusade was going to mean my own personal fulfillment, my own self-realization, what I had always longed for throughout my life—to develop myself, to become, to be, to give my all within a structure that I believed in, for a society I had always dreamed about, to give everything I had—which you know, quite frankly, wasn't a whole lot. More than anything else I can say it was my enthusiasm, my ability to work hard, my passion, my commitment.

The people who came to the first workshop came with this same spirit. They understood the crusade as a challenge to their lives, as almost the consecration of their existence, of becoming, of creating, of re-creating themselves as people—of all that they could not become under Somoza. We were a beginning. [Alemán 1980]

Workshop 1

On the eve of the first workshop, a feeling of nervous excitement could be sensed among the members of the national staff. As became the norm for the entire crusade, the materials were not ready on time. At the last minute, the personnel joined forces to staple the piles of training documents coming off the cranky mimeograph machine, which kept breaking down at inopportune times. Work continued until dawn. At that moment, some of the staff members wondered whether the program would be able to meet the immense challenge.

The first group of participants came together in Tepeyac, a simple mountain retreat, famous for its honey, on the side of a volcano. Run by nuns, it had served during the 1970s as an educational center for community development and union organizing activities sponsored by church activists. Under Somoza, many people who had participated in Tepeyac programs had been arrested and persecuted, and some had been killed. In December 1979, Tepeyac served as the birthplace of the crusade's educational staff.

One of the outstanding characteristics and strengths of the first phase of training was the way in which problems were confronted and how, ultimately, they led to the enrichment of the workshop. The educational philosophy espoused by the leadership—learning from problems that emerge from practice—became a reality in Workshop 1. However, as explained by different members of the national team, many of the problems that surfaced in Workshop 1, while serving as valuable lessons for participants, affected the subsequent operation of the crusade and were never fully resolved. They reflected the inherent and ingrained problems and challenges of an educational and social system in transition. The deep structural transformation being attempted raised issues, both personal and political, for all people involved in the process and for the new structures they were attempting to create. In the context of the crusade, these problems were a part of the learning process—to be studied, analyzed, and responded to. As Francisco Lacayo, special executive assistant to Fernando Cardenal and subsequent vice-minister of adult education, liked to say: "In creating the Crusade we didn't make it work in spite of all the contradictions and problems we faced. No, we did it with the contradictions, learning from the problems and mistakes, immersed in the process—trying to find answers, becoming aware" (Lacayo 1980).

In the first workshop, the central problems and subsequent lessons that were gained from confronting them arose from essentially three situations: (1) the predictable tension between the students and the teachers over political and professional questions, (2) the lack of consensus among the pedagogical staff members about the crusade's educational scope, and (3) the evolving nature of the program's methodology. The situations were interrelated, one generating discussion of another, and they were exacerbated by time pressures, a lack of coordination, and common definition. During the previous months of October and November, the general planning activities had been so intense, the tasks so compartmentalized and demanding, that the members of the Pedagogical Division had only been able to meet once as a staff to discuss basic educational questions. They, likewise, had been unable to meet with the Organizational Division staff to discuss these issues. Therefore, they had not developed an integrated pedagogical approach that incorporated all the different aspects of the program. Each small group tended to work independently of the others, although the training and research teams did collaborate on several mutual projects and were in close agreement on issues. There had been no time to develop a common understanding of adult learning principles overall or to reflect collectively about the meaning of a liberating, revolutionary education system. Nor had there been time to discuss the relationship between those two aspects or the implications of that relationship for the campaign. On a more specific level, the time pressure, and a feeling on the part of some of the staff members that a common approach to training was not a priority, had made it impossible for the different pedagogical teams to develop a coherent strategy for training.

As originally designed, the first workshop might not have been affected by this lack of consensus because the training team was to have run the entire program without the participation of the curriculum staff. But as the first day of training approached, it became clear that the materials were not going to be ready on time and that the training team was not going to be able to familiarize itself with them. Consequently, the curriculum team members would have to present the package themselves. During the workshop their presentation caused considerable tension among the workshop participants, but the conflict served as a rich educational experience. It was a clear example of what Francisco Lacayo meant by learning from contradictions. The first major presentation of the materials was scheduled for the sixth day of training. By that time, a climate of camaraderie, cooperation, and creativity had been established among the workshop members, and a style had also developed of learning by discovery, doing, discussion, and analysis. Participation and enthusiasm were high.

Because the members of the curriculum team had not attended the first five days of the workshop, nor had they been involved in the design of the training methods, their style of presentation was radically different from the participatory approach the workshop group had become accustomed to. This situation was to occur at other times during the workshop as well, such as when a lecture on art was given by representatives from the Ministry of Culture. For the presentation of the primer materials and methodology one of the senior members of the curriculum team, a long-standing member of the Ministry of Education, gave a lecture. She expounded the program's teaching package at great length, and questions or contributions from the audience were not solicited. Many members of the workshop found this approach and accompanying attitude to be paternalistic in nature and reflective of the oppressive past. A long debate and discussion on methodology ensued. The formal evaluation of the workshop, drawn up by both trainers and participants, details this problem as follows:

> Certain tensions were revealed during the presentation on curriculum regarding the concept of literacy. The vertical and directive style of the presentation was in contrast with the approach that had been used in the rest of the workshop.
> For curriculum, participants were expected to learn already elaborated documents, not to analyze or criticize them in order to contribute to their development as they had with all other materials.
> The workshop methodology was "learning by doing" and not academic expositions. When the approach and style of work used in the curriculum presentation finally changed, valuable criticisms and contributions were made. [Cruzada Nacional de Alfabetización 1979a, 7]

In the discussion about methodology, tensions surfaced between student and teacher participants as well. One of the members of the research team identified some of the contributing factors and recognized some of the mistakes made by the Pedagogical Division.

> The participants, in their discussion and evaluations, made us see our mistake in dichotomizing and isolating our work. For besides the tension with the curriculum group, it became clear that all teams contributing to the workshop thought that their materials were the most important. Consequently, we often overloaded people with information both in quantity and in the fact that information was fragmented and unrelated to other presentations. From their evaluations you can see that the participants sensed that there were two different visions of what literacy was all about. We had started out by presenting one method of learning—of creating, discovering, analyzing, re-creating—and then curriculum presented them with another, something already completed, expository, the purpose of which was to be assimilated and nothing more. They resented it. . . . This situation also generated a certain division between teachers and students. [Suarez 1980]

Luis Alemán went on to spell out the tension between student and teacher participants in detail, emphasizing the reasons behind it.

> This conflict was a very serious problem. But in the end, it was handled and confronted with great maturity by both groups. There were moments, however, when the teachers took one side and the students the other. What happened really was this. The woman who gave the presentation was an older professor who had taught pedagogy courses in primary school education to many of the young teachers present. During her exposition a good sector of those teachers returned to the past. They were in the days of yesteryear with their respected professor; they admired her gestures, her way of speaking. They had gone back in time. This caused a tremendous conflict because the university students saw the presentation as imposing, as traditional, as an example of "banking" education. We saw it as the perfect example, the maximum ideal of the teacher of the past.
>
> It was an enriching, if painful, experience for all of us, for it served as a means of discussion and serious reevaluation. We realized that we all were at fault. We had not communicated or coordinated well, but we also realized that the problems we were facing were natural and inherent to a process such as the one we were involved in—a process that had no set fixed path or clear answers but a process that we were creating along the way. What we had to do was confront the problems we encountered with responsive solutions, solutions based on specific situations and the concrete reality of the program, not on an idealized version of what was happening. [Alemán 1980]

In the formal evaluation of the workshop, the participants concluded that despite, or indeed on account of, the problems encountered, the training had achieved the desired goals well. They were particularly positive about the workshop's organization and structure—which allowed for maximum involvement and participatory methods of learning, which promoted cooperation, analysis, and creative critical thinking—but they stressed the need for more discipline and a greater integration of the training coordinators into the study/work groups. They felt that the workshop time schedule needed to be followed more closely and tardiness punished. The members also wanted the coordinators to participate more actively with them in their learning groups. When the workshop participants departed to begin their field experience, they felt sufficiently prepared to handle the program's materials. They had found the idea of community-action research especially useful but mentioned specifically the need for more practice in its application, as well as for more practice with the field diary and the ways to promote dialogue and *concientización*.

For Luis Alemán, the most important result of Workshop 1 was that the participants had gained a spirit of initiative and invincibility, a sense of confidence in their own skills and an ability to confront and solve problems. As he expressed it: "Thank God, we were able to instill and affirm a spirit, an enthusiasm, a hope, a faith in themselves, a belief that they could accomplish anything no matter what the challenge or problem. Because if the crusade was to be a success, they would have to accomplish what seemed the impossible, and they would have to do it all" (Alemán 1980).

Laboratory, Stage 1

After completing the workshop, the group of eighty entered into the next phase of their preparation—the teaching-learning laboratory. The overall goals of the laboratory were twofold: to provide a teaching-learning experience in literacy work and community-action research, which would improve the skills of the workshop participants as trainers, and to allow for a better planning of the subsequent workshops through a careful evaluation of Workshop 1 in the light of the laboratory work. Supervised by the national training team, the practicum lasted from December 18, 1979, to January 17, 1980, and was conducted in small villages throughout the country. In the practicum, the workshop participants became experimental *brigadistas*, simulating the living, learning, and teaching situations that the volunteers would face during the crusade. Toward the end of the laboratory period, three participants were called to Managua to help the national office staff mount the infrastructure for Workshop 2. The original team simply could not handle all of their responsibilities without additional staff. A five-day evaluation, held in

Tepeyac from January 19 to January 23, concluded the first stage of the laboratory. The second phase continued until the crusade's start, and it was staffed by those participants who were not selected to be trainers for Workshop 2. This stage of the laboratory involved the same literacy groups the participants had originally been working with.

The first proposal for the teaching-learning laboratory had emerged from the October planning meeting, but because of other demands on the training team, no one had had time to develop the idea. Although the need for a field experience was quite clear, it was only during the workshop that actual planning for the laboratory took place. Delegates from the ATC (the Farmworkers' Association) who had come to participate in one of the workshop presentations on the new citizen and labor groups were asked to attend a meeting the same day in order to help organize the laboratory program. They indicated the areas of the country that were most appropriate for the field activities and where the basic support infrastructure also existed. Locations were decided upon, and the ATC agreed to contact its local chapters so that they might prepare the way for the workshop participants, finding lodging for them and informing the villages of their arrival.

During the laboratory period, this relationship with the ATC caused a certain tension to develop between the crusade staff and the Ministry of Education. Because the field experience had been improvised during the workshop, the training staff had bypassed the provincial ministry offices and had organized the laboratory by working directly with the ATC. It was an understandable mistake, since the laboratory sites were to be in remote places where there were no schools, but many directors of education only found out about the presence of the workshop participants in their province through the grapevine, and they complained that they had been neither informed nor consulted. A few of the directors continued this initial resentment throughout the entire campaign. This strain may have been in part exacerbated by the natural tensions resulting from the profound structural transformation that was occurring in the nation. The ATC was made up of peasant farmworkers and was a direct consequence of the transformation process, while much of the ministry staff, especially outside of Managua, was made up of educators from the old system.

Four days after Workshop 1 ended, the practicum began. The participants were sent to rural areas in five different provinces—Río San Juan, Matagalpa, Nueva Segovia, Chinandega, and Chontales—and for organizational purposes, one squadron was assigned to each province. Each squadron was made up of about sixteen people and was then broken down into nucleus groups of four. The nucleus was finally divided into pairs—one student, one teacher—and sent to different communities to teach. Embarrassing, unexpected situations sometimes ensued when the pair consisted of a man and a woman. The peasants naturally thought they were husband and wife and in some instances, as a special honor, gave them the matrimonial bed to sleep in. Sometimes the two did not want to say anything at first for fear of hurting the people's feelings, and it was only after one or two nights of feeling very uncomfortable, and scarcely sleeping, that they explained the situation.

Weekly meetings were held by the squadrons in the ATC headquarters of the provincial capitals, and using their field diaries as a basis for discussion, the participants shared experiences, analyzed progress, discussed problems, proposed solutions, and evaluated the group activities. The results of this collective evaluation were compiled into one document, which was later used for further analysis in the final evaluation meeting, where the next phase of training was planned.

Originally, it was thought that the national team would maintain close communication and actually participate with the field teams in their work. However, because of the pressing tasks regarding the next level of workshops and the relatively long distances to some sites, only one major visit was made. In retrospect, the team saw that its attempt to replicate the geographic spread of the actual crusade in the teaching-learning laboratory experience was a mistake. If the practicum sites had been closer to Managua, the staff could have been more involved in the process and better used the lessons being learned in the field in the further development of the program.

Learning through problem solving became the slogan for the laboratory The many difficulties encountered served as the basis for a rich educational experience for the individual participants and the training team alike. Unfortunately, because of the separation that existed between the pedagogical teams and the lack of time to systematize or discuss the information collectively, these lessons—many of which applied directly to improving the program's materials—were not acted upon until later during the campaign when the problems became massively evident. Even though the problems and insights were discussed throughout the laboratory period and during the evaluation workshop, the suggestions could not be incorporated directly into the primer or the teacher's guide because those materials had already gone to the printers in Costa Rica. (Nicaragua did not have enough paper or presses large enough to do the job economically and fast so a Costa Rican company was given the contract.)

Despite this situation, though, corrective measures such as supplementary, updated teachers' instructions could have been developed as the problems with the original material became evident. The failure to do so is one more example of the kinds of difficulties that are inherent in putting such a massive project together so quickly. Time pressure, logistic demands, and structural limitations affected the staff's ability to respond to this situation, as did the division of tasks and lack of opportunities for communication among teams.

All of the difficulties that were first encountered by the laboratory participants were magnified during the crusade. As pointed out by the national team in interviews, some problems could have been tempered if more attention had been paid to insights gained during the laboratory experience. The problems, a number of which were inevitable and unavoidable, involved questions of logistics, communication, politics, motivation, health, and difficulties with the primer and the teaching method. The first problems were with the logistics of getting the teachers to their sites. Long treks over rocky mountain paths were common, two people got lost, and one university student fell off a mule into a cactus patch and ended up spending five hours removing needles and putting iodine on his wounds. In some cases, no one was expecting them at their sites; in others, no preparations for lodging had been made. When adequate information had been provided, the people were expectant, more ready to participate. In other situations, people were reluctant to become involved, often shy, or in some instances, fearful that the pair were Communists coming to take away their land and chickens. In the majority of cases, it took some days to overcome hesitancy and resistance. Home visits, village meetings, and a smiling persistence on the part of the experimental *brigadistas* helped them to gain the confidence and acceptance of the communities.

But life in the countryside was harder than expected. Many teachers got sick, all got badly bitten by insects, some lost weight. Others, especially in more remote sites where no organizational support existed, were profoundly lonely. Despite these difficulties, most teams had started their literacy work with enthusiasm and community support after one week. In Río San Juan, one member of the crusade told of one peasant's reaction to their arrival: "When we told the assembled group of people the purpose of our work, one man stepped up to thank us. Using the words of a famous Nicaraguan saying he told us, 'Now "the dawn of a new day is no longer a temptation" beyond our reach. You have come to us like the rays of that new sun'" (Campos 1980).

The laboratory participants saw their tasks as essentially being to test the program's materials, methodology, and community organizing activities and to identify strengths and weaknesses so the next level of training could be better designed. They carefully scrutinized all aspects of the program, and their evaluation reports contained revealing conclusions that predicted the ultimate strengths and weaknesses of much of the campaign. They concluded, as had the participants in the pilot project, that despite the problems with the materials and teaching methods, literacy skills could be taught and learned but that the difficulties and weaknesses in the approach presented serious obstacles to learning and hindered the full development of *concientización*.

The most widespread concern centered around the generation of an effective, participatory critical dialogue. The pictures of Sandino and Fonseca that had been chosen for the second and third dialogues were not conducive to an analytical discussion. Because Somoza had suppressed information about the two men, most people could not recognize either figure, and even if they did, such recognition did not usually lead to a discussion that was intimately related to the learners' immediate world. There was one exception—a village near the Honduran border where Sandino had worked and fought. The peasants there told the story that the general had hidden some documents with them, burying the packet and warning the peasants not to reveal the whereabouts of the papers until all the village knew how to read. In that place, there was a lively critical discussion of the photograph as the people believed that Sandino knew that it would be safe to reveal the documents only when they had learned to read because that would mean a popular movement had gained power and was fulfilling the original promises of the peasant leader.

Overall, however, the photographs led to a formal exposition on the part of the literacy promoter and an inability to move beyond discourse to analysis and participation. Every squadron pointed out this difficulty and the literacy teachers' inability under the circumstances to facilitate participation. Their concern about the situation was deeply felt because they saw it created resistance on the part of the learners toward taking part in further dialogue within the context of the specific lessons. The training staff suggested that to overcome this difficulty, instead of trying to analyze the photographs, a quote from each man might be used, especially one that related to the participation of the poor and the peasants in the struggle for liberation. On the whole, this idea proved too abstract, and when it was attempted, it did not generate discussion.

Outside of the two-hour literacy sessions, however, in the events of everyday living, animated discussions and dialogue did take place. In fact, one of the most positive aspects of the laboratory experience noted by the *brigadistas* was the generation of participation through the community-action research program. Activities such as town meetings and sociodramas were held in order to discuss and confront community needs and problems. Many of the squadron members became involved in community organizing as a result, and they felt acutely that the literacy workers should be community organizers as well.

Other specific lessons gained through the laboratory experience principally involved questions of materials and teaching methods, such as the widespread problem every group mentioned involving the second syllable family taught—sa, se, si, so, su—and its inverse syllables—as, es, is, os, us—and the compound ones—sas, sis, ses, sos, sus. Other problems identified were (1) there was a tendency on the part of some learners to spell out letters they had already memorized during some past educational experience rather than to sound out syllable families, (2) the learners had difficulty creating words from the syllable families they had learned, and (3) the laboratory participants had problems in writing appropriate analytical field diaries.

Many of the groups found that the aspects of artistic and cultural expression and community-action research were especially effective in stimulating participation and helping people overcome their shyness and sense of inferiority. As Luis Alemán has explained:

> The volunteers organized bonfires, town meetings, piñatas, assemblies. People began to work with sociodramas, couplets, songs, poetry, chants. It was art, but not in the traditional, formal artsy fashion, rather in a natural way—used by people as a means to express their own reality, their own needs. And the kids from the workshop knew that it wasn't a matter of making it formal, fancy, or professional. It wasn't a drama or play with a set script, no, it was inventing and creating on the spot, a permanent meeting of expression and creation. . . . And the results were incredible. The peasants loved to express themselves this way. Some were tremendous actors, playing their roles so well that they amazed even the group from the workshop with their creativity and ability to learn and apply new concepts. In one area where two communities had been feuding for years, the group actually got the two together for a cultural activity. They held a bonfire and sang songs, recited verses, and gave speeches. Can you believe it? The whole thing actually ended with handshakes and even pats on the back. [Alemán 1980]

Evaluation and Planning Meetings

With the rich and moving laboratory experience behind them, the squadrons returned to the mountainside retreat of Tepeyac—cocky and confident and with a deeper commitment to the project and an exuberant enthusiasm for the challenge ahead. They had proved to themselves and to the crusade staff that the training had been effective and, more important, that the campaign would succeed. They returned as know-it-alls. They came back, as one national team member described, like "Tarzan's mother," as if they had actually born and bred the jungle hero. And they returned with criticisms and suggestions. However, the first day of the reencounter was a disaster because the national team broke its own educational principles.

A five-day evaluation workshop had been designed with three basic purposes in mind: (1) to assess the effectiveness of the training materials and methods in light of the first laboratory experience—which, by implication, meant the assessment of the literacy materials and methods as well; (2) to program the next phase of training; and (3) to select from the group of eighty the trainers for Workshop 2 and the researchers for the second laboratory stage. The national training team came to the encounter with all the pressures and worries of Workshop 2 in mind, and the group of eighty arrived with the extraordinarily profound experience of the laboratory vivid and beautiful in their memories, eager to share and analyze. The national team began the meeting with an exercise to evaluate Workshop 1. Enthusiasm sputtered and hit bottom. As one team member has recalled:

> What a hell of a mess. It was as if we had erased their field experience from the map—the experience that had meant the most to them, that was the freshest in their minds, a time that had given them a treasure of memories and a rich source of learning material. We wiped it from the map with our worry about programming and planning the second workshop. It was like we were saying to them, you never went to the mountains to teach and if you did, it was only to evaluate Workshop 1. What a tub of cold water we dumped on them. We soon realized we were going upstream against a strong current. [Suarez 1980]

The flexibility, sense of respect, and sensitivity of the members of the training team allowed them to listen to the participants and to reevaluate and reschedule on the spot, thus recovering the lost momentum.

> They made us realize that we had just broken the first educational principle we had espoused in Workshop 1—that of beginning with the most concrete, direct, motivating experience that people share. Then, they went on to challenge us by saying that we didn't know what we were talking about, that we were idealists and romantics who didn't really know what was happening out there, how hard it was. Distances were great, roads terrible, food scarce, people had to be convinced to participate, and the method and primer had problems. In all fairness we had done everything possible to make time to visit them, but given our other responsibilities, it was difficult. Those were the days and nights of no sleep, of long hikes into the mountains, of bug bites and sunburn. We got dizzy sometimes from so much walking in the sun and disoriented and lost when it got dark. But they were right. . . . we hadn't been there, we had managed to visit them once or twice, but we hadn't participated

on a daily basis. Next time, at least one member from each national team, pedagogical and organizational both, should work alongside them to be able to share and learn from the experience. The program would have been much improved if we had.

That first day back was awful but through a sociodrama and discussions we worked out the problem and reoriented the meeting. It turned out very beautiful, really. In order to begin the process of sharing with us and each other, they produced a newspaper of their experiences, a literary collection, really, including poems, songs, anecdotes, legends, and stories from their peasant companions and their own reflections. [Suarez 1980]

In a more systematic fashion, the group then proceeded to evaluate the lessons learned from the laboratory experience, make suggestions to improve the next workshops, and based on that analysis, plan Workshop 2. This evaluation affirmed several basic educational principles—those of learning by doing and discovery and of creating and re-creating knowledge through the integration of theory and practice, testing and analysis. The group also established the validity and importance to the training process of cultural expression, community research, the theoretical background papers, and the active participation in and promotion of community organizing activities.

Two issues evoked passionate discussion—community-action research and the role of community organizing in the literacy crusade. The workshop and field experiences had proved to the participants the importance of the concepts presented in community-action research, and their practice in the field had shown them the urgent need for community organizing. They returned fervently believing that these two aspects had to be fully integrated into the campaign. "To understand this," explained one of the team members who helped develop the research plan, "you have to go back to Workshop 1."

There, we presented the participants with the concept of community-action research. For us, research was the process of knowledge building, of acquiring understanding, of reflecting, of people forming opinions about their life situations so that they could plan, define their objectives and actions in order to transform their world. At the end of the workshop, after they had a lot of practical, concrete learning experiences and exercises, we gave them a document explaining the idea and approach. They discussed it, analyzed it, and found it fascinating but more for the theory than for the methodology. They found that it helped them understand the more global aspects of the revolution, it fit into the analytical framework they had been developing as a result of their practice. But we pointed out to them that besides analysis and theory, the methodology—the community participation—was also vital.

They went to the field with an extraordinary enthusiasm and excitement about the research process because they saw it as the cornerstone, the very foundation of the program. They saw it as the way to enrich the content and methodology of the primer, as the way to involve the people in developing their skills, their ability to analyze and reflect over their world in order to transform it. They went to the field and tried it out. The results of their efforts were on the whole very favorable, some quite extraordinary.

First, in their literacy groups they had begun by helping people to reflect over their lives in order to discover and analyze their reality. Then later, they worked with the community in general. They organized town assemblies to discuss the area's needs and problems so that people could address the situations more effectively. They were beginning the slow process of social transformation. [Suarez 1980]

and that of their own sociali- zation

However, some members of the national staff felt that the trainees, in their enthusiasm, had forgotten the massive nature of the campaign. In its actual operation the crusade would depend on young, inexperienced people, many of whom it was felt would be incapable of understanding the concepts involved in the approach or of generating such a development process. Moreover, giving the volunteers increased responsibilities might distract them too much from the priority task—teaching people how to read and write. Concern was great on the part of some members of the pedagogical staff that the quality of literacy skills acquired would be seriously limited by such an approach. Others argued the opposite, stressing that the integration of reading and writing with community development activities was vital to learning and to revolutionary transformation.

The debate continued during the course of the actual campaign, and eventually, a resolution was reached in the field. Because of the volunteers' natural interest and the overwhelming needs of the rural people, many of the *brigadistas* became involved in organizing with the support and approval of the EPA. In a midpoint evaluation congress, the representative of the *Frente* emphasized that the community organizing aspect was one of the most important activities of the campaign. In varying degrees, the staff members who had been dubious about integrating literacy with community work changed their minds during the crusade. Several had become active, articulate proponents of the integrated approach by the time the campaign ended.

In the Phase 1 evaluation meeting in January, after much debate and eloquent testimony, the group of eighty finally convinced the crusade leadership of the importance of integrating development organizing with literacy and of including community research in the rest of training. They emphasized the postitive and creative effects of the process in

affirming a sense of personal dignity and promoting community participation, analytical skills, and a commitment to the programs of the
revolution. Fernando Cardenal, despite some initial reservations, was
impressed with the participants' arguments and convictions. He supported their position and agreed to its inclusion. In the final teaching
guide, however, because of a restriction on the number of pages and
the rush of last-minute activities and responsibilities, the program of
community research and its supporting theoretical analysis had to be
presented in abbreviated form, and it lost much of its original force
and purpose. Consequently, although the laboratory experience had
proved the creative potential of such an approach, the crusade did not
test its viability on a massive scale. It should be noted, however, that
in some cases during the campaign, the volunteers used the approach
naturally in their work with communities.

The evaluation meeting ended with the team's selection of forty-four
of the eighty to be the training coordinators of Workshop 2. The other
participants were given the responsibility of continuing the field testing
of the training process in stage 2 of the laboratory. The stage-2 researchers
met on January 28 and 29 to plan the follow-up program, review the
initial structure of the EPA, and revise the documents on community-
action research.

Phase 2

In the last week of January, after the evaluation/planning meeting,
the twenty-two pairs of newly prepared trainers proceeded to the
countryside to oversee the final arrangements for the second tier of
workshops. The spirit of initiative and creativity that had been engendered
in these participants by Workshop 1 would be sorely tested during
Phase 2 but ultimately found resilient, strengthened by the many problems
the trainers would encounter and resolve. They arrived in the nine
provinces that had been chosen as training sites and found that in many
cases, arrangements for the workshops either had not been made or
had been only partially made. In some instances, the newly selected
provincial coordinators had not responded to their assignment of setting
up the sites effectively; two were replaced for poor management as a
direct result. Undaunted, the training facilitators forged ahead, confronting
problems, big and small.

The spirit, sense of confidence, and analytical skills that had been
acquired in the first workshop gave the new workshop leaders the ability
to solve the problems creatively and quickly, as did the authority bestowed
upon them by the national office. Since the workshops were to begin
in less than a week, that ability and authority were crucial. Without

this capacity on their part, the program could well have floundered seriously, placing the entire multiplier process in jeopardy. The response of the trainers under fire was decisive in guaranteeing the rest of training. They identified problems, took initiative, and organized Workshop 2 on the spot. In Managua, for example, the facilitators themselves had to find the workshop locale, buy the food for ninety participants, and double as cooks during the first few days of training.

As Luis Alemán has said, they were the foundation of the entire process:

> The group was fundamental. Without them the crusade never would have succeeded in capturing the imagination of the public. During those days the provincial coordinators had just been named and really didn't have a sense of the campaign's spirit or knowledge of literacy. Into that situation march the kids from the group of eighty. The crusade had no atmosphere then, no appeal beyond an ideal, no body or bones. It was just an embryo, but with the *mística* they possessed, that vital need to become and to do, they did. Off they went to the provinces two or three days before the workshops were to begin. What do they find? The coordinators had not been able to do much really. In some places ANDEN had a group of teachers ready, but there was no food ordered or no place to meet. The kids moved mountains, hustling and bustling everyone—the coordinators, ANDEN, Juventud, the ministries, everyone. We gave them the authority and responsibility to do whatever they had to, come hell or high water, but to get those workshops moving. Without their insistence and initiative Workshop 2 wouldn't have happened. With its completion the spirit of the crusade took actual shape and form. An ideal was becoming real. [Alemán 1980]

As a result of the facilitators' work, people began to believe that the campaign was more than just a promise. The pledge was going to be kept. However, the thrusting of this vital organizing upon the workshop facilitators had some negative repercussions as the crusade advanced. Often, given the urgency of time pressures, they had to give direct orders to the provincial coordinators. The training personnel, of course, saw themselves as the most knowledgeable of the staff. Their preparation had been extensive, covering all aspects of the campaign, while the coordinators were newly hired and had had only a brief two-day orientation. In certain cases, this situation caused resentment and friction and affected the future working relationship between the Organizational and Pedagogical Divisions.

Workshop 2

Despite the difficulties, Workshop 2 started on time almost everywhere. As the training began, the facilitators were joined by representatives from the national pedagogical team who were to serve as support staff, but more in an observer role than an advisory one, intervening only when absolutely necessary. The goal was to give the trainers as much experience on their own as possible.

Workshops took place anywhere shelter could be found—in schools, church retreats, haciendas of ousted National Guard officers, and mansions of the deposed Somoza elite. One group even met beside an empty swimming pool in a caboose car that had served as an elegant private bar during the former regime.

Originally, Workshop 2 had been designed for 280 primary school teachers, but in planning the program in November, the national team had realized the importance of expanding the number of participants so that an effective selection process could be conducted. The number had been increased to 630 in order to provide what was thought to be an adequate pool of candidates from which to choose the most capable facilitators for the next level of training. The national team also felt that including more university students was important to the process because of their experience during the war, their openness to educational change, and their commitment to the revolution. The group of 630 was mixed—about 60 percent were young teachers, almost 30 percent were university students, and a little more than 10 percent were members of citizen and labor organizations, ministries, and private organizations. (The ATC sent one delegate; the Sandinista Labor Federation [CST], thirteen; the Nicaraguan Women's Association [AMNLAE], seventeen; and the CDS, twenty-five.) Once again, the selection process was not as rigorous as the national training team would have preferred. In some provinces, ANDEN attempted to choose who it sent according to criteria based on potential capacity and commitment, in others, no. Attempts were also made to select participants according to a regional distribution so that once the crusade was in operation, these people could form the basic pedagogical support structure for each municipality.

Because the specific purpose of Workshop 2 was to prepare more trainers for the multiplier process, the participation of representatives from the citizen and labor associations was limited, and this limitation had its costs. With hindsight, it is clear that if the program had involved more organizational representatives at this juncture, the workshop would have been enriched by their presence, and the citizen and labor associations would have been able to participate more effectively in the crusade from the beginning. As it was, in general, their members did not receive any preparation until Phase 4, so their participation in the organizing stages of the campaign was sporadic and not as strong as it might have been.

As one national team member has pointed out: "We did not really incorporate the citizen and labor associations into the training process until Workshop 4, which was the last stage and the most problematic. We limited our focus to preparing trainers. If we had included the associations at the beginning, the provincial commissions would have been greatly improved and more involved in the process" (Suarez 1980).

But there was another, far more serious problem—the lack of participation in Workshop 2 on the part of the provincial coordinators combined with the fact that no internal training on the educational aspects of the crusade ever took place within the campaign's Organizational Division. This situation led to a lack of coordination and coherence in the overall program and exacerbated the same separation between the Pedagogical and Organizational Divisions on the provincial level that existed on the national level. A common shared understanding of the program's pedagogy and its political scope did not exist. Consequently, the changes that the new pedagogical approach implied in educational roles and methods could not be implemented in an integrated fashion.

Selected in December and January, the provincial coordinators had received no preparation or background on the pedagogical aspects of the crusade. Despite the insistence of the national pedagogical team, many never did, a situation that frustrated Luis Alemán. "We had always planned to give them training, but the Organizational Division said there was no time" (Alemán 1980). It was true that the coordinators' responsibilities were heavy and urgent, so the organizational leadership did not consider that training their personnel in the educational aspects of the crusade was a priority. Some coordinators did participate in Phase 4 on a very informal off-and-on basis, but because of the quality of those workshops and the sporadic nature of the coordinators' attendance, they did not gain the understanding necessary for an integrated, coordinated implementation. As one member of the pedagogical team has explained:

The fact that the provincial coordinators began with such overwhelming responsibilities taking up all their time resulted in a certain programmatic weakness that was never really overcome. Many coordinators never received the workshop because there was so much else to do. They could not develop a real commitment or become incorporated into the educational program, nor could they grasp its full significance. This problem was somewhat addressed in the fourth workshop when certain coordinators more or less attended the training sessions, but there were others who never did. This remained a problem throughout the crusade. In part, it was responsible for the lack of coherence present in the many dimensions of the literacy program. Because for all the explanations you might give people, what really gave you the total sense of the crusade were those first workshops with their special dynamic environment—their participation, excitement, their methodology of learning by doing, discovery, creation, analysis, and re-creation. Those workshops joined together all the different aspects of the program—the objectives, methods, and materials—with the spirit of the campaign—its creativity, *concientización*, and commitment. [Suarez 1980]

The problems were many, and those in one province were somewhat different than those in the next. When asked what their greatest difficulties had been in Workshop 2, the facilitators most frequently mentioned the following: logistics, the provincial coordinators, and the poor selection and orientation of the participants. In one or two instances, health was cited as a problem since vaccinations had been given immediately prior to the workshop, causing fever in many cases. As usual, the materials did not arrive on time, nor in sufficient quantity. One mimeograph machine broke down and the counter on the other malfunctioned. Luis Alemán would shrug his shoulders as if to say, "What can you do? It's chaos, yes, but we're doing the best we can." Despite the problems, the learning climate and the sense of cohesion generated by Workshop 2 were reported to be similar to those of Workshop 1. The levels of commitment to the revolution were not as high, but an enthusiasm for the crusade was instilled in almost all of the participants.

Decentralization enriched Workshop 2. By being regionally dispersed, these workshops were better able to reflect the problems and conditions of the provinces and the concerns of the local people. In the process, they acquainted the crusade personnel with the regional situations. Enthusiasm among the participants for the new educational methods was great—simulations, sociodramas, songs, fishbowl discussions, and debate energized the sessions. Most groups participated with zest. The level of creativity and quantity of artistic expression and cultural production remained high through Phase 2. Workshop walls were covered with examples of poetry, songs, drawings, and drama. As in Workshop 1, training facilitators had some problems in establishing and defining their new educational role. Many acted as master of ceremonies, presenting or announcing activities and then standing back and watching them take place. Others were more directive and domineering. That there was difficulty in developing problem-posing situations and in presenting the dialogue could be noticed as well in some of the workshops.

The creativity and sense of commitment and criticism that were manifested in many of the Phase 2 workshops can be demonstrated by one example of the participants' artistic expression. One workshop group developed its own radio program and patterned it after the clandestine station, Radio Sandino, that had been so important during the war. The programs were designed to animate, criticize, inspire, and improve the workshop, and they were broadcast by using tapes that would suddenly begin running at mealtimes and during recreation periods.

> RADIO ALFABETIZAREMOS—RADIO LET'S TEACH LITERACY—broadcasting to you clandestinely from its secret location somewhere in Nicaragua. We will be transmitting on the following frequencies: 600 megahertz and 1300 kilohertz. Our mission is to orient, suggest, and bring to you the concerns identified in each of our squadrons. . . . a few people when it comes time to participate do so passively, conservatively, adopting only a receptive role; others are individualistic, challenging people on personal grounds, never admitting their own responsibility. . . . Criticism is not just pointing out errors and mistakes. It involves an analysis of a given situation, showing its virtues and weaknesses, its truths and untruths, but at the same time proposing the means, the alternatives that can solve the problem or defect identified. Criticism is only one part, it is a beginning. It obliges us and bestows upon us the duty of self-criticism, of admitting our weaknesses and responsibilities. It obliges us to ask ourselves, To what extent have we personally contributed to overcoming the problem? . . . Let us give the best of ourselves. Let us participate and work on behalf of our brothers and sisters, the peasants and workers of Nicaragua, who today are still imprisoned in the jails of ignorance. [Aurora Workshop 2 1980]

Workshop 2 was further enriched by informal discussions about life in the countryside and actual literacy teaching. Because of their laboratory experience, the training facilitators could speak with authority about these aspects. They were able to provide participants with valuable information about the cross-cultural aspects of actually living in a rural situation. For example, after a simulation in which a female *brigadista* had given a peasant student, a male, an encouraging pat on the back, the facilitator cautioned that women in the country can be very jealous. Innocent gestures of affection can be misinterpreted and cause resistance to both the *brigadista* and the program. This important cultural component was missing from the rest of the training because even though the training team wanted to include a laboratory experience for this second group, last-minute changes in the next level of training made it impossible to do so. This lack of actual experience lessened the authority the next set of facilitators could speak with, and given the composition of the next group of participants, mostly teachers, this was unfortunate.

About two-thirds of the participants from Workshop 2 were selected to become Workshop 3 coordinators. They were chosen by the Workshop

2 facilitators for their capacity to communicate, lead, and handle the learning materials, methods, and discussion themes. Ideally, they were to be paired—one teacher, one university student. The rest of the Workshop 2 participants became municipal advisers.

Laboratory, Stage 2

While Workshop 2 was being conducted, the second stage of the laboratory continued with the participation of the Workshop 1 members who had not been chosen to be Workshop 2 trainers. These laboratory participants served a dual role: researcher and *brigadista*. By the end of February, their work and behavior were providing some valuable lessons about what the crusade was going to face when actually in operation. Problems of food, discipline, health, safety, labor migrations, and communication were revealed. For example, the laboratory *brigadistas* would leave their sites without asking a supervisor's permission to visit Managua on weekends. Letters would arrive from parents, and a mail delivery system had to be set up. Counterrevolutionary bands of former National Guardsmen harassed and threatened teachers and students alike.

In terms of educational aspects, it was discovered that the laboratory *brigadistas* had to divide their literacy groups to accommodate the students' different rates of learning. By the end of this second field experience in March, the lab participants had found that after lesson nine, learning accelerated. This information was valuable and should have been incorporated into the program's calendar to emphasize the fact that if *brigadistas* worked hard to consolidate skills in the first nine lessons, the rest would go quickly. Again, because of time pressure and lack of communication, it was not. The supervisory team also noted that the *brigadistas* needed more practice in such methods as sociodrama and dialogue.

Phase 3: Workshop 3

The words of a member of the group of eighty, Alonso Cano, reflect the difficult transition between Phases 2 and 3. "We thought we had problems in Workshop 2. In 3, we had an avalanche of them" (Cano 1980). From 22 workshops in Phase 2 the number jumped to almost 400 in the next phase—a quantity that was both unexpected and unplanned for—from 630 participants to approximately 12,000. Originally, Workshop 3 had been designed to prepare approximately 7,000 university students and a small contingent of carefully selected teachers as training coordinators for Phase 4, a plan that implied the early dismissal of university classes that semester. However, certain decisions were made just prior to the launching of Phase 3 that resulted in profound changes in the selection of the participants and the design of the workshop. These decisions, which would also have serious consequences for Workshop 4, originated in the highest spheres of government.

The country's leadership, facing the staggering problems of reconstruction, was, of course, concerned about the development of skilled professionals and technocrats who would be capable of handling the urgent challenge of rebuilding the economy. They wondered about the wisdom of closing the universities almost two months early (as called for by the training design), especially in light of the fact that in the previous several years, classes had been continually interrupted and often suspended because of the war. This thinking and a certain lack of confidence in the potential of students as workshop coordinators led the government leaders to reconsider the original training proposal and decide not to close the entire university. At that time, perhaps in part because of the ambivalence felt by the country's leadership about university-student participation in the campaign, enrollment in the program was not as high as had been anticipated. But in all, some 1,000 students were given permission to finish their studies early so they could participate in Workshop 3. Students preparing for careers that were considered vital to the nation's development, such as medicine, agriculture, and engineering, were required to finish the semester.

This decision, made some ten days before Workshop 3 was to begin, initially provoked minor panic among the members of the national training team, but by that time, problems were second nature to them so the panic subsided quickly. In the rush of reprogramming, there was little time to dwell on the decision's implications, but they were considerable. University students had been chosen originally to be the major participants in Workshop 3 and the trainers of Workshop 4 for important reasons—both pedagogical and political. The team had felt that the university students would be more open and capable of understanding the new educational approaches to be used in the campaign than the traditional teachers who had been educated and brought up under the Somoza system. Moreover, from experience, the team knew that it is very difficult for teachers of children to grasp the special nature of adult learning, its different teaching styles and student-teacher relationships. It was felt that the teachers would resist the structural changes that were the very underpinnings of the program, whereas the students would welcome the participatory approach.

But perhaps what concerned the planners most were the political and psychological implications of using teachers as the principal group of trainers in Phase 4. On the whole, teachers in Nicaragua were considered to be very conservative, both in their pedagogy and in their politics. Becoming a teacher was a means to climb the social ladder toward economic advancement. Many of the teachers had come from the lower classes of society. Their families had scrimped to pay for their studies, and as students, many of them had worked hard. They felt their place in society was well deserved, won by arduous labor and study. This attitude often led them to belittle or feel superior to others who had not made it—namely, the peasants and workers, the very people who were to be taught literacy skills. If these teachers were used as *brigadista* trainers, they might subconsciously, if not openly, convey this negative message to the young people. Politically, the more conservative of the teachers could use the training to undermine the campaign by not preparing the students adequately or by encouraging them not to participate. It would be impossible for this type of teacher to inspire the commitment, excitement, and sense of purpose that volunteers would need in order to get the maximum benefit from their training.

University students on the other hand offered a different perspective. Some had participated actively in the war and were firmly committed to the revolution. Others had not fought, but were sympathetic to the Sandinista vision of a new, more equitable society and wanted to participate in its creation. It was felt that as a group, the students held ideals, albeit often vague and unformed, that were compatible with the goals of the campaign and that they would be more open to recognizing and affirming the potential of the peasants and the workers. During the long struggle against Somoza, many of the students had become at least rhetorically imbued with a commitment to the poor and to the goals of social transformation that were espoused by the FSLN.

The national training team feared that without this spirit and openness on the part of the trainers, the goals of the crusade could be seriously compromised, not only that of teaching literacy but also of helping people develop an awareness of themselves as creative, competent citizens committed to building a new society. Pragmatically, the team members also sensed that although many of the student volunteers welcomed the crusade as a personal challenge, as an adventure, many of the teachers saw it as a burden, a separation from their families. The teachers had been informed that they would be serving as educational advisers to the volunteers, but they had not expected to be involved until the final stages of the training program, in mid-March after school was over. Moving up the date of their participation unexpectedly, when classes were still in session, would decrease their already shaky commitment and motivation and surely weaken the training program for the *brigadistas*. These arguments, however, probably did not affect the government's decision, because no representative from the training team was present during the high-level discussions. The crusade delegate was not aware of such issues and therefore could not present them. This situation is another example of the difficulties of coordinating the many sectors involved in the campaign and points to the particular problems of a new government's trying to mount such an effort in a short time during a period of transition.

The last-minute decision triggered fundamental revisions in the actual design of the workshops in regard to length and participation. Although the national team had recognized the advantages of residential programs for developing skills and commitments, such as in Workshops 1 and 2, the budget and lack of infrastructure did not allow for more of this type of concentrated training. So, as originally conceived, the Phase 3 workshops were to be nonresidential, but they would be conducted full time—eight to nine hours a day. However, when the decision was made not to include many university students, even the ability to conduct a full-time program was affected.

Because the training would be held while classes were still in session, the workshops became, by necessity, a half-time effort—four hours per day. (Exceptions were made in those rural areas where the teachers worked at great distances from each other. In these cases, the school year ended early.) This half-time pattern broke the rhythm of the sessions and limited the ability of the trainers to create a congenial and spirited learning environment. The optimum flow and processing of activities depended upon eight-hour periods—a concentrated time in which to develop the skills, attitudes, and type of participation that were required for the maximum functioning of the workshop. Learning was diminished by this half-time schedule, especially since the teachers also had all the worries and responsibilities of finishing school on their minds—final examinations, grading papers, and record keeping, among others.

Increasing the number of participants in Workshop 3 by some 5,000 people also meant that more trainers had to be found, and Workshop 2 participants who had not originally been selected to become coordinators were now recruited. The group of eighty was called on as well, so their work in developing the educational support structure for the campaign in the provinces was suspended. Despite this additional recruitment, there still were not enough facilitators. Many of the coordinator pairs, therefore, had to conduct two or three training sessions a day—morning, afternoon, and evening. The difficulties all the facilitators faced were enormous, as Luis Alemán has explained.

Once the decision was made not to close the university, the only answer was to carry on with the teachers. But what that meant—it was awesome. The teachers [were] one of the most difficult and challenging sectors of society—so many without any sense of real commitment, little concern, without any love for their work. Unfortunately, the Somoza system had done its job well, too many people only cared about themselves. On top of everything else, that decision meant we had to organize the entire teaching profession in the whole nation with only ten days advance notice. Thank the Lord, there was more support from ANDEN and the provincial offices of the crusade by then. But we still had to run around to all the municipalities in order to locate the teachers, inform them of the changes, make lists, find training sites, etc., etc. Those people from Workshops 1 and 2 were heroes. Some had to coordinate workshops morning, noon, and night with three separate groups. We knew what it was like to conduct one workshop—you get exhausted. To conduct three at one time must have been terrible. But they were tremendous—the tasks they faced and no real supervision. Once they got beyond the provincial capitals, no nothing. [Alemán 1980]

After Workshop 2, the new training coordinators were deployed throughout the nation to each province along with representatives from the national office to act as team leaders. After one day of rest, the first task of each was to meet with the provincial crusade coordinator, the literacy commission, the director of education, and delegates from the *Frente*, ANDEN, and the citizen and labor associations. They met in order to discuss the Phase 3 work plan and to define final tasks and time lines. The training facilitators then headed for the municipalities to work with the local commissions in overseeing the final preparations for Workshop 3. They were kept busy—assuring adequate sites, delegating responsibilities for logistic support, enrolling teachers, assigning them to specific workshop sites, and imparting the crusade's spirit of enthusiasm and national pride to the communities through town meetings and cultural events.

On February 23, they were due back in the provincial capitals with their reports in order to coordinate the activities throughout the provinces so that Phase 3 could be launched. Materials were distributed, and last-minute details were ironed out. Two days later, on February 25, workshops began all across the land. Some started a little early and some a few days late, but they began. Those religiously inclined called the fact that they began on time a miracle; everyone agreed that it was an extraordinary demonstration of commitment, determination, cooperation, and plain hard work.

The national adviser to one of the more isolated regions, Río San Juan, has described the team's adventures and accomplishments in that area.

We arrived and the situation was unbelievable—a place totally abandoned and forgotten by the outside world. We were two days late because the cattle barge we were originally going to take did not leave as scheduled.

The cows never came. So we hitched a ride on a rice boat. It took us twenty hours finally just to get there. Once in the provincial capital, the only transportation was by jungle path and river. It was so bad that I even ended up as part trainer. We broke all the rules. I had to send off the coordinators to the municipalities permanently. We closed the schools two weeks early. The distances and mobilization were so difficult that we sent off two facilitators up river and didn't see them again for fifteen days. I stayed in the capital receiving messages by boat, mule, and canoe. We sent out all the materials to them in the same way. [Suarez 1980]

Workshop 3 began, and the problems flourished. In Managua, a special meeting of all teachers with members of the National Board of Directors of the FSLN, to have been sponsored by ANDEN as part of the workshop, was canceled on the day of the event because of inadequate communication on ANDEN's part. The cancellation caused division among the teachers and bad feelings in general. An opportunity to inspire and challenge people to excellence for the difficult moments ahead had been lost. One of the provincial supervisors has described other difficulties.

Given the massiveness of the program at that moment, all the problems we expected with the teachers surfaced and flowered. If we thought we had serious difficulties in Workshop 2, it started out as chaos in 3. In some places, workshops had to be suspended temporarily while negotiations were held between ANDEN and the Ministry of Education. Certain teachers, despite the fact they were being paid for their participation, refused to attend. At that moment we realized the extraordinary human limitations we were going to have to work with. [Suarez 1980]

According to all reports, the first days of Workshop 3 were discouraging and in some cases downright disastrous. Among other problems, the teachers resisted the university-student facilitators. They considered them to be lacking in education experience and knowledge and too rigid and unforgiving politically. As a result, some teachers challenged the primer's design, insisting that their traditional teaching methods were better. Some complained that the program was a Cuban invention. To clear the record, representatives of the national team were called in, when possible, to explain the theoretical basis and authentic Nicaraguan roots of the crusade's program. As the workshop continued, these difficult situations mostly improved, although some of the participants continued to oppose the effort and refused to cooperate in workshop activities. One national team member has remembered:

Starting with the first days of that workshop, when the teachers arrived with their pencils and notebooks, ready for long lectures and boring sessions of note taking, I watched them grow and develop. But at the beginning, it wasn't easy for the training coordinators. They had come from the rich, full exciting experience of Workshop 2 to chaos. Those first days they would come to me desperate, some even crying with frustration. "How do we shake up those people? How do we get them involved? They're impossible!" But after about the third day attitudes began to change. By the end, a large number of the teachers had captured the sense and spirit of the campaign. [Suarez 1980]

As Luis Alemán has explained: "Even though the workshop was conducted on a massive scale, its approach had an appeal. Some of the teachers saw that the methodology was different, was effective, and realized its validity. They recognized it would require changes in their teaching style, but the dynamics of the workshop caught their imagination, and they became involved. They liked the participation. They felt they were worth something" (Alemán 1980).

Although it cannot be determined how widespread or deep this change in attitude was, it occurred to some extent in all regions of the country. One report pointed to the internal organizational structure of the workshop—the small study groups—as having helped promote involvement. In the few instances in which workshops were held for members of the citizen and labor associations, they were much better than those for the teachers, with participants showing, as was to be expected, greater levels of enthusiasm and energy. The most difficult workshops seemed to be those for the secondary teachers, who demonstrated a sense of superiority and self-importance in regard to the younger and less-educated primary school teachers.

One of the clearly positive consequences of Phase 3 was the development and growth of the training facilitators themselves. Certain problems did exist, however. There were some problems when one coordinator in a pair was more active and energetic than the other, and sometimes personalities influenced decisions more than they should have in the final selection process. But in the face of adversity, it was felt that the facilitators had responded well as a group. As one report concluded: "The development of the coordinators was one of the most outstanding and inspiring results of the workshop—the positive and qualitative way in which they responded and grew through the process. The university students and especially the young teachers jumped in and dedicated themselves completely to the work with great initiative and responsibility" (Nicaragua, Ministry of Education, National Literacy Crusade 1980, 3).

Because of the massive staffing needs of Phase 4, the selection process used to choose the next tier of trainers was limited simply to excluding the most reactionary participants. Although most members of the national pedagogical team felt that Workshop 3 was the point at which the training suffered a severe collapse, especially in terms of the pedagogical and political aspects of the program, they also recognized that the effort had its positive results. The next level of training was clearly weakened, but the national team also felt that many of the teachers had, through the workshop experience, overcome their stubborn resistance and become committed to the process and the campaign. Many also joined ANDEN, which the team considered to be a positive result. In this way, Phase 3 had helped strengthen one of the citizen and labor associations, an important goal of the crusade.

Phase 4: Workshop 4

If people thought that Phase 3 was an avalanche, Phase 4 was clearly an earthquake. As it began, some staff members were not sure how the program would withstand its tremors. One national adviser put it this way: "The massiveness of Workshop 4 caused us incredible problems. Well, God help us, frankly it started out one hell of a mess" (Suarez 1980). Certain program specifics had not been resolved until the last minute, and this situation created the same kind of unexpected problems that had occurred during Phase 3.

During the course of Workshop 3, the Ministry of Education had announced that the entire eligible student population (those twelve years old and older) would participate in the one-week's training to be provided by Workshop 4 even if they were not going out to teach. The feeling was that given the extraordinary historic significance of the crusade to Nicaragua and to the rest of Latin America, all students should have an opportunity to at least take part in the preparatory training activities. In addition, participation in the training program would acquaint the students with the learning techniques and approaches that were to form the basis of the new educational system. It was also thought that in the process, some of those who had not yet decided to participate might choose to join their classmates as volunteers. This result did occur in some cases, but probably not to the same extent as if the training program had been run by more committed and enthusiastic university students.

In the few days between the termination of Workshop 3 and the beginning of Workshop 4, much had to be done. The provincial and municipal offices were filled to overflowing with busy people compiling long lists and counting stacks of materials. Across the country in crusade offices everywhere, members of the group of 630 were madly trying to match teachers with workshop locations. They sat at tables, on desks, on the floor, on porch steps—everywhere—making lists. Small but important details absorbed them. For instance, a typical interchange went like this (Miller 1980):

> "Nidia Hidalgo will be assigned to the Divine Shepherd High School."
> "Check."
> "Nidia de Gonzalez to the Carlos Fonseca Institute."
> "No, wait a minute. Nidia Hidalgo and Nidia de Gonzalez are the same person; de Gonzalez is her married name."
> "Hey, it is Isabel Arias or Iriabel Asías?"
> "But, just a second, Ana Lorena is eight months' pregnant, and you just placed her in Las Flores when she lives way over in the valley in La Nuca. We have to change her. With Ana's luck, well, it would be just like her to have the baby on the way up the hill to the first day of training. We've already got twenty extra workshops to mount, we can't afford to lose her! We need every able bodied soul we can find. Oh, blessed virgin, may that baby wait at least nine more days."
> "Ana Lorena to La Nuca."
> "Check."

Work lasted until early hours of the morning, sometimes until dawn. While lists were being checked and double-checked, other staff members were out in the communities checking on training sites and material distribution and locating more facilitators for last-minute increases in enrollment.

On March 14, most Phase 4 workshops began—over 5,000 in all. They had two separate schedules: one for those people who had volunteered for the urban corps and one for teachers not yet trained and all students of twelve years of age and above. The student and teacher programs were full time and lasted eight days; the others lasted ten days and took place evenings and weekends. It was necessary to have two separate schedules because many of the urban volunteers worked and could only participate part-time. When possible, secondary teachers were assigned to coordinate and facilitate the student workshops. Supervision was handled by members of Workshops 1 and 2 and representatives from the provincial literacy commissions.

As the coordinator of the national training team, Luis Alemán, said: "There wasn't an hour of the day or night practically when a workshop wasn't functioning somewhere in the country—in every village and school, in every province and municipality, in every corner of the land" (Alemán 1980). The avalanche had indeed turned into a national earthquake. Tremors reverberated throughout the program, but in the end, the foundation stood, for in just ten days more than 85,000 crusaders would be on their way to homes and villages throughout the country.

However the problems that had to be overcome before the actual campaign could begin were significant. The traditional antagonism between students and teachers, which had been aggravated by the war and by the separate structures of the EPA and ANDEN, caused one kind of problem. For example, in several instances, entire schools had refused to accept their teachers as facilitators. Negotiations took place, but in some cases, the tensions were so severe that teacher transfers had to be made and different trainers found. Other problems were created by teacher facilitators who wanted to accelerate the training program in order to be able to finish early. They began to eliminate all the participatory activities from the schedule—discussion periods, sociodramas, and simulations—but as soon as this tendency was detected, students in the sessions were asked to act as monitors to prevent any further deviations from the original workshop design.

As was to be expected, the age of the participants also made a difference in the way the workshops functioned. Junior-high-school-aged students were much less disciplined and attentive than the older groups were, and although the widespread problem of discipline confronted in training was due in part to age, it was exacerbated by the structure of the workshop. An analysis of the roots of this problem probably provides one of the most valuable lessons to future planners of campaigns like the crusade who wish to involve an entire student population in the training phase, regardless of later participation. The success of the training program rested on the willingness of people to participate in the learning activities; essentially, it depended on their commitment or potential commitment to the program. The original training design had contemplated the participation of only one group—those people who would actually be going out to teach or to supervise the literacy teaching. Thus, the inclusion of the entire student population and the implications of such an action had not been considered, and no contingency plan had been made. Since there was no time to assess the significance of this decision, the training went ahead and both types of students participated in the same workshops, except in isolated instances when the coordinators saw the problems this combination was likely to cause and separated the two groups.

The students who were not planning to go out and teach did not, of course, have the same interest or purpose in attending the workshops as those who were. The attendance of the former was compulsory, but the training activities were geared for those people who were going to become literacy teachers, not for those who were going to stay at home. The latter group often got bored during the sessions—ready to participate in any distraction or diversion. As was to be expected, their behavior frequently disrupted the flow and spirit of the training, especially among the younger students. In the senior high group, the seriousness and sheer numbers of those going on the crusade held the others in check, creating an atmosphere in which effective participation could take place for those who were interested and so inclined. In the groups composed of younger students, especially those without the will or commitment to become involved, the educational principle on which the workshop was founded lost its validity for the very functioning of the workshop depended on participation. This problem could have been overcome by dividing the workshop participants into two groups and providing separate training for each. As one national team member has explained:

> The primary obstacle to an effective training program wasn't so much the fact that we had gone from a process of selectivity to one of massivity, but rather, it resided in the internal structure and basic principles of the training itself. The workshop was designed as a revolutionary experience—creative and participatory. Without participation it couldn't work.
>
> The fundamental ingredient that must be present for that participation to occur is motivation, the human will, the personal commitment. And so what happens? The student who is not going to teach doesn't have that commitment, that political will, that motivation to participate in the workshop. But without the participation of everyone, there can be no effective workshop, for a participatory approach is precisely the basis, the very foundation, of training.
>
> Once the Ministry of Education wanted to include the entire body of students in the workshop, a different structure was needed—one separating those students who weren't going to be volunteers from those who were, giving those who weren't their own particular training program. For example, those not joining the crusade didn't need so much emphasis on the primer or the teaching methodology. They weren't going to use them. What they needed fundamentally was really a chance to discuss their own situation—why they weren't going on the crusade—to express themselves artistically in sociodramas, to confront their own problems and decision. [Suarez 1980]

Besides the fundamental problems of participation and discipline, certain specific weaknesses in the use of the materials and methodology were identified during the training process. The time allotted for learning simulations and analysis was not enough. Not all participants got a chance to conduct a literacy session and receive feedback on their effectiveness. On the whole, the dialogue process was difficult for people to master. Many workshop participants demonstrated a condescending, patronizing attitude toward their peasant students in teaching simulations. Not able to get beyond the basic description questions regarding a photograph, they would launch into a short speech or skip the rest of

difficulties

the dialogue process entirely. A minority, though, had a natural facility for generating analytical discussions. Without prompting or practice, they could establish a dialogue and a relationship of camaraderie with their "students" as learning partners.

The training worked best under two sets of conditions. When the teachers were committed and excited about the program, their attitude was conveyed to the participants and generated a sense of purpose and seriousness. When participants entered the training with that enthusiasm and purpose, they demanded the best from their workshop facilitators and, consequently, established a more effective learning environment in which to acquire skills.

Workshops for university students were perhaps the most effective because of the seriousness and dedication of the participants. Unlike the primary and secondary students, the university students entered the training on a volunteer basis. One U.S. observer described the university workshops.

> The education workshops were surprisingly like ones in the States. Volunteers studied in groups that were no greater than forty. Within each group, studies and discussions were carried out in smaller groups, which allowed for maximum individual participation and improved discussion and communication. Time was well scheduled. Agendas were posted and approved by groups. Schoolteachers played low-key, facilitating roles and skillfully kept the groups active. Time was taken out for playful breaks, fatigue was softened by a game, and spirits were lifted by a song.
>
> Nicaraguans are confident orators by tradition, and the animated discussions were rarely dominated by a minority. In my visit to workshops, I constantly witnessed the same scenes: students who could explain easily why it was a privilege and a responsibility to participate; a quiet schoolteacher, proud to watch the students talk with a visitor; an atmosphere of delight at learning and exercising new skills. Almost all of the students were eagerly anticipating the kind of work that youth have traditionally wanted—work that is meaningful, creative, and satisfying. [Trueman 1981, 5]

Amid the turmoil and chaos of Phase 4, something happened, something intangible and contagious. Despite all the problems and resistance, a spirit was building, gaining force even among some of the more stubborn teachers. This spirit was many things—a sense of national pride; a spirit of community service, of Christian duty and solidarity; an excitement for adventure; and a sense of participation in the making of history, in the building of something new, something better. A challenge of hope began to move people.

The force grew. By the end of Workshop 4, fewer complaints were heard from teachers. They, along with the students, rushed to make last-minute preparations—buy toothpaste, mend underwear, kiss grandmothers, watch last television shows, go to the movies one more time, and attend good-bye parties. Some, of course, still resisted, trying to find excuses not to go to the mountains, but ultimately, many were caught up in the magnitude and significance of what they were about to undertake as a nation. Although Workshop 4 had not fulfilled its purpose as well as expected, it did contribute toward building a spirit of enthusiasm and laying the foundation for essential skill acquisition. It also provided a common starting point and a basis for the next phase of training—a stage that until then, had not been contemplated.

Phase 5: Workshop 5, Saturday Workshops, and Daily Radio Program

The fifth level of training was not contemplated originally but emerged from the continued need and demand for further preparation, both to train new volunteers and to reinforce the skills of those already in the field. The first innovation was the implementation of Workshop 5 for all those people who had not been able to attend the training program given during Phase 4. This part of Phase 5 followed the same schedule of activities that had been outlined for Workshop 4 and continued until the beginning of May, with workshops being offered on a weekly basis.

The weakness of Workshop 4 in terms of adequately preparing the majority of the volunteers in the skills of literacy teaching led the members of the national team to reconceive the training process as a permanent, in-service program of continual development and preparation. This reconsideration once again demonstrated the crusade team's ability to confront problems, to learn from them, and to create ways to respond to them on the spot. Two ideas emerged from this reevaluation: (1) the Saturday workshops, an outgrowth of the all-but-forgotten weekend meetings that had been held during the laboratory practicum, and (2) the use of radio as a means to provide specific pedagogical instruction to the volunteers.

The Saturday workshops for *brigadistas* in the field became the cornerstone of the entire training process and started, depending on the location, about three to four weeks after the campaign began. As one of the national training team members has explained:

> In the course of the campaign, we realized that the Saturday workshop was the essential foundation of all training, the axis around which the entire process revolved. It was a program of permanent preparation and

evaluation—bringing together theory and practice, action and reflection, in a constant process of growth and development, overcoming problems, improving pedagogy, discussing social and political issues, practicing dialogues, and preparing lessons for the following week. [Cendales 1980]

The same emphasis on group learning and a pedagogy of shared responsibility that had been stressed during the previous levels of training were the basis of the Saturday sessions as well. As specified in *Tareas Permanentes*, the document explaining the functions of the Saturday workshops,

> The workshop is not made up of a teacher who teaches or a student who studies, but rather, its foundation is a learning group who, through reflection and work, produce their own knowledge, acquiring learning skills—the ability to know. The workshop is a center for reflection and action in which the traditional separation between theory and practice and school and work place is overcome. [Nicaragua, Ministry of Education 1980b, 5]

The principal objective of the Saturday workshops was to reinforce the skills and knowledge that had been acquired in Workshop 4. These workshops were to be a means to oversee and orient the educational, political, social, and cultural aspects of the program. Specifically, they were designed to incorporate the individual volunteer into a group so that collectively, problems could be identified, discussed, and resolved. Through group analysis and the special assistance of the supervising teachers, difficulties in applying the teaching methods and in adapting to a community were confronted and overcome where possible. These workshops were also a means to build morale, to help people feel they were part of a broader process.

In urban areas, the volunteers usually met with their squadrons and technical advisers in schools, but any location large enough to accommodate the numerous Urban Literacy Guerrillas would do. In San Juan del Sur, the lovely seaside resort near Costa Rica, they even used Somoza's former beach house, a modern mansion of brick and tile complete with empty swimming pool and old-fashioned gazebo. In the countryside, *brigadistas* gathered together in groups as much as distance allowed. They met in rural schools and churches, along riverbanks, in backyards, and on patios and porches. The idea was to bring people together in as large a group as possible at regular meeting times so that municipal and township advisers could visit them more easily. Of course, in most rural settings, the distances were so great and the geography was so isolating that the Saturday workshops tended to be small and visits difficult.

Although the teaching advisers were responsible for conducting the training sessions, they also worked in conjunction with a weekly planning group that was made up of all the technical advisers and the EPA squadron leaders in their surrounding area. This cooperation was significant, because it was the only major attempt to integrate the EPA students with the teachers into a coherent structure that would allow for effective cooperation and communication. When the teachers and students were responsible, flexible, open, and concerned about the advance of the program, they usually got over their traditional antagonisms and, after a sometimes rocky start, managed to work together effectively. This cooperation, however, did not always materialize. Some students demonstrated rigid, uncompromising attitudes toward the teachers, and some teachers remained aloof and irresponsible, never fulfilling the duties assigned to them by the crusade and never becoming involved in the life of the community.

In all, each Saturday workshop was designed to last from four to five hours and to use the same small-group, participatory style that had been used in the other workshops. Role playing, simulations, sociodramas, and criticism/self-criticism were among the methods that were used. The majority of the time, some two hours, was devoted to improving what was called the political-pedagogical aspects of the program. International and national current events were studied, analyzed, and sometimes role played, as were the discussion themes of each lesson. Simulations were conducted and critiqued in order to practice and improve teaching and dialogue techniques.

In most cases, the simulations were only an acting out of the next week's lesson presentation, but in some instances, they were more systematic and focused, with the themes for the role plays emanating from a discussion of actual problems that were being confronted in the field. In those cases, a conscious process of collective analysis was used in which *brigadistas* would describe their difficulties, discover common problems, and develop simulations to practice overcoming them. This process closely reflected the learning principles and philosophy of the crusade—the dynamics of practice-theory-practice and of action-reflection-action.

Discussions were often rambling, sometimes insulting, and as the campaign progressed, frequently thoughtful and instructive—provoking serious questions by and dialogue among the *brigadistas* themselves. In discussing how to teach lesson eighteen, "We are forming work brigades to construct and improve our housing," and its accompanying photograph, which showed people working on an urban housing project, one group had the following discussion.

"I like these themes. They're a lot easier to understand, not just blah, blah. Anyway, my cousin worked on one of these projects out behind the sports arena. Now they've got their own house."

"Yeah, that's fine for the city, but where's the land going to come from for the campesinos?"

"Something's got to be done, though. Don Luis keeps saying how they're poor and all—and they are. But you know what? They live better than we do. The only thing is, we have electricity. Aside from that, my sister's house, where we all live, is in lots worse shape."

"But I mean it. What about the land? . . . In the country, you can't even talk about housing until you talk about land reform."

"There's a problem here. . . . Because the dialogue's supposed to be about people's experience, right? Well, most of the campesinos won't understand what this picture's about because they've never seen buildings like this."

"Sure they have. There's lots of them in Matagalpa."

"Not everyone here can get to Matagalpa like Doña Angela, stupid."

"You're stupid. Anyway, anyone can tell you what this is."

"Remember, friends, Chico said we should stop calling each other names. And remember, Jorge, lots of the women and kids never get out of here. It's all right to tell them what it is, isn't it?" [Hirshon 1983, 178]

During the sessions, elementary pedagogical principles were also discussed in relation to the learning difficulties the volunteers were encountering. One hour was dedicated to providing specific instruction on the next week's lessons, and another was devoted to conveying general information from the other sections of the crusade, the EPA, the ministries, or the citizen and labor associations. Approximately the first hour of every session began with gathering statistics and studying the volunteers' progress reports on such items as attendance figures, causes of absence, lessons mastered, and learning difficulties encountered. At this time also, suggestions from the radio program were communicated, field diaries discussed, and the teachers' reports on the positive progress of each volunteer presented.

The principal problems and obstacles of the Saturday workshops involved poor attendance (especially in urban areas), parental weekend visits, and a lack of educational advisers in some rural areas. The last difficulty was in large part overcome during the course of the campaign by selecting outstanding *brigadistas* to become advisers. Although it is difficult to judge the nationwide effectiveness of the Saturday workshops, they generally began slowly and were received with a rather cavalier attitude by the *brigadistas* . However, reports from observers in the rural areas indicate the seriousness with which these sessions were held in the final weeks of the campaign, and great improvement was also confirmed by supervisors. According to these observations, even some of the younger *brigadistas* discussed and attempted to find solutions to the learning difficulties of their students with the sincerity and authority of committed, seasoned teachers.

The training support provided by the *Puño en Alto* radio program, which began in mid-April, was small at first because it was limited to some five minutes of specific teaching instruction per broadcast. However, the amount of instruction increased during the final months of the crusade. As the official campaign radio program, *Puño en Alto* was under the direction of the Ministry of Culture, and it was dedicated principally to communicating messages back and forth from children to parents and vice versa. Some tension over programming and style occurred when the campaign staff began to increase the amount of teaching instruction. The Ministry of Culture officials resisted the change because they felt such revision detracted from the original purpose of the program. Another radio program developed separately from the crusade. The Catholic radio school designed a supplementary program for campaign participants, and it was broadcast two hours each evening on the Catholic station. It consisted of a day-by-day presentation of a dramatized literacy class based on the methods and materials of the crusade. However, many international experts considered it stilted in its dialogues and condescending toward peasants.

Summary

From design to implementation, the campaign training program prepared some 100,000 volunteer teachers and staff members in less than six months. Using a five-stage, decentralized multiplier process, the national training team began by preparing 80 volunteers in a two-week formal workshop, which was followed by a month-long practicum in the field. The training pyramid multiplied and expanded as follows: Teaching teams from the group of 80 trained some 600 people in a program that lasted fourteen days; the 600 prepared 12,000 in one week; and in a like amount of time, the 12,000 trained over 100,000.

The program's philosophy—based on learning by doing, problem solving, participation, and reciprocity—was reflected and implemented throughout the entire training operation, especially during the initial stages. Committee structures within each individual training group, the system of rotating leadership, and a variety of participatory learning methods reinforced this philosophy.

The success of the first stages of training was demonstrated by the frank and open relationship that was maintained between national staff members and regional personnel, one of candor and camaraderie that allowed for quick and creative responses to the inevitable problems that occurred throughout the campaign. This close and critical relationship, based on mutual respect that was forged during training, facilitated the vital organizational decentralization and the establishment of a system of open and responsive communication. However, this process was somewhat hampered by the fact that all program personnel had not participated in the complete program of workshop preparation.

The major problems in training resulted from last-minute political and economic decisions that were made without input from the national team. Instead of including a combination of teachers and university students in the third phase of training as originally planned, university students were generally excluded so they could complete their course work. This change affected the political and pedagogical balance that the national trainers were hoping to achieve—teachers being, on the whole, a more conservative force, and university students a more progressive sector. As a result, the fourth stage of training was not as dynamic or effective as it might have been. Another factor affecting the quality of the fourth stage was the decision to involve all students in the training program, not just those who had volunteered to become teachers. The final phase of training was ultimately the most important of all because it was carried out in the field and, consequently, could most directly respond to actual problems experienced by both teachers and learners.

6

The Campaign in Operation

It's difficult sometimes. Tomasita is smart and wants to study, but her baby cries a lot and she can't put him down. I visit her three times a day just on the chance she'll be free, but . . . she's only on lesson four. . . . Camilo doesn't seem to assimilate his sounds very well. Of course he does need glasses. He's sixty-seven. . . . Socorro and Joaquin are way ahead on lesson fourteen, but Julio left to pick coffee and Catalina's in bed with malaria. . . . Vicente has improved incredibly since he fell off his mule. He was really a lazy bum before. But now, with his broken arm, he's quite serious and dedicated, even though he's had to learn to write all over again with his left hand.

—Guadalupe Rivera (1980)
Brigada Enoc Ortez

March 23, 1980

On March 23, in town plazas across the nation, over 50,000 high school and university students displayed their crusade uniforms: blue jeans, gray peasant shirts, rubber rain boots, and knapsacks of every color and hue—fuchsia pink, gold, green, purple, and blue. Standing with their classmates and teachers they pledged, as did the almost 30,000 urban recruits, to carry out their responsibilities as literacy volunteers with honor and respect. In Managua, rousing speeches were given by Carlos Tunnerman, Fernando Cardenal, Sergio Ramirez, and Bayardo Arce. People cheered, flags waved, bands played, mothers cried, and the students—shouting and laughing with excitement—scrambled for transportation. Some climbed into buses or trucks; others boarded boats or trains. The roads were clogged for three days. As the caravans of volunteers passed through towns and villages, people waved and offered up bananas and oranges and words of encouragement.

The *brigadistas* from the major cities were transported to regional centers where they sometimes had to wait in order to receive their teaching assignments alongside volunteers from the local area. Confusion reigned; town plazas across the country were jammed with eager impatient kids and frustrated supervisors.

"When are we going?" "Let's get moving!" . . . "Attention! Your attention please! The Ricardo Morales Squadron from St. Lucas's school, advisor Mrs. Leona Castillo, has been assigned to the hacienda El Tepeyac on the road to El Tuma. Please gather your group and get ready to board the truck." Where is it? What road? Which truck? "Please, *compañeros*, we're doing the best we can to get the transportation organized. Be patient." "We want to inform the Arlen Siu Squadron from the Ruben Dario Secretarial College that you will not be leaving until tomorrow." Groans from the kids; smiles from already frayed teachers. [Hirshon 1983, 8]

Up into the mountains and back into the jungles, the volunteers continued their journeys. Some were dropped off along the way, and some went on to road's end. With their brightly colored knapsacks bulging, they trudged off into the hills. A few groups got lost, and most of the walkers got blisters. Some were welcomed warmly; for others, acceptance took longer. The crusade had begun.

Mobilization

During the massive mobilization, some 60,000 volunteers and advisers were transported, 136,000 gallons of diesel fuel and gasoline used, and 950,000 kilometers covered (Pastran 1980, 2). To accommodate such large numbers of people with the limited resources available, the teaching brigades and support staffs were dispersed gradually, their departures staggered over a four-day period. The crusade office worked in coordination with the Ministry of Transportation, the Farmworkers' Association, and the army to carry out the massive operation. Together, these groups located, deployed, and coordinated every available means of transportation. In small caravans and large, they mobilized buses, boats, ferries, trains, dump trucks, jeeps, ox carts, horses, mules, donkeys, canoes, rafts, and finally, feet. From road's end or riverside, some volunteers had to walk for two or three days to reach their assigned communities. In all, approximately 1,900 vehicles and other forms of conveyance were used.

The journeys were not without their problems. One squadron trucked in through the mountains of Matagalpa got lost for several days during the hike down to the jungles of the Atlantic Coast. Back roads were treacherous, and many of the drivers were unaccustomed to the dirt and gravel surfaces and steep grades. Despite the problems, the first phase of the massive mobilization was completed with no serious mishap. However, during April, in a smaller effort to transport new recruits, one bad accident occurred. Three volunteers who had been singing, perched precariously in luggage racks, were seriously hurt when their bus slid on a steep mountain road and tipped over. They spent most of the campaign in the hospital. However, given the proportions of the effort, the overall mobilization went extraordinarily well. One volunteer described her experience this way:

> I arrived here in this mountain top yesterday on the back of a mule. . . . We left Saturday from Managua at 3 A.M. in a caravan of seventy buses and dump trucks, about 1,500 university students in all, complete with a gasoline truck and an army escort to protect us during the twenty-hour journey. We spent most of the time singing, shouting cheers, and waving. It was incredible, really! Even though it was nighttime in every village and town along the way, people left their homes to wave at us. Of course, they knew we were members of EPA [the literacy army]. Women would offer us oranges and bananas, shout up at us, "Take care! See you when you return. We love you!" They would throw us kisses too. One old man, he must have been at least seventy, ran beside the bus smiling up at us shouting EPA, EPA, EPA. I didn't know whether I was crying from the dust, the cold, or the wind, or the emotion I felt at seeing what a revolution can really mean. [Selser 1980, 2]

People were mobilized from every province across the nation. From Managua alone, in the initial March effort, 1,646 volunteers were sent to Madriz; 3,542, to Rama; 1,369, to Chontales; 1,354, to Boaco; 3,974, to Matagalpa; 3,599, to Jinotega; 833, to Puerto Cabezas; 1,194, to Bluefields; 3,600, to Estelí; and 542 to Nueva Segovia (Pastrán 1980, 4–5).

First Month

Within one week, the vast teaching corps was in place. Excitement and chaos were common. On the day of one brigade's arrival, a farmer ran up to the teaching supervisor in Wapa shouting that he had seen the *brigadistas* in the nearby town on their way. "They're coming! I saw them in town today! All boys. They'll be here by afternoon at the latest. . . . Late today, they said. . . . Remember, we're at your service for anything you might need" (Hirshon 1983, 30). That afternoon, the *brigadistas* arrived with never-ending questions for their teaching supervisor, whom they affectionately called *profe*, a Spanish nickname for "professor."

> "Is this it?"
> "Yay! We're here at last!"
> "Profe, we spent five days at our school waiting for our placements! How come it took so long?"

"Profe, they didn't give me a hammock."
"Profe, we don't have any pencils, only the other group got them."
"What happened to my brother? He got on the other truck by mistake."
"Profe, can we go now?" [Hirshon 1983, 30]

The first weeks of the campaign were marked by the expected confusion inherent in the launching of a national effort of such unprecedented scope and magnitude. Supervisory visits conducted by the national pedagogical team throughout the country revealed the nature of the problems and the challenges being encountered.

Placement of Teaching Brigades

The first bout of confusion began with basic organizational matters—the placement of the teaching brigades. The brigades that were sent from the larger cities, such as Managua, León, and Granada, to rural sites outside their provinces encountered the most difficulties. In many instances, the teaching assignments had been made from the central offices in Managua, so precise coordination with regions had been difficult, and information had not always been accurate or complete. In the process of placing volunteers by long distance, guidelines were unintentionally broken. Young women often ended up being sent to the more remote sites while young men received more accessible assignments. As a result, once in the field, entire brigades had to be relocated in order to meet the crusade guidelines. In Bluefields, one contingent, some 500 strong, arrived unexpectedly without the previous knowledge of the provincial office so no arrangements had been made for their placement or temporary lodging.

The original plan to house women together in squadrons was not always feasible. Sometimes when the plan was strictly adhered to—in one case, for example, by a nun—it meant that *brigadistas* had to travel two to five kilometers daily on foot or mule to reach their students. If the squadron had been divided, volunteers could have been placed in twos or threes in homes nearer their teaching sites. In some instances, the EPA structure, organized according to school and class, also had to be altered because of the geography of a region or because of the previous placement of other brigades in a given area. On occasion, these relocations and changes in structure caused serious friction between out-of-province EPA officials and the provincial offices of the crusade and the EPA. In some cases, city brigades felt that the local EPA was being given preferential treatment. However, these tensions had usually smoothed out after the first month or two.

The initial relocations caused concern and consternation among some city parents who had been given the specific location of their children before they had left. During the first two or three weeks of the campaign, before new site lists could be made, some parents who sought their sons and daughters in the countryside found, much to their dismay— sometimes after walking great distances—that their children had been relocated. What had been in part a way to alleviate parents' concerns, providing the *brigadistas* with specific site locations before their departure, turned out to be unworkable in practice. Placement of the volunteers in urban areas was the least problematic, although people had to be encouraged to teach outside their own neighborhoods when it became evident that certain areas had a surplus of volunteers and others had a greater number of students than could be accommodated by local recruits.

The number of educational supervisors was inadequate to cover the needs, and in certain cases, their distribution was unbalanced. Brigades from Managua, for example, sometimes arrived without sufficient supervisory staff. In response to this problem, some advisers were relocated, and new people were recruited. Fifth- and sixth-year students of education were drafted, and outstanding *brigadistas* were chosen to fill the gaps.

To better supervise and manage the program, each provincial literacy crusade office divided its territory into zones, usually according to traditional municipal, township, and neighborhood boundaries, but in certain instances, difficulties of terrain and transport made it necessary to establish new geographical districts. Each zone was assigned support personnel to act as liaisons with the teaching brigades and to provide them with educational assistance and supervision. In some of the more remote, isolated municipalities, a peasant coordinator was chosen to serve as an additional liaison with the crusade offices in the municipal center and townships. Given the geography of some regions, it made more sense for other provinces to take care of outlying areas not officially under their jurisdiction such as sections of Boaco, Matagalpa, Zelaya, Chontales, and Río San Juan.

With the task of mobilization behind them, the literacy commissions entered a stage of consolidation. When the citizens' associations, labor organizations, and government institutions were strong, the commissions functioned rather well, although one relatively common problem that affected the coherence of their work was the fact that most member groups did not assign a permanent representative to the commission.

Parents' groups served as effective advocates for their children and helped the national crusade office by identifying the regions in which supply distribution was deficient. Through letters and visits, they kept the appropriate staff members informed of which brigades were lacking what supplies. Sometimes, however, promises were made that were not immediately kept, thus causing some mistrust. For example, *brigadistas* going to the Atlantic Coast were promised mosquito nets for their immediate use, but it took a month to acquire and deliver them.

A New Census, Encouragement, and Motivation

During the first days of the program, it became obvious, both in the cities and the rural areas, that the original census was no longer accurate. It also became clear that people needed to be further motivated, inspired, and encouraged to join the program. In searching out the names on their assigned lists of tentative students, volunteers found many discrepancies. Some people had moved or migrated temporarily in order to look for seasonal farm work. A few had died; others were ill. Some were hesitant to participate, expressing fear of communism or of threatened reprisals from former National Guardsmen. Others simply were disinterested; still others were shy. After this initial response, volunteers immediately began a new census, encouraging and cajoling the less convinced members of the communities to participate.

Sometimes it seemed as if the problems that the brigades were up against at this early moment were going to swamp them before they could even begin. One teaching supervisor explained the situation this way: "Someone who is drowning in a glass of water is drowning just the same as if he were doing so in the open sea. Viewed from a distance, perhaps the difficulties we faced seemed like mere glasses of water, but submerged inside them, they were drowning us just as effectively as if they had been the widest ocean or the deepest sea" (Von Rechnitz 1980, 3). The same supervisor described the comments of his *brigadistas* concerning their cer.sus and enrollment efforts.

> So-and-so doesn't want to study because he would have to walk half a block to whatchamacallit's house and they haven't spoken to each other since the pig of the latter ate the chicken of the former along with all her newly hatched chicks.
>
> The guy down the road isn't going to participate. He almost died yesterday because he went to a tooth puller who yanked out two molars at once. He's spent the last two days bleeding from the the gums with a pain that's about to drive him crazy. And if that weren't bad enough, he suffers from epilepsy. In the last two days he's had three attacks. . . .
>
> So-and-so is a farmworker and has to migrate soon with the winter crops. He'll only be in class for a few weeks. . . . His brother won't participate because the first time he ran into difficulties in class, he burst out crying saying he was too old at forty-five and he was nothing but a useless donkey anyway. Despite the words of encouragement from the volunteer, he lost all hope and has refused to come back. . . .

The owner of the house on the hill was arrested in Tipitapa for being drunk and disorderly. His relatives don't want to have anything to do with the government until he's let go. [Von Rechnitz 1980, 3]

Women with families felt that study would be difficult, if not impossible, because of child care duties and daily homemaking tasks. They frequently resisted the first invitations of the volunteers. However, as people began to see the seriousness and persistence of the young *brigadistas* who were living in their communities, often in their very homes, enrollment figures rose. The key to motivation resided essentially in patient but persistent cajoling on the part of the volunteers and a basic sense on the part of the participants that the program offered them an extraordinary, once-in-a-lifetime opportunity to learn practical and useful skills.

The volunteers brought their new students together, and when it was immediately available, gave them the initial test to determine their literacy level. Many people discovered at this time that they had serious vision problems and needed glasses.

The woman next door can't participate even though she's enrolled because when she took the initial test her eyesight was so bad, why she couldn't even see three men on a donkey, much less one. It's surprising the enormous quantity of peasants with serious vision problems at such an early age. The perennial malnutrition, the totally unbalanced diet, and the little use they give to their eyes has wreaked havoc on their vision. [Von Rechnitz 1980, 3]

Personal motivations for enrolling in the learning program differed.

I want to learn because . . . that way you wake up your mind.

Not knowing how to read and write, well, it's as if your eyes were covered with a hood and you had to walk with a blind man's cane. We need to see. Don't you agree?

I want to know how to read and write because when you don't know that, even though you may have good feelings inside your heart, you can't express them.

I want to be a man who understands.

I'm a foundry worker, and I want to know how you get ahead.

I'm a sixty-year-old grandfather and have nine grandchildren—five boys and four little girls. I want them to know that everyone can learn—even me. You see, when I was young, I didn't have a chance to get an education. Now if they see me studying and see that me, an old man, can learn, well maybe they'll study harder. Then, they can do better and go farther with their lives than me. I'm a gatekeeper at the factory across the road. When I go home now my grandchildren stand beside me and watch me practice.

. . . not to be deceived ever again.

Before I had to use my thumbprint to sign for my salary. I want to be able to write my own name.

I work in the fields. The best farmer is the peasant, you know. So I want to learn more about the technical part of agriculture to be even better.

So someday . . . well someday . . . so maybe I can learn how . . . to fly. [Citlali and Miller 1980, 1–3]

Teaching and Holy Week

In both the cities and the rural areas, the student-teacher ratio was high—in some places averaging ten to one and, on occasion, reaching as high as twenty-five to one. Different class times were set in order to teach the large numbers of students in a manageable and effective fashion. As a result, some *brigadistas* taught as many as three different sessions daily. Classes were most frequently held during daylight hours, both for reasons of security and because the lanterns had not arrived on time.

In many cases, Holy Week interrupted the beginning of teaching activities. Orders from national headquarters called for the continuation of work throughout the holidays, but resistance on all sides made this plan difficult to carry out. In a few instances, parents came to take their children away for the traditional Easter week vacation, but teachers were, by far, the worst offenders, and many of them encouraged their young charges to return home so they could leave their supervisory posts with a clear conscience. Some peasants also resisted the idea of attending study groups during the holiday week. In one province, almost the entire literacy corps and supervisory staff returned home for several days during this time. Despite this resistance to working through the vacation, the majority of the groups remained at their sites and began study activities as planned. This same kind of problem recurred on Mother's Day and on the first anniversary of the revolution. To counter the temptation for the volunteers to leave their sites, local celebrations were encouraged.

During the first several weeks, staff members on all levels, from national to local identified two specific educational needs that required immediate attention. More technical preparation for the supervisors was necessary, especially concerning the specifics of how to carry out their functions; for the volunteers, more attention to the teaching methods was needed, particularly those related to the dialogue. Confusion over responsibilities and areas of authority among the crusade staff, ANDEN, and Juventud was also detected. Tensions between teachers and EPA members were common.

Volunteer Adjustment

Before going to the countryside, many volunteers, despite their enthusiasm and excitement, were also plagued with questions and fears natural to such an adventuresome undertaking.

> We all feared the unknown, sharing an unspoken worry that would have been secret had it not been so general: "Where will we be sent and how difficult will it be? Will I live where they only eat tortillas and salt, where the water is contaminated, where letters from Mom won't reach me? Will I get sick? Am I brave enough? Today [in training] we learned how to recognize malaria symptoms. What if I get malaria? Are the counterrevolutionary death threats serious?" [Trueman 1981, 6]

In their adjustment to rural life, the *brigadistas* found the answers to some of their concerns. They faced the problems of everyday country living and survival under conditions of stark poverty. Poor health and isolation probably affected the *brigadistas* the most. In areas adjacent to volcanoes, constant seeping gases caused sores, headaches, and throat irritations. Soothing hard candies became a favorite purchase of the volunteers at the village store. At least one brigade left its site because of serious health problems: Tuberculosis was discovered to be widespread and until proper medical precautions could be taken, the group was relocated nearby. A scarcity of water was a problem in some regions. One young boy's first message home to his family (Parajón 1980) reflects the nature of the situation and his hopeful, if rather individualistic and unrealistic, solution.

> Dear Mom and Dad,
>
> I am fine. I arrived safe and sound but please send me twenty cans of grape juice. The well is filled with mud, and the river is far away. . . .
>
> Love, your son

During the dry season, a shortage of water was common in certain southern provinces. Some volunteers, accustomed to at least one bath or shower a day, now had to walk five kilometers for their one wash per week. In extreme situations, water was trucked into villages, but often, the roads were so bad that after one trip the drivers refused to return. When water finally arrived, some brigades went without until every family in the community was first provided for.

In some of the poorer regions of the country, until provisions could be obtained, volunteers went days without eating or simply survived on a diet of bananas. Some desertion occurred because of this lack of food. An emergency food distribution program was instituted immediately under the auspices of a government agency—the National Basic Grains Distribution Program. Insects and amoebas attacked the city-bred volunteers with an unanticipated ferocity. Loneliness did too. The adjustment period had its harsh and maddening moments. One *brigadista* wrote to his parents what was felt throughout the country by rural and urban volunteers alike. "The mosquitos are driving me crazy. Whenever I talk they fly into my mouth. They say the mosquito nets are coming soon. I sure hope so" (Julio Ramirez 1980).

One *brigadista* supervisor summarized the initial problems facing the rural teaching corps.

> Despite all their goodwill, their strong political and Christian spirit, their commitment to the poor, the first eight days for every literacy volunteer are quite simply hell—for city dwellers think that the countryside is just like the beautiful scenic tourist posters hung in travel agencies. They are in for a rude awakening. The majority of the volunteers get intestinal infections from the water they drink and continue drinking. But at least after the first eight days, it doesn't give them the awful diarrhea it did at the beginning. Others get bad colds and high fevers because the contrast in temperature here between day and night is tremendous. The humidity just increases the risks of such illnesses. Thank God, the coughing and the diarrhea didn't coincide. Some kids ended up as veritable human sieves thanks to the efficient daily labor of the fleas and ticks that have clearly decided not to cooperate with the crusade.
>
> The hardest part for the volunteers is the loneliness and isolation, finding themselves suddenly living among strangers with whom, at least up till now, they have little in common. The feeling is one of anguish and insecurity. Thank God, because of their political spirit and Christian faith, none of my *brigadistas* have deserted. Everyday they seem to adjust and find themselves enjoying life here more. [Von Rechnitz 1980, 3]

The transition also had its tender and beautiful moments. One young university student woke on her first morning in the countryside to a surprise.

> I was exhausted from the long journey—twenty hours by bus, boat, and five hours on a mule up and down steep hills. I slept soundly that first night in a little one-room bamboo house of my new family. They adopted

me quickly. At dawn I woke up, and the entire household was surrounding me, watching me quietly. I was startled and a little bit unnerved. Then the father of the family smiled and said gently, "Don't worry, little one. We will watch over you. Go back to sleep. You are so beautiful we just like to look at you. Sleep. We will protect you. Never fear." [Selser 1980]

The primitive, subhuman living conditions touched many of the *brigadistas* profoundly. One described the arrival of her group at a small squalid hut in the jungle where they were to teach.

There were eight children, completely nude. The pigs and cows were living with the people. There was no difference between the animals and the children. The only water was dirty. It was so striking, the contrast between the exuberant jungle outside and the conditions inside that tiny house, lit by one candle. Everything was silent as we looked at each other. One after another, we began to cry. We were so sad to see with our own eyes the poverty of our people. [Perez-Valle 1980]

Supplies and Logistics

The most common complaint heard during the first months of the crusade centered around logistics and supply distribution. Some problems had been foreseen, like transportation; others arose unexpectedly, despite thoughtful planning. For example, the first-aid supplies, which had been carefully calculated to last five months, usually ran out within two weeks because when confronted with the extent of illness and disease in the countryside, many *brigadistas* placed their first-aid kits at the service of the communities. Medicine was immediately shared with their adopted peasant families. As a result new supplies had to be ordered and special medical brigades formed to attend the pressing health needs.

The difficulties in transportation drove some of the more dedicated provincial and municipal staff members to desperation. Wanting to be out in the field supervising and advising, they were frequently stymied and stranded by a lack of vehicles. Public transportation was slow, sporadic, and unreliable, so they hitchhiked, begged, borrowed, and on occasion, threatened to steal in order to obtain transportation to oversee the program. One early morning conversation with a frustrated fellow staff member bemoaning his woes went like this:

It's too much. I swear I'm about to do something drastic. First, we got a jeep from the Agrarian Reform Institute, but it had a flat tire and the spare was being fixed in the garage. My uncle was going to let us use his car, but he had to go to Managua. Finally, the Health Ministry loaned us a truck, but wouldn't you know it, the blasted battery is dead. We are trying to recharge it now, but so help me, if it doesn't get fixed in the next fifteen minutes, I am ready to steal the nearest car I see. [Canales 1980]

Attempts were made when possible to coordinate trips with other government institutions, but cooperation was not always feasible. Transportation remained a problem during the entire crusade, especially for the provincial and municipal support staffs as they needed to reach entire regions quickly and efficiently.

For the brigades and their advisers, transportation was an inconvenience but also an appreciable part of local color. As one adviser has related:

> Traveling in the crusade was all of a great adventure. You would go to the road and see what you could catch. Sometimes a lumber truck loaded down with freshly cut tree trunks from Nueva Guinea would stop for us. Other times someone from a government agency might pick us up. But sometimes, and this is when the adventure would really get interesting, a supercrowded bus would go by. When you would ask people from around here, Where do you catch a bus that goes to such and such a place? sometimes they would say, "You see that pile of people that's coming down the hill? Well, the bus is inside!"
>
> Getting on to one of those relics is a real accomplishment. First, you have to pass over and through a jungle of human legs, hundreds of packages and sacks, and usually two drunks; then you travel between a man who looks like he's being squashed to death by a giant watermelon in his lap and a woman with two children in her arms and two pigs under her feet. [Von Rechnitz 1980, 3]

Materials and equipment did not always arrive on time, and when they did, they were not always what had been ordered. The hammocks arrived on schedule but were too short for many of the volunteers. With the extraordinary Nicaraguan ability to turn the most bleak situation into a joke, the size of the hammocks became the source of crusade humor. Their smallness was attributed to one of the most beloved and charismatic figures of the revolution, *comandante* Tomás Borge, the only surviving founder of the FSLN. Because the crusade was political, the jokesters said, the hammocks were made just the right size to fit Tomás, the oldest political leader of the nation (*commandante* Borge, even with his boots on, measured at most five foot one).

Boots for the volunteers arrived in wrong sizes and late, as did the Coleman lanterns. After some initial problems with the lamps' pumping mechanism, it was found that *brigadistas* needed practice in their care and use. Old-fashioned kerosene lanterns supplemented the inadequate supply of modern ones. Pencils and notebooks did not arrive in sufficient quantities at first, so pages were shared and pencils broken in half. On the whole, the crusade staff tried to cooperate in meeting the logistic needs of the campaign, but there was one notable exception. The brigades sent from Chinandega to Nueva Segovia were told by the Nueva Segovia provincial coordinator that all their requests for equipment would have to be handled by their home provincial office in Chinandega. Loud complaints were heard from the volunteers and their parents. This coordinator was soon replaced, and the out-of-province brigades attended to as required.

When food scarcities and *brigadista* hunger became apparent, the crusade staff put together an emergency system that was seriously handicapped by poor staffing. Food supply and distribution were carried out under the direction of ENABAS, the government's basic grain and food distribution agency. In many places, the system became notorious for its inefficiency. One brigade would receive five drums of cooking oil, one bag of beans, and no rice while another would get five bags of rice and no oil. An informal system of barter was established by the volunteers, and, as reported by a government official, "when ENABAS failed, MAMA-BAS worked" (Gorostiaga 1980). Mothers supplemented their children's diet by sending frequent food packages, and during the campaign, the crusade's logistic staff was increased to help with the food distribution.

Daily Living and Learning

Life during the literacy campaign was hard work. Some *brigadistas* came prepared for the worst. "I am really impressed how some of these kids came prepared and equipped. One of the boys looks like he is ready to fight the crocodile that always shows up in the jungle movies wanting to eat Tarzan. Another one has all the trappings of a walking Boy Scout store. It's a sure sign of how ignorant most of us are about how people live in the countryside" (Von Rechnitz 1980, 3).

Days were long. Besides teaching and promoting community organizing activities, the volunteers were expected to help with the daily chores and the field work of their host families. On the other hand, the literacy learners, in addition to their normal everyday labors, needed to spend two hours in class and extra time in personal study.

Chores with the family began the day. "None of us in the family I was living with liked doing tasks alone. Fourteen-year-old Santos and I got up every morning at three A.M. or four, if we were feeling self-indulgent, to build the fire, put on the coffee, mill the day's corn and make the tortillas. Everyone else got up at five or six" (Trueman 1981, 6). Perhaps a bath followed. "It was cloudy on top of the mountain this morning and freezing. We got to the well at sunrise and bathed, screaming with each gourdful of water—then on the way back, we slipped in the mud. So much for cleanliness! The path is incredibly steep" (Vasquez 1980).

Housekeeping tasks and productive responsibilities usually filled the morning and early afternoons until class preparation and study began. Although well intentioned, the help provided by the *brigadistas* to the peasants was sometimes of rather questionable merit, at least at the beginning. "I'm learning a lot. I now know how to milk a cow and plant vegetables. The other day I was with Don Demesio roping a steer, but I'm so stupid that I frightened the thing, and we had to work twice as hard to catch it again. . . . The rains are constant. The soles of my boots came unglued, and I had to sew them with a needle they use to make sacks with" (Ramirez 1980, 5). The peasants became the teachers of the *brigadistas;* city youngsters learned the skills of country living. In the process, bonds of friendship and family were developed.

> Since the *brigadistas* proved to be almost foolish about how to survive in the country, the mastery of new skills became the work of everyone together. The *brigadistas* mastered the cow's teats, the making of tortillas, and the chopping of wood. They learned to swing the machete, pick coffee beans and carry water buckets on their heads or hips. They learned to follow routes that were so untraveled that they had never become paths. They learned to look for new kinds of landmarks, or mark the paths with machete cuttings in the trees. But the campesinos (peasants) knew what they knew because of their lifetime in the country. Few *brigadistas* could learn, in five months, to hike without muddying themselves unnecessarily or to pass under and over barbwire fences with enough grace to keep one's place and to protect one's clothing. Few learned to recognize all the bits of food that the mountain woods offer, or to hear far away sounds through the mountain's silence. Few could tell in the morning whether it would rain in the afternoon and the most unfortunate were those few who didn't learn how to bathe in a river without drowning. And so the campesinos cared for and protected us *brigadistas* as if we were long lost relatives who'd come home, but who hadn't fully left behind that other world beyond the nearest village. [Trueman, 1981, 9–10]

The volunteers found that the actual task of teaching literacy was fraught with difficulties, surprises, and moments of inspiration (Hirshon 1983, 104, 105, 108).

> Doña Bernarda . . . just doesn't have any memory. . . . I give her classes at short intervals all day long, but nothing stays.
>
> I ask questions and my class just giggles.

I talked for awhile with Doña María. She'd written her name in chalk all over the kitchen, together with Don Agapito's and the syllables sa, se, si, so, su, "so I can learn something while I work."

Some volunteers were humble and others openly honest in assessing the success of their teaching efforts (Flora et al. 1982, 15, 17, 21).

The experience of being a teacher is neat, but sometimes it ceases to be so nice because there are peasants who don't understand—they don't understand anything. You have to take it calmly and repeat again and again. Teaching requires a lot of patience and I don't have much patience.

There were plenty of problems in class. Rural people tend not to have a firm hand; they can't make the letters. One must take their hand and trace the letter, trace over it again, with the patience of Job. At the beginning, everything was difficult for teacher and student alike. They thought they would never learn to read or write. One day they would know all the vowels; the next day you would ask them and they wouldn't know anything; we would start all over again. We would spend as much as a week on one thing until it "stuck." And reviewing; every day we gave them a new point and reviewed the previous day's work so they wouldn't forget it. Slowly, their hands became more flexible, they were learning more and more, and finally you felt more and more satisfied because they were assimilating more rapidly.

I learned from the dialogues because my pupils lived certain experiences which I had not. According to the lesson plans, the dialogues were to last ten minutes, fifteen minutes but I usually carried them on for an hour because they had so much to tell me that I didn't know. Mostly I learned things from their personal experience; the little which I knew I transmitted to them.

Dialogue in class, when it was effective, allowed people to express themselves and to think about the world in new and thoughtful ways.

"Doña Auxilladora, what does ignorance mean to you?"
"Ignorance means that I don't know anything about who I really am or very much about this world that I live in."
"Why do you want to learn to read and write?"
"Well . . . to wake up my mind."
"And you, Asunción?"
"Learning to read and write. . . . we're going to be able to participate more in the benefits of agriculture. Now we're going to have the tactics, that's what I call them anyway, the tactics to work the land better. Somoza never taught us to read—it really was ungrateful of him, wasn't it? He knew that if he taught the peasants to read we would claim our rights.

Ay! But back then, people couldn't even breathe. You see, I believe that a government is like a parent of a family. The parent demands the best of his children, and the children demand the best of the parent, but a governor, like a parent, that does not give culture and upbringing to the child, well that means he doesn't love his child, or his people. Don't you agree?" [Rivas 1980]

But conducting the dialogue in class was often difficult. The students were unaccustomed to expressing themselves in such a setting, and most of the *brigadistas* did not have the training, educational supervision, or patience to meet the crusade's high expectations. Questions tended to elicit short answers, and discussion was usually limited. Some interchanges were exceptionally brief and superficial. However, no matter how short or stilted the answers were, it was often the first time people had had an opportunity to express their ideas publicly and to receive affirmation of them.

> "What do you all see in this photograph?"
> "Great happiness."
> "Yes, that's true. They are smiling. Remember that day? And you Chilo, what do you see?"
> "It's a picture of the triumph celebration."
> "Who is in the picture?"
> "People." "Sandinistas."
> "Who do the people triumph over?"
> "The Somoza dictatorship."
> "Right." [Miller 1980]

Some question and study themes seemed to touch more directly on issues of personal emotion and meaning, and they evoked longer responses.

> "This picture—what do you see in this photograph?"
> "A guardsman and a guerrilla who is behind him, leading him."
> "What would you say the difference was between the two? What motivates them? Who received money?"
> "The guard."
> "Why didn't they want you to read and write, don José?"
> "Because we would have described what they were doing; we would have told about their badness."
> "Marta."
> "We would have found them out and become angry."
> "And doña Alma, what do you think?"
> "Before, only children could learn to read and write but today, it's different because of the revolution. Now we can too."

"Luis?"

"Well before, Somoza had us repressed in everything, there were no jobs. Food was expensive. We've got problems and needs still, but that's because Somoza took everything with him. Now, we have a beginning. Now we live in peace." [Miller 1980]

Some responses offered opportunities for interesting discussions that were not pursued. For example, in one rural area, a young *brigadista* dictated the words "the moon" (*la luna*) to a student. The peasant wrote the words correctly but capitalized them both and was curtly told that they should be written in lowercase. La Luna was the name of the hacienda the man had worked on for the past seventeen years and where the classes were being held. The rich history and meaning behind the uppercase form, La Luna, were never probed.

Conversations and discussions outside the regular study sessions, however, helped people develop their skills of expression and analysis in a more complete, natural way—affirming their individual worth and intelligence. These informal exchanges became the core of the shared educational experience for student and teacher alike. The peasants had many ideas and sometimes surprised the *brigadistas* with their wisdom and creativity.

> In spite of his isolation and his poverty he had hundreds of ideas he wanted to talk about. Noon faded into evening as I listened. He had one book in his house, an almanac which included a copy of the United Nations' Human Rights document. He liked the document very much though he was quick to point out that no country in the world guaranteed all those rights.
>
> He added: "Most of those rights have as little to do with me right now as the right to own and ride a bicycle. I have no money and there are no roads here."
>
> We talked about the future. He had a lot of ideas about what community organizations could do to change the conditions under which people live. "Everyone in this area should pick up their house and move to one central place. Among the bunch of us," he figures, "there would be enough money for a truck that could take us out to the fields. If we could have a small town here instead of widely scattered houses then education and health care would be easier to provide. None of us would have to walk two hours to take advantage of services." Neither of us knew that some farmworkers groups in another part of Nicaragua were actually organizing around that dream. [Trueman 1981, 15]

Poetry and literacy skills were practiced and reinforced in heartfelt salutes to the volunteers:

To my literacy teacher and compañero: Guillermo Briones Cisnero

My friends, Nicaragua is free.
The oppression of Somoza is defeated.
For with the rumbling of bullets,
    Anastasio and son
    ran far away.
And now with the shouting of ABCs
    ignorance flees and
    joins them in Paraguay.
These verses I do recite
    in honor of Guillermo,
    my friend and compañero,
Because I respect him like no other
    and love him
    like an older brother. [Hurtado Lopez 1980, 1]

Fear and courage marked the lives of all people participating in the campaign. Rumors had been spread prior to the crusade to instill horror and doubt in people, stories of terror and torture circulated everywhere, and death threats were common. During the campaign, there was harassment of volunteers and participants, especially along the borders where Somoza's ex-guardsmen often made incursions into Nicaraguan territory. Houses were stoned in the middle of the night, women *brigadistas* were raped, and seven volunteers and staff members were assassinated. One volunteer has described her peasant family's reaction to the violent threats:

Genaro and Jacinta told me they had heard that counterrevolutionaries would kill any family who accepted a volunteer. The neighbors had not participated in the program at first because of that rumor. The Torrez family had signed up anyway. "When else would we have such an opportunity?" Jacinta told me. "Death threats or not we want to learn and we want our children to learn." But even with that sort of resolve, we worried. Voices of strangers in the night, men stumbling along a nearby midnight path, froze my family into rigid silence; the lights were snuffed out and everyone sat still . . . listening for familiar tones amidst the mumbling. [Trueman 1981, 8]

News broadcasts and letters tell of the fear and the commitment that was demonstrated in response to death.

Eight ex-national guardsmen crossed the border from Honduras yesterday and murdered the literacy teacher Georgino Andrade. [Radio Sandino, 19 May 1980]

The struggle is long and sometimes cruel. What's needed above all, my dear friend, is love and commitment. Remember, "The freedom of a people is not won with flowers." We are young, and we are called upon to build the new, to create what our heroes and martyrs would have wanted. Put yourself in the place of Georgino Andrade. You wouldn't like it, if out of fear, the cause you gave your life for wasn't continued. [Sandinista Youth Association 1980, 5]

All volunteers, of course, did not share this type of commitment and spirit of self-sacrifice, nor did all of their advisers. Some were immature, some arrogant, others apathetic or resentful—students and supervisors alike. On occasion, male *brigadistas* would become involved with local girls or other volunteers, and sometimes scandals would result. A small minority drank excessively or used drugs. Although the bureaucracy frequently was slow, when major infractions were detected, the violators, whether *brigadistas* or teaching advisers, were ultimately dismissed from service.

In general, however, the *brigadistas* carried out their tasks with concern and a sense of responsibility that grew as the campaign progressed. They took on many roles in their communities and learned invaluable lessons about planning, organizing, and working in groups, as did their teaching advisers.

We were actors, masters of ceremonies, folk dancers, sign painters, survey takers and public speakers. We made rice punch for a hundred people and planned a day of children's games where children had never before been brought together in their own honor. We learned how to make decisions about how to do all these things. We learned to challenge each other when traditional sex roles were defended (who should cook the rice for the punch) when tasks were carried out haphazardly and when some people got bossy or offensive. [Trueman 1981, 10]

In some areas, the people of the communities learned leadership skills through the development and creation of local organizations.

The campesinos (peasants) had organized to receive us and part of our work was to help those first committees expand into community organizations, farmworkers' associations, women's groups, and the people's militia. . . .

Carrying out community projects called for social gatherings and planning sessions. . . . Many people had their first experience of speaking at meetings, holding an office, working as a community leader, or publicly sharing their art.

One man, don Wilfredo, who had to stand at a meeting and introduce himself as the committee-head for the farmworkers' association, was assisted by an old friend—my campesino father, don Genaro. Don Genaro saw the nervousness in don Wilfredo's toothless smile and stood up behind him with his arms wrapped around don Wilfredo's arms and chest, hugging him from behind while don Wilfredo found the words to tell us who he was and what his responsibilities were. [Trueman 1981, 8]

To help with the communication between the *brigadistas* and their families, radio stations set aside specified times during the day for parents, children, and sweethearts to send messages through the program, *Puño en Alto*, run by the Ministry of Culture. The crusade office used the system to convey important information to staff members in remote areas.

To Rodolfo Diaz in Tonolá from your parents. Please have two burros waiting for us at the crossroads on Sunday. We're bringing your sister and your birthday cake.

Urgent. Urgent. Brigadista María René Nuñez of Kilambé near Wiwilí. Your grandmother is very ill. Please return home as soon as possible. Your Father.

For Tilo Santos in San José by the lake. Received your letter. Do not worry. My malaria improving. Am returning next week. Thanks for yellow flowers. As always, your fiance, *Brigadista* Victoria.

For the technical adviser María José Calderón of El Diamante, Jinotega. Stopping by to pick up the statistics on Tuesday. Please have ready. Signed Chico Montenegro. Chief of Statistics, Jinotega office.

Urgent. Urgent. *Brigadista* Carmelo Blanco Reyes in San Martín. Pick up package at post office in Muy Muy. Did you receive other one? Please write. Haven't heard from you in two months. Signed, your Mother.

Religion played a significant role in the life of the campaign, a role that went beyond the fact that the three top crusade officials were Catholic priests. This phenomenon was an important one. Many of the campaign leaders were committed Christians—for example, over 300 priests and nuns served in the program as *brigadista* supervisors or on the crusade staff—and because many of them had previously worked in rural development programs for the poor, they often came to the job with a special understanding of the people the campaign was intended to serve. However, problems did arise.

Depending on the attitudes of the individual supervisory teacher or the local religious leader, the role religion played on the community level could be either complementary or antagonistic to the campaign's goals. Conflict occurred when differences in faith or in commitment to the revolution were strong. This was a particular problem in communities that were divided along religious lines between Catholic and small fundamentalist Protestant sects or in brigades in which the teachers wanted to use the campaign as a means of religious proselytizing. There were cases reported of the lessons in the primer being replaced completely by readings from the Bible.

In the majority of instances, however, religious tensions were not seriously disruptive, although in the areas where they occurred, divisiveness did result. But when of the same faith as their adopted families, *brigadistas* and advisers sometimes shared Sunday services with the community, thus enhancing a closer personal bond as well as establishing a positive association of revolution with religion. One Sunday in Las Parcelas, a poor village in southern Nicaragua, is especially illustrative of the complementary relationship that sometimes developed.

Twenty-two *brigadistas*, many wearing crosses around their necks, came together to celebrate mass with the villagers of Las Parcelas in their new community center, a large open-air structure they had built jointly during the campaign. The people sat in a circle: some on chairs or logs, others perched on tables. A few leaned against the rough-cut tree trunks that had been used to hold up the roof. The priest, a soft-spoken gray-haired man, had fled to Nicaragua from Guatemala where the government had expelled him under threat of death. Many of the villages in which he and his colleagues had served had been burned and the populace killed by Guatemala's army. He sat on a stool, his head bowed. The mass had begun.

A villager read the scripture; a *brigadista* sang a hymn she had written. Father Gurdian began the homily, relating the story of good seeds and bad, and drew from the members of the group their individual thoughts and comments about the Bible reading. Villagers and *brigadistas* contributed, some more hesitant than others, but each expressing his or her own personal views, and each receiving words of affirmation and encouragement from the priest. One older woman commented, "Like the gospel says, Father, there are bad seeds and good seeds, weak ones and healthy ones. Yes. But all seeds need water and sun to live and well, maybe if the weak seeds got enough, well maybe even they could do better, like us, like now. Before we didn't get education, but now even, well even we can grow. And who knows, with the right fertilizer some of the bad seeds might become good" (Miller 1980).

A small political minority, representing the richest economic interests in the country, opposed the campaign, labeling the effort "indoctrination" and "domestication" and attacking its political nature. "The literacy campaign is pure indoctrination. It was designed as a political project when it should have been conducted as a social campaign with political and economic benefits" (Robelo 1980). The head of the Superior Council of Private Enterprise summed it up this way: "Look, it's meant to domesticate the minds of the poor, to numb them. Instead, the campaign should be selling freedom and democracy" (Dreyfus 1980). In contrast, the U.S. ambassador, Lawrence Pezzullo (1980), complained about an anti-U.S. bias and what he called "heavy Cuban input," but he said, "It's more nationalistic than anything else." There was "nothing really wrong or fearsome about it. If they were indoctrinating, it would be of concern." The director of USAID, also worried about Cuban influence, nevertheless called the campaign an "excellent contribution and a good delivery of services" (Harrison 1981).

The members of the opposition, however, refused to allow their children to participate and often sent them out of the country for a summer abroad in the United States or Europe. Most Nicaraguans believed this to be a particularly ungenerous act. Other parents were encouraged not to give the needed permission for their children's participation. Bitterness escalated when Alfonso Robelo, a millionaire industrialist and a member of the junta, sent his own children abroad. Tension increased even more when he resigned from office and began speaking out directly against the government and the crusade, encouraging peasants to drop out of the program as an expression of their political freedom. After one such speech in the town of Matiguás, several female *brigadistas* teaching in the surrounding area were raped in the weeks immediately following his apperance there. It was commonly believed, rightly or wrongly, that Robelo's words incited these acts and that he deserved personal blame. This kind of confrontation exacerbated the growing antagonism between those people who supported the revolution and those who did not. Robelo lost public support as a result of his opposition, and such political events were curtailed by the government, a decision that led to considerable international criticism of the FSLN leadership.

On a community level, problems with local landlords sometimes disrupted the program's operation. One peasant leader explained to the teaching supervisor:

> This woman, my patrona, my boss Doña Cloris, she wants to get rid of me for having a brigadista in the house. First she comes in the middle of class and dumps everything off the table—the books and everything. Then she begins yelling at everyone: "Let the counterrevolution come," she screams, "so all these damned brigadistas will be hung!" Can you imagine that? . . . She doesn't like it that I'm with the farmworkers' union,

that I complain when things aren't right. First she was after me about some pigs I had, and now this. And she says she won't rent me the land to work this year. And, anyway, she's not paying me right. The last time, she gives me the money and I says, "Wait a minute, let's look at this sum." "Oh, no, it's fine," she says. But sure enough, I figure it up and she owes me fifty córdobas more. She gets all upset and everything, but of course I'm right, and she has to pay up. That's cause I learned math. With someone else she would have got away with it. [Hirshon 1983, 63]

Although tensions between social classes were aggravated during the campaign, the crusade clearly helped many people confront their differences and overcome strong antagonisms. As an example, one young man who had been an active Sandinista combatant during the insurrection proudly explained how he learned to appreciate a co-worker as a result of their participation together in the campaign. They had grown up in the same small town but had had limited contact.

I came from a very poor family and Illiana from a very rich one. My mom didn't even have enough money to get me pencils for school; my dad left us when I was little. It wasn't the happiest of times. When we were teenagers I remember Illiana—she was always the best dressed girl around. Stuck up too. She never paid any attention to us, so when I saw that I was going to have to work with her in the crusade I wasn't too happy. Frankly, I was suspicious. I didn't want to have anything to do with her. After having spent almost two years fighting, watching friends die, well you get rather hard sometimes. You question people who didn't participate that way. You wonder, . . . How could she be sincere? How could she be trusted or worthy of such responsibility? I thought sure she would cave in under the pressure and quit. Spoiled little rich kid, I thought, but do you believe it? I was wrong. She was the most dedicated practically of all of us. She tromped through the mud, walked to villages in the pouring rain, worked until dawn, always smiling and enthusiastic, and what's more she didn't quit when she got pregnant until the day before the birth. And two days after the baby was born, she was back at it. Now that's what I call dedication. Without airs or pretension, she showed all of us what it means to be committed and selfless, simply by her actions. I'm damn proud to be her friend, and you know that baby's going to be something else. The way his mother carts him around, he's going to know these mountains better than most anybody. [Canales 1980]

National Activities

Organizational Division

During the first month of the crusade's operation, the Organizational Division responded to the most urgent needs identified in the field. An emergency plan was implemented in cooperation with ENABAS to distribute food supplies and equipment to the *brigadistas* in the countryside before winter rains made much of the road system impassable. To improve the distribution operation and record-keeping system, business students were recruited to work with the logistics support staff on the municipal level. A special adoption program was organized through which each government institution adopted a different provincial teacher corps and worked to raise funds and collect food and clothes to help the volunteers and their host families. New volunteers were recruited to meet the unfulfilled demands for literacy facilitators. Health brigades were organized, then trained in a one-week seminar by the medical faculty of the university, and deployed in teams of four or five to serve each municipality across the country. Medical supplies were reordered and eyeglasses requested and distributed.

Bureaucratic bottlenecks were also on the agenda for action. To address the difficulties and lack of clarity as to functions and lines of authority between the Pedagogical and Organizational Divisions and among the crusade staff, ANDEN, and the EPA, operational documents were developed to clarify the distinctions and responsibilities of each group. To facilitate cooperation among the organizations, a coordinating body made up of representatives from each participating group was formed on the municipal and community levels. To better integrate Ministry of Education officials into the crusade, the regional and provincial directors of education were put in charge of the urban literacy activities.

During the campaign, the Organizational Division put together three national "emulations" to stimulate more effective and dedicated efforts on the part of the staff and participants. The emulations consisted of a series of contests that promoted a lively rivalry among regions. Winners were announced in public meetings to fanfare and applause, and colorful banners served as the symbolic prizes to spur improved performance.

A new department was formed under the auspices of the Organizational Division. Called the Internal Technical Secretariat, it was responsible for keeping the personnel and participant records for the entire crusade. The Statistics Office was placed under the authority of the Organizational Division as well. With the assistance of the Bureau of National Statistics and Census (INEC) and a selected group of technical students, the campaign staff designed the statistical forms and organized and trained the municipal and provincial statistics personnel. The Organizational Division kept the provincial coordinators informed of policies and information requests through monthly meetings held in Managua and through daily radio contact with the provincial offices. During the final weeks of the crusade, the organizational staff gathered and verified statistics, distributed diplomas, and organized the demobilization effort.

Pedagogical Division

The Pedagogical Division took on a temporary identity during the first two or three weeks of the crusade. The different sections—Curriculum, Training, and Research—merged into one supervisory structure in order to provide assistance to the provincial offices in assessing the initial functioning of their operations. This information-gathering effort lasted some fifteen days, and the entire division was needed in order to cover the nation within the short time period. Originally, it was thought that once the crusade was in operation, the majority of the Pedagogical Division would maintain this supervisory role, but unexpected program demands required that the sections continue working in their designated areas of training, curriculum, and research. Supplementary materials and training had to be designed for the crusade, plus planning for a follow-up adult education program had to be begun. By the end of June, the entire pedagogical staff was dedicating most of its time to the design of reading materials for the transition period between the campaign and the more structured adult education program.

Because tasks were more extensive than originally thought, new personnel had to be located. Consequently, after the first field visit in April, four technical advisers from the group of eighty were recruited to work with two Pedagogical Division team members. They formed the Supervision, Oversight, and Advisory Work Group and were charged with visiting the regions on a monthly basis to assess the pedagogical aspects of the program and to consult with, inform, and advise provincial offices on new policies and approaches. This group's reports included information on the campaign's problems, weaknesses, and achievements, and its work, under the direction of the Research Section, was especially helpful in determining the educational areas that needed to be strengthened and improved. Organizational weaknesses were also identified in the process. However, because of inadequate coordination and poor information channels, the group's efforts did not contribute as effectively as they might have to the decision-making process.

The initial two-week visit conducted by the Pedagogical Division staff and the subsequent visits made by the special advisory team were carried out in close cooperation with the provincial pedagogical staffs—members of the group of eighty. These conversations and site observations uncovered the first major educational problems of the campaign—the lack of adequate preparation of the volunteers as well as the same for the support staff. The first was an expected problem; the second came to some as a surprise. The pedagogical team responded to both. The Saturday workshops were designed to help further prepare the volunteers, and materials on the dialogue, the reading process, and learning games were developed. Seminars on how to run the workshops and present the materials were provided for the teaching supervisors.

The second problem had clearly been an oversight. In the educational program, the pedagogical team had not considered the need for any staff development of the professional teachers. It was quickly found, however, that for people to be able to assume the specific planning and supervisory functions of the crusade it was not enough that they know the procedures for carrying them out. In the first month, therefore, the Pedagogical Division developed a draft booklet, *Permanent Tasks* (*Tareas Permanentes*), which outlined the specific responsibilities of the crusade's educational supervisory staff and provided some suggested ways to accomplish those tasks. In mid-April, a four-day workshop was held for all provincial-level pedagogical personnel to discuss the problems they were confronting in the field, examine possible solutions, critique the draft of *Permanent Tasks*, and plan for municipal-level training on the same issues. In May, a workshop was held on the math text to prepare provincial staffs in its use, and the math workshop was subsequently duplicated throughout the country on the municipal and community levels by the provincial pedagogical teams.

Permanent Tasks contained information on how to conduct the following activities: (1) supervision of and support visits to the literacy groups, (2) staff meetings of the Pedagogical Division, (3) Saturday workshops, and (4) planning sessions. It also provided background material on the reading process and specific instructions on how to teach writing and on generating a dialogue.

The relationship between the national Pedagogical Division and the provincial teams gave unusual strength and vitality to the educational program and allowed for a responsiveness and creativity that were unique in a government bureaucracy. The national pedagogical staff saw the provincial personnel as being directly in touch with the everyday reality of the crusade and considered them vital participants and necessary co-creators of the educational materials that were being planned to improve the program. Therefore, materials and information were always critiqued and evaluated together so the program could be best adapted and applied to the actual situations in the field. The process used has been described by one member of the national staff:

> We would sort out the burning issues and problems from the real life experience of the crusade acquired through the visits of the supervision team and the contact with the group of eighty. Because of our close relationship with them, they were always open, frank, and critical with us. We would then categorize the problems, design a response, and finally convene a workshop during which we would discuss the problems identified,

evaluate them in relation to the proposed solution, redesign and improve the proposal based on the discussion with the group. We would conclude by planning the next stage of the multiplier training process for the municipal staff. [Suarez 1980]

This technique was used effectively during the entire campaign. It overcame the bureaucratic pitfalls of a totally centralized system of control and avoided the resulting mechanistic application of policies that often have little to do with real life situations. The process functioned well because of the basic trust, commitment, and shared understanding of the campaign that had been developed among the group of eighty and much of the national team during the first training workshop in December 1979.

Unforeseen Duties

Beyond the extensive, often exhausting duties of the national office, Father Cardenal and his staff were confronted with the painful, unforeseen task of responding to the deaths that occurred during the campaign— about fifty in all. Seven were a result of assassination by counterrevolutionaries, others were from illness, but the vast majority were from accidents such as drownings or being struck by lightning. Although such problems had been anticipated and the *brigadistas* had been constantly warned about swimming or crossing rivers alone, the staff had not really considered in a practical way how it would respond to deaths. The idea was too abhorrent. Each time a death occurred, the national office was shaken; every death was felt personally.

The crusade staff worked to get government compensation for families and legislation passed by the Council of State that would severely punish anyone who harmed literacy volunteers. At the beginning of the campaign, the staff had instituted an emergency airlift service that was able to save all those victims who survived the initial accident. (Helicopters for the service were first requested from the United States. When that request was refused, the Mexican president sent his official helicopter along with several others. The USSR also sent two.) For those people who did not survive the accident, the staff was deeply concerned about how to help family and friends through the time of mourning and how to assign the responsibility for attending the survivors among the members of the national office. Their sense of mutual caring and support sustained the members of the national team in these times of grief and allowed them to share in the consolation of the families.

Late one afternoon, the division coordinators met in Father Cardenal's secretary's office to discuss how they were going to respond to the fact that a *brigadista* had drowned.

"The helicopter left this morning so the body should be arriving soon. Father Fernando insists on going to the airport, but he's exhausted; he just got back from visiting some brigades in the north and hasn't slept for several days. He was dozing in his chair so we brought him a cot and he lay down without saying a word. You know how tired that means he was."

"He feels so responsible. It's too much for him to go. He needs to rest."

"I'm not going to wake him."

"I'll go instead."

"But, Padre, you're exhausted too. When do you sleep? You stay at the shortwave radio all day and all night just to be sure there are no urgent messages."

"No, I'll go and get Father Roberto to come with me so we can be with the family, stay with them tonight, and help make the funeral arrangements. You stay here and get your rest. Tell Fernando where we are, so he can come as soon as he wakes up." [Miller 1980]

One incident, which became known as the crusade's special miracle, had an unexpected ending. A young volunteer took ill suddenly in a remote mountain village, lost consciousness, and stopped breathing. A helicopter was radioed for but could not land because of fog. As was the custom, a wake was held. Candles surrounded the body, dimly lighting the one-room house where he had taught. The villagers came to pay their last respects. As the grandmother of the house bent over to pray, Manuel's eyes flickered and then opened. She screamed, everyone ran, and Manuel sat up. He recovered from the illness and eventually became one of the best-loved workers in the national office of the adult education program, which followed the campaign. Manuel always had a smile for everyone; his enthusiasm was boundless. "Boy, was I lucky that helicopter couldn't land. They would have packed me in lye, covered me in plastic, and that would have been it. Thank the Lord that the saints were with me and so was the fog. The only thing I regret was scaring that poor lady. Doña Chepita will never be the same. But I think she forgives me; she sent me a chicken last week" (Morales 1980).

First National Congress: June 9–11, 1980

At the crusade's halfway point, a series of evaluation-planning meetings were held on all program levels—community, township, municipal, provincial, and national. In all, it is estimated that more than 100,000 people participated formally in the activities. The culminating event, a three-day National Congress of some 700 delegates, included program participants and crusade supporters. It involved people who were learning to read and write, their literacy teachers, supervisors, logistic support personnel, technical advisers, provincial coordinators, national staff members, Ministry of Education officials, representatives from the citizen and labor associations, delegates from the government and the FSLN, international volunteers, UNESCO experts, and representatives from Nicaraguan solidarity groups from all over the world. CELADEC sponsored the National Congress.

From community-level gatherings to the national encounter, the meetings began with a discussion of program needs, problems, deficiencies, and achievements. On the provincial level, discussion was enhanced by role plays and poetry. This analysis led to the second phase of discussion, which was dedicated to examining the solutions that would improve the work and refocus it in terms of the goals and objectives of the crusade. The congress meetings were structured into three commissions: pedagogy; citizen-labor associations and administrative organization; and statistics, regulation, and logistic support.

The encounters stimulated participants to move beyond their particular limited view of the crusade and gain a broader national vision of the program's problems and achievements. Through this process, the participants were able to acquire a clearer understanding of and dedication to the priority needs and challenges of the campaign's final phase.

Before the congress, only the provincial and national pedagogical staff had a global perspective of the campaign. During their meetings and workshops, they had confronted the totality of the national experience through discussions and analysis. But the provincial administrative coordinators, the *brigadistas*, the representatives from the citizen and labor associations did not have the kind of vision that a national perspective gives you. They hadn't had the opportunity to discuss and understand the way we had. . . .

It was reassuring for people to discover that some of their problems were shared, that they weren't alone in their difficulties. It gave them a greater spirit of unity and sense of purpose to confront them and find solutions. The congress was a national assembly where all sectors of the population were represented. It was an opportunity to take the pulse of the crusade, to discover the most urgent problems and issues confronting the program, and provide effective responses to them. It was a three-day encounter where everyone was enriched. We felt we were participating in something new, something unique. The first congress really was more than just a conference. It was one immense workshop of national expression and creation. [Suarez, 1980]

One international teaching adviser who had participated in a provincial-level congress described her surprise and satisfaction at reading the report about the National Congress. The document served as a stimulus to spur more effective work.

> Within each commission they had studied the comments that had come up from the local and regional congresses, dividing them by categories and pairing each "difficulty" with one or more "suggestions" to resolve the problem. . . . I had to admit I was impressed. In my more cynical moments I had suspected that the careful programming of our own congress would be boiled down into broad generalities and the solutions would amount to exhortations to try harder. I should have known better. In each commission, the difficulties went on for pages, and from somewhere along the chain of contributions some solutions had popped up that were not only practical and feasible, but downright creative. . . . It was very reassuring to leaf through the pages and see once again that we weren't alone in our problems. . . . It was also nice to see that there were some problems we didn't have. [Hirshon 1983, 152]

Concluding Month

By the first anniversary of the revolution, July 19, 1980, over 100,000 people had passed the final literacy test and earned their diploma. To celebrate the first anniversary, a national contest was held in which prizes were awarded for composition and creative writing to participants in each of the crusade's six battlefront areas. The national winner was from Ticuantepe, a small town near Managua. In her essay, she wrote:

> I feel very happy to be part of a free nation, a land without anguish or oppression. We have attained many achievements in our revolution like the literacy campaign and many other things as well.
>
> It gives me greater pleasure to tell you that I now know how to read and write. I am fulfilling the dreams of my son, the same dream that was shared by Carlos and Sandino, the dream that we all learn to read and write.
>
> Carlos, the seed that you planted has borne the fruit of your dreams. [Landez 1980, 1]

Final Offensive

To guarantee the maximum number of literates before the conclusion of the crusade, a program of accelerated intensive study was instituted. It was named after "the final offensive," the wartime military operation that had led to the victory over Somoza. The final offensive of the National Literacy Crusade began on July 22, but on the day before, a counteroffensive was also launched against the *brigadistas* by ex-National

Guardsmen who wished to paralyze the campaign. During the final month of the crusade, five *brigadistas* and staff members were assassinated.

In the week before the final offensive began, representatives from the national pedagogical team fanned out across the country. They spent two days in each province, presenting the program plan to local crusade staff and commission members and working with them on the details of its implementation. The final offensive was to be a means to accelerate learning without sacrificing quality. During the remaining four weeks of the campaign, the volunteers' efforts were to be dedicated solely to teaching literacy and organizing the follow-up program. All other activities, such as work in the fields or community organizing, were suspended. Classtime was augmented by two hours, Sunday sessions were added, and individual tutorial study was provided. Saturdays were dedicated to intensive volunteer workshops and the radio program was devoted totally to pedagogical instructions. Parental visits were discouraged, and *brigadistas* were given permission to leave teaching sites only for dire emergencies. *Brigadistas* whose students had passed their literacy test were relocated to provide assistance to other study groups. Specific orientations were given to help accelerate the rhythm of learning by eliminating some of the more superfluous learning exercises from the final lessons. Many new literacy graduates took on a monitor role in their groups and provided individualized attention and practice opportunities to fellow students who were still finishing the primer. Many provincial and municipal staff members moved into their offices in order to be on twenty-four-hour call.

The level of work and dedication was intense. Late one night, in a municipal office in the north, two members of the local pedagogical team were writing up their work plan for the final week's community visits. Suddenly, without warning, their small electric generator went out, and the office was plunged into darkness. A chicken had tripped over the cables, gotten caught in the tangle of wires, and was squawking in loud complaint. While the municipal coordinator went out to fix the damage, the two continued their work in the dark without a pause except for a softly muttered "damn." One pounded away at the ancient manual typewriter while the other dictated from memory.

On the community level, brigade meetings were held to assess possibilities and to develop a concrete work plan for everyone. The situation of each *brigadista* was surveyed, and questions were asked. "Who, exactly, is studying with you? What lesson are they on? Who has finished? Who has dropped out? Who might be coaxed back? How many will be finished by August? We counted the lessons and exercises that remained for each student and divided them into the time remaining, emerging with a rigid day-to-day schedule" (Hirshon 1983, 181).

Although the enthusiasm and spirit of the crusade staff were boosted by the urgency of the final offensive, the literacy students did not always greet the increased activity with similar dedication. Often there was resistance to classes on Sunday. The most committed learners enjoyed the added attention and opportunities for study, but for some of the students, Sunday continued to be a day of relative rest. However, surges of learning did take place all over the country, because by early July, most students had reached lesson nine, the point at which significant breakthroughs occurred in reading comprehension and the learning process. Several *brigadistas* described the increased momentum, and one well-known, but reformed, hooky player teased his supervisor, Sheyla, as he asked for a reward visit to his family, knowing full well that such trips were strictly forbidden during the final offensive.

> "They're making progress, Sheyla, they really are." "Three of mine are about to finish. Of course, they turned out to be superintelligent." "We're coming along fast at Don Chavelo's. Going through a lesson every other day. And I'm still trying at Doña Jacoba's even though I can't get anywhere. Three shifts, Sheyla! Don't you think I deserve a few days in Managua for all my good efforts?" [Hirshon 1983, 163]

Despite the teasing, a new seriousness and sense of purpose filled the young volunteers. The realization that time was short affected them, as did the knowledge that to get academic credit for their teaching, they would have to produce results or at least demonstrate that they had tried. One *brigadista* proudly told his teaching supervisor about a meeting that had been held with the EPA representative while she had been away at a municipality meeting. "You'll never guess what! We had a meeting with Chico when you weren't here, and it was the best meeting we ever had. Everyone came, and everyone was serious, and nobody goofed around or anything" (Hirshon 1983, 166).

Teaching supervisors were especially burdened during this time. Besides their normal tasks, they now had the additional responsibilities of overseeing the literacy testing, collecting final statistics, supervising the selection and training of local people to replace the *brigadistas*, and organizing the follow-up community study groups that would carry on the learning efforts of the campaign after the *brigadistas* had left. Supervisors were often caught between competing demands and conflicting directions from the national office. The Pedagogical Division emphasized the importance of organizing the follow-up program and of keeping educational standards high, while the Organizational Division stressed the testing and statistical aspects of the campaign and believed that all participants should have the opportunity to take the literacy test, whether or not they had finished the twenty-three lessons of the primer.

Graduation

On Saturday August 2, Nandasmo was declared the first municipality in the nation to be victorious over illiteracy. Close to 95 percent of its campaign students had completed the final literacy exam successfully. After that first declaration, municipalities and townships across Nicaragua were added to the list daily. Celebrations were held. In gleeful marches to town cemeteries, marked by mock solemnity, wooden caskets carrying the corpses of ignorance were mourned and buried once and for all. Graduation ceremonies were held in village squares, town plazas, school yards, coffee sheds, factories, and open fields. On the coast, on mountain tops, and in jungle valleys, people sang, cried, and cheered. Proud graduates walked shyly and humbly up to makeshift stages in order to accept their diplomas. Dogs barked, babies misbehaved, and in San Juan del Sur, wayward pigs interrupted the final rousing speeches by barging through the audience, upsetting chairs and guests. Women screeched, then everyone laughed. A confused pig ran through the band and knocked over the tuba. The ceremony was over. The tuba was returned to its owner, and the dancing began.

Ceremonies were deeply emotional for everyone and brought back memories of the past. Two celebrations in the north of Nicaragua illustrate the depth of feeling and sense of history evoked by the experience. Adriana stood tall before the group of literacy graduates, a gangling about-to-be-pretty thirteen year old. Tears shone in the corners of her eyes. Behind her sat the small corps of young literacy volunteers— eight classmates from the same junior high school. With them sat their teacher who had spent the five-month campaign living and working at their side. Emotions of joy and sadness covered their faces. Adriana smiled shyly as she called the names of her students, six laborers from the surrounding coffee plantation meticulously groomed for the occasion, their unruly hair wetted down and combed carefully in place. One by one they went forward—each to receive the literacy diploma and a hesitant awkward kiss on the cheek.

Adriana's mother sat on a bench at the edge of the open coffee shed, silently crying and absently petting a blond dog sprawled at her feet. Her carefully applied mascara slowly blurred and dissolved in tears of pride. "She has grown so much. How proud her uncles would be," she said quietly. "Nicaragua is finally free." She looked off over the hills to the mountains near Pancasán, the place where her brother had died fighting Somoza's guardsmen thirteen years before. Her gaze continued beyond the mountains on to Condega, the home of her husband's family.

Painful memories returned. Late one evening a little over a year before, the National Guard had broken into their living room and massacred the entire family, infants and adults alike—nine in all. Some were machine gunned, and some pierced with bayonets. Adriana and her mother had been visiting them that same afternoon but had decided to make the long journey home instead of staying the night as they frequently did. They had left at around six; the family was killed at ten-thirty.

The dog nudged her leg, interrupting her thoughts. She looked down and smiled affectionately. "His name is Campana," she whispered. "A young fighter left him here during the war last June, right before a battle with the guard. He said he would be back as soon as he could and asked the people on the plantation to keep the dog safe. The dog was his friend. He never returned."

The enthusiastic off-key singing of the National Literacy Anthem broke her reverie and signaled an end to the graduation. Adriana ran up to kiss her mother. She was smiling, tears almost forgotten. "Mom, I didn't tell you what happened last week. I thought my teaching had been completely useless, that my students weren't going to be able to graduate, that I had failed. It was awful." She laughed. Adriana explained that she had gone to town overnight to pick up the final examination forms. When she left, her students were on lesson twenty-one, but when she got back, they had somehow mysteriously regressed to lesson five. "I was so upset. They couldn't read anything. Then one of them turned to the last page of the book and carefully began to read the final story. In the two days I was gone, they had taught themselves lessons twenty-two and twenty-three. They wanted to fool me," she chuckled, "and they did!"

Laughing, she took off her red and black bandana, and tied it around her mother's neck. "I'm going to miss them, and I think they are going to miss me too. Do you know that José and Pedro didn't come to graduation today because they said it would be too sad?" Her face turned serious. "But Jaime promised to take my place as coordinator of the group. I had to convince him because he wasn't too enthusiastic, but he's been to school and works on the plantation too. If he takes the job seriously, he should be able to keep the group going so when we come visit at Christmas they won't have forgotten anything. I hope so." Jumping up, she ran over to help the others get the food ready for the celebration. Campana barked and chased after her (Miller 1980).

Over the mountains, about twenty-five miles away, another graduation ceremony was taking place on the outskirts of Wiwilí, a small town that was well known as a haven for Sandino's army and as a center for his agricultural programs. When the U.S. Marines left Nicaragua in 1933, Sandino, along with many of his men and their families, returned to the region and began farming and working the cooperatives they had established during the seven-year struggle. After the general was assassinated by the National Guard in 1934, the U.S.-appointed commandant, Anastasio Somoza García, immediately sent troops to Wiwilí to eliminate all vestiges of Sandino's peasant cooperatives—men, women, and children.

Forty-six years later, in the same valley, a poor farmworker stood before his community and read a poem calling forth the memory of Sandino in honor of the literacy crusade and of his young teacher Maira. Before the ceremony, Maira had copied his poem neatly in her own hand on a clean sheet of paper so the letters would be clear. But Juan Velasquez chose to read his own carefully written words. "They were easier to read," he said. Haltingly at first, gathering force as he proceeded, Juan read:

> One day, over there, yonder by the mountain top
>> where only the songs of the Jilguero bird are heard
> I came upon a garden of Sandino's carnations—
>> flowers long asleep that have blossomed once again,
>> a garden filled with the fragrance of harmony,
>> flowers whose seeds Sandino planted
>> once a long time away,
> Over there, yonder by the mountain top
>> near the peak of Kilambé.
>
> As I looked at their colors, reborn once again,
>> the flowers spoke.
> They told me that they had been waiting for the sunrise to come,
>> nothing more—
>> the new dawn of a people,
>> a sun that now shines like never before.

He looked up and said to the gathered volunteers, "I give you my poem in honor of the crusade to take with you, so you and the campaign will never forget this poor mountain man."

As he finished, a fine mist began to fall. The men of the community mounted their horses and mules; the rest of the crowd headed for the porches. Mules bucked trying to toss their riders, volunteers ran in the rain. The festivities began—games, dancing, and feasting. Strung between two trees hung a line decked with ribbons. The horsemen raced under the rope attempting to lift the specially tied bows with a stick. Those who successfully managed the feat offered the ribbon to the woman of their choice and were rewarded by a kiss and the first dance.

As the games started, a radiant, smiling volunteer slipped in the mud trying to cross the road. "This is nothing", she laughed, "You should have seen me when I first tried to climb Mt. Kilambé to get to my village. I had mud up to my ears." As she turned, her face became clearer. Faint scars marked her cheeks, and a large scab covered the side of her nose. She had mountain leprosy, a common rural disease that weakens and disfigures its victims. The crusade's medical staff had sent her back to Managua to recuperate, but she had asked to return for the graduation ceremonies and the victory celebration. "How could I miss this," she said. "We won!" (Miller 1980).

Demobilization

Transporting the thousands of rural volunteers and their teaching advisers back home safely was yet another challenge. The poor network of roads and almost total lack of bridges exacerbated the problems that are inherent in any massive transfer of people. By August, the winter rain had made many roads and rivers impassable; the lovely streams that the *brigadistas* had crossed on foot during the dry season had become swollen torrents, and the dirt roads had turned into muddy swamps. What had been a two- or three-day walk in March was now often a five- or six-day journey.

A carefully orchestrated eight-day demobilization program was put into action. At each point along the way, the community organizations provided accommodations and hospitality for the footsore *brigadistas*. From the most remote sites, the young volunteers walked to area transportation points. From municipal centers, they were transported to provincial capitals, where they rode through the streets shouting and singing, waving to the cheering crowds. By the time they reached their final assembly points, the exhaustion on their faces was clear. They looked like members of a ragtag army, ready for a long rest.

In rare cases, some *brigadistas* were accompanied by their students to the provincial capital. Farewells were painful, and some *brigadistas* wanted to prolong their departure as long as possible. Before the bus loads of *brigadistas* left the northern town of Jinotega, one young man entered the cathedral to pray with his student. Afterward, on their way out, the student walked over to the side of the church and traced the engraved words on the wall, softly reading the verses of scripture as his hands touched each letter. The *brigadista* stood next to him smiling with quiet pride.

Brigadistas who lived in the immediate area simply proceeded to their homes. Those from cities such as Managua or León waited until all their fellow *brigadistas* arrived at the provincial assembly points so they could all travel home together in caravans. The arrival scene in Managua was tumultuous. Every afternoon for one week, the capital's main plaza was filled with happy, anxious families waiting to welcome their sons and daughters. The volunteers returned in caravans organized by regions along the six battlefronts. As the buses and dump trucks arrived, cheers went up. Torrential rains sometimes drenched the crowd, but nothing could dampen the collective enthusiasm. The *brigadistas* clamored down from the vehicles, throwing knapsacks to the ground; juggling pets, presents, and guitars; hurrying to hug family and friends as soon as they could be found in the crowd. Tears and smiles marked their faces. Although there were many blistered feet and sunburned cheeks, everyone arrived home safely. One jeep did turn over, but the only casualties were two chickens and one parrot.

The demobilization was more difficult, however, in some areas. In one region, the volunteers had been trucked into their communities from the Pacific side, but by August, the roads in that area had been washed away. Since the easiest and safest way was to walk to the other coast, a column of *brigadistas* marched several days to the Atlantic Ocean. There, they were ferried upriver and transferred to trucks for the final journey home.

Volunteers returning from the Atlantic Coast were especially loaded down with pets, jungle animals and birds, that had been given to them by their grateful peasant families and students. Despite instructions to the contrary, the volunteers found it difficult to refuse the gifts. In the final caravan from East Coast, two entire trucks were devoted to transporting pets as well as a good number of chickens, wild turkeys, and iguanas. One boy even brought home a baby jaguar.

August 23, 1980

On August 23, rural *brigadistas* and urban *guerrilleros* from all over the nation came to the capital to celebrate the achievements of the campaign. An afternoon of parades, speeches, and songs drew a massive concentration of volunteers, their families, supervisory teachers, and new literacy graduates to Managua's largest plaza.

One person stirred the crowd especially—a market woman, some fifty years old, from the cotton-producing area of Chinandega. Short, strong, stout, and outspoken, María Ulloa de Alaniz had been chosen to represent the hundreds of thousands of new literates. She won the day with laughter and thunderous applause for her spirit and her poetry. Her poem went like this:

Good-bye to Ignorance, good-bye.
Ignorance, good-bye forever,
    because I will never see you again.

I bid you farewell,
   feeling a little sad it's true,
Because quite frankly, Ignorance,
   I couldn't do a thing with you.
But with this literacy crusade,
   I surely could.
Satisfaction I found, and it was good.
So I turn to all those *brigadistas*
   who, with honor and glory,
   helped us fulfill this great mission,
We salute you.
We toast you with congratulations,
   because you knew how to overcome this stagnation.
You used your minds and your hearts,
   and even risked your lives for our liberation.
So from my grateful soul,
   I want to bid you good-bye,
   because now in Nicaragua,
   Ignorance has been overcome.
Forever we have won.

The festivities, and laughter, went on throughout the evening, and people danced until dawn.

Closing Congress

A second National Congress was held to assess the achievements of the crusade and to analyze the lessons that it provided. The insights and information gathered from the two-day encounter were to help lay the groundwork for the follow-up adult education program as well as an entirely new educational system. The national meeting was also considered a contribution to other nations that might be interested in mounting a similar venture. On September 5 and 6, more than 800 delegates participated in the proceedings, which were held in the imposing red-carpeted, marble Rubén Dario Theater, which had been built by Somoza.

Among the participants were students of the literacy campaign, peasants who had recently learned to read and write. The spontaneous speech given by one of them at the conclusion of the congress probably best describes the spirit, pride, and interest that had been generated by the campaign. The master of ceremonies asked the audience if anyone had anything else to add to the presentations that had already been made. He paused briefly, then continued with his closing comments as he did not expect anyone to come forth from the large assembly. Surprise marked his face when he saw a young peasant rise and walk to the stage. Juan José Mercado, complete with clean white T-shirt and red baseball cap perched precariously on the side of his head, gave a speech that won the day.

Good afternoon, fellow *compañeros* of the city and the country. I feel very moved to be here with you today. My name is Juan José Mercado, and I am a new literate from Nandaime, Montegrande Occidental, province of Granada. I stand here before you not ashamed to admit that I didn't know how to read. I am not ashamed, *compañeros*. It is true.

When the *brigadistas* arrived in our village, they were strangers to us. They came to our house and told us, "We are here to serve you and to teach you how to read." "What do you mean?" we answered them. "Take this book and this pencil and see, we are going to teach you how to use them." I'll never forget him. Ramón Romero Ruiz is his name. I took the book and held it upside down, and I am not ashamed to tell you, friends. I did. Ramón said to me, "No *compañero*, not that way, this way." And I began to read my very first letter of the alphabet.

I work on the San Albino farm. I have worked there seven months in the dust and in the rain. There I worked and there I learned under the guidance of Ramón who daily was at my side, teaching and encouraging me. I am not ashamed to say it because they told us we Nicaraguans should never be ashamed, and tomorrow when they ask me, "Who was your teacher?" I will be proud to tell them. He is the reason I am here. He has helped me earn the respect of my *compañeros*.

Ramón invited me to come. He said "Let's go. I invite you to the congress." And so I came. I had never heard of this theater before with its beauty and its magnificence. I have come and contemplated lovely things. I had never been to this place before, and I am not ashamed to admit it. Coming here has given me very great joy, and I will tell my *compañeros* at home to continue studying so that tomorrow, sometime in the future, we can reach greater distances with this revolution, we can go farther. That is what we ask of this government.

And I am not ashamed to say that when I first arrived in Managua, I got lost; my people are from the countryside, so frankly we don't know our way around here. I had to ask directions because I didn't know which way was up or what was what. And when I finally got here, I was amazed to see such a marvelous thing as this Rubén Dario Theatre. This is the first time any of my family has stepped on these grounds, walked on this grass, or entered this beautiful place. Not my parents, who are very old now, not my brothers or my sisters. Nobody. They would be proud. The fact that I am here today is due to the strengh of the revolution, the revolution that is everywhere with us, teaching all that it can. May it continue to do so. That is what I ask.

They are few, the number of words I have to say today, because I have never been in front of so many people before, and I'll tell you quite frankly, I am nervous. My body is trembling. It doesn't bother me to tell you though because you are my *compañeros*. . . . Thank you. I wish you happiness as does the revolution. May you never tire of teaching us. Don't get tired and don't stop because now I am responsible for teaching fourteen *compañeros* in the follow-up program. With the little bit that I have learned, I'm teaching the others who still don't know how to read and write very well. We want to learn many things. [Tape of speech]

As he finished, to pounding applause, tears could be seen in some of the eyes of the listeners. For them, Juan José was what the campaign had been all about. His words affirmed their mutual victory over the silence of poverty and powerlessness.

Follow-Up

From the beginning of the campaign, the literacy crusade had always been considered only a first step in the long process of education and social creation. Crusade leaders were well aware that the basic reading and writing skills that were mastered by the hundreds of thousands of Nicaraguans during the campaign were fragile. Five months of intensive study provided an educational foundation that needed to be reinforced and consolidated. A transition program between the crusade and the permanent course of adult education was designed to provide people with a time to practice and strengthen their literacy and math skills. The challenge was awesome. Nicaragua had scant financial resources available, and well-prepared human resources were also limited.

For a time, the follow-up program seemed to face insurmountable obstacles until the practical experience of the campaign pointed toward a workable solution. The inspiration for the transition program arose from a natural phenomenon that had occurred within the literacy groups. As the most advanced students had finished the primer, they had taken on a new role in their study group and had begun to concentrate on helping fellow students practice and master the skills. The transition program drew on this community resource. Outstanding literacy graduates or educated members of the community were chosen by the *brigadistas* in conjunction with their teaching supervisors to continue the work of the learning groups when the campaign terminated.

After being given some basic training by the crusade's teaching supervisors during the last month of the campaign, the new educational "coordinators" were provided with a carefully designed teaching guide and a set of follow-up reading materials that stressed collective study, composition, writing, and action projects as the fundamental basis for community learning. The focus of the study groups was twofold: to help those people who had not finished the primer complete their studies and to help the new graduates finish the math text and consolidate their reading, writing, and comprehension skills.

These community learning groups were supported by the network of mass citizen and labor organizations. The work of the coordinators was bolstered by specially selected traveling "promoters," itinerant teacher supervisors who served as liaisons with the regional adult education offices and provided the community groups with encouragement, orientation, and extra learning materials when available. The weekly Saturday workshops, which had begun during the crusade, were continued under the direction of the promoters. Rounding out the support activities was a radio show that was oriented especially toward the study groups and broadcast twice daily on all national channels, with a special Saturday program geared to the workshops. During the first months of operation, the show received more than 2,000 letters.

The story of one individual coordinator gives an idea of how the follow-up program worked in one area.

> Pablo is up every morning at five and while he sharpens his machete, he listens to a radio program which continually reviews points about how to teach. "You, as the teachers must be the most humble member of the group," advises the announcer who explains how to recognize and affirm an individual's progress, and how to overcome common learning difficulties. Preparation for the lessons also gets very specific, and Pablo often puts his knife aside to open the workbook and follow orientations about a particular exercise. [Trueman 1981, 16]

Pablo's *brigadista* explains his background and the extraordinary significance the appointment has for him.

> Pablo and I had some months before wondered sadly if his new reading skills would ever be put to much use. Unlike the rest of the family, 24 year old Pablo had grown up in a town and had finished the third grade. With that background he was able to advance through the lessons quickly. "Gee," he would say, "I've just begun to realize that reading is more than being able to mouth the printed words, I'm just learning to interpret what I read. If I had stayed in school maybe I'd be a teacher now. . . . If the Crusade were only five months longer . . . if you could only stay, maybe I could finish the fifth grade and maybe . . ."
>
> During my visit in November, three months after the conclusion of the campaign, Pablo and I recalled these sorrowful conversations that we'd had during the Crusade, looking back with amusement and appreciation. We had been so pessimistic then; so sure that good things were happening "too late" for him. Some of the conversations had, for Pablo,

followed a desperate day of drinking locally made moonshine, and once the discussion ended with his sobs. So little time had passed since then, yet here he was, not only continuing to learn but he was the teacher. [Trueman 1981, 16]

A support system provided Pablo with basic assistance and encouragement.

> Pablo is visited at least once a week by Faustino, the volunteer area coordinator. Faustino is also a campesino with very little formal education. He walks several hours every evening visiting study groups in the valley. If he doesn't leave before dark he stays the night. He makes sure classes are happening regularly and he encourages those who miss classes to take learning seriously. He reminds them that if Nicaragua is to be governed by the people, they must be literate. "When we know how to read well," he tells them, "we'll be able to form better community organizations, we'll study better farming techniques, we'll learn to plant more foods and to eat and live better."
>
> Every Saturday Faustino and Pablo and the other group facilitators meet to review the past week's work and plan for the coming week. Their meeting is guided by the same radio program that they listen to individually during the week. Instructions are given slowly and are interrupted with musical interludes which the groups use to discuss the instructions.
>
> The announcer comes back to talk about problems encountered by study groups across the country. Shortages of radios and lamps are among the most serious problems. . . . Possible solutions are discussed in the program and Faustino, Pablo, and the others who listen feel proud to be doing as well as they are. [Trueman 1981, 17]

Crusade Achievements

More than half a million people, students and teachers alike, participated directly in the campaign as learners—some 460,000 as students of literacy and about 95,000 as students of the nation's reality, its problems and potential. During the course of the crusade, all participants became students of the revolutionary process and of the national program of development. According to official statistics, some 406,000 literacy students demonstrated their mastery of elementary reading and writing skills by passing a five-part final examination. From an effective rate of 40 percent, illiteracy was reduced to some 13 percent. Besides reading and writing skills, students also had the opportunity to develop mathematical and analytical skills and to express themselves in public while studying history and the national development program.

The fact that so many people were able to develop and master such skills in a five-month time period, no matter how basic, is quite remarkable. In conventional terms alone, this must be considered an extraordinary achievement, but the campaign involved more than mastering simple literacy skills. Because the program was conceived of as a mutual process of learning and human development, the teacher corps and support staff were also learners. To varying degrees, these people acquired new depths of understanding about the problems of poverty and the challenge of development.

It is generally agreed that the volunteers and support staff members who worked in the rural areas, some 65,000 in all, gained the most from the experience. They lived and worked alongside the peasant families they taught. From that close relationship, many learned to appreciate for the first time the traditional culture of the rural people— their songs, dances, and poetry; their predominant values of humility, honesty, and respect; their intelligence; and their capacity for survival in the face of extreme deprivation. In the intimacy of everyday living, the volunteers saw the effects of misery and underdevelopment. Rural poverty touched them personally and, in so doing, moved many of them to a deeper commitment to the revolution and to working with the poor. Their families were often affected in similar ways by the experience, especially those who visited the volunteers at their teaching sites. As a result, new bonds were developed between people of the country and people of the city, new understandings were reached, and new relationships were established.

The Nicaraguan literacy crusade was part of a national process of social transformation that was designed to redistribute power and wealth, a development process that was oriented especially toward favoring the poorest section of society. Although it is difficult to find quantitative measures to evaluate how well the campaign contributed to redistribution, overall qualitative judgments can give a general picture of some important achievements. Besides helping people gain basic skills, knowledge, and attitudes conducive to transformation, the campaign had other specific results that contributed to national development, participation, and the consolidation of the new balance of power and wealth. During the campaign, for example, volunteers worked with the people of their newly adopted communities in establishing a nationwide malaria control program and participated in countless local development projects. They also gathered valuable information for future national development planning. Literacy brigades and specially trained university research brigades conducted several surveys to collect important agricultural data. Cultural brigades interviewed community people, and in such conversations, recorded national history and culture—thousands of local stories, legends, and histories. This information was to form the basis of future educational materials. Medical brigades made a country inventory and a distribution map of rural diseases to be used for more accurate health programming.

Women's participation, both as teachers and as students, was high. Over half of the EPA was female, as was some 50 percent of the literacy students. The separation of EPA squadrons according to men and women increased the leadership opportunities for female *brigadistas*. If the organization had been integrated, men would probably have dominated the structure because of the ingrained deference given to them. The campaign experience provided young women volunteers with the opportunity to test their skills and to live independently from their families. In the process, many gained a new sense of identity and confidence and decided upon new career directions in rural development, careers that had been traditionally closed to women. Women literacy students were highly motivated, but they needed assistance in child care in order to be able to attend classes consistently. Although many of these women students were chosen to become study group coordinators for the followup program, fathers and husbands sometimes discouraged them from taking on this leadership role.

The crusade had a profound effect on the nation's new institutions as it increased the opportunities for community involvement in development. Through participation in the campaign, the citizen and labor organizations expanded their network of affiliates and tested and improved their operational capacities. Members not only acquired basic literacy and math skills but gained valuable practice in organizational and planning activities as well. Government agencies discovered serious bureaucratic bottlenecks in their operations and were able to design corrective strategies to make their services more responsive to the community. In the process, officials fine-tuned their skills in planning and administration.

In all, more than one-fifth of the population participated directly in the campaign, and through family and friends, almost the entire nation was affected by its efforts. Despite program problems and weaknesses, significant learning took place in relation to both literacy and development. The success of the crusade was due to many factors. The political will and national unity that resulted from victory over the dictatorship provided the necessary impetus for the effort. The momentum and hope engendered by that triumph made it possible for many campaign participants, both students and volunteers alike, to overcome the unresolved weaknesses of the educational program and the personal difficulties of living in desperate poverty and discomfort. The overall sense of responsibility and openness on the part of many of the staff members fostered a climate of unusual creativity and cooperation and a working style of remarkable flexibility and responsiveness. As part of a national program of development and transformation, the crusade was able to mobilize necessary resources, but more important, it was able to challenge people to excellence.

Perhaps the voices of people who were involved in the crusade can give the most articulate and accurate assessment of the experience.

I was raised here in these mountains and started earning a living when I was twelve. My parents were very poor and had no money to send us to school. I grew up and went into Sandino's army. That was when I was fifteen in 1931. The National Guard was after us and called us "bandits"—I fought on the Atlantic Coast, and when peace was declared, I handed over my rifle. Then I got married, and in this last war, they found out my son was Sandinista. The guard took him and killed him, but I must accept his death because I know it's God's will. And now we're learning to read and write. They're coming to teach us. I thank God because nobody has ever done that before and it makes me very happy.

> Don Ciriano (1980)
> peasant from Nueva Segovia

Do you know, I am not ignorant any more. I know how to read now. Not perfectly, you understand, but I know how. And do you know, your son isn't ignorant any more either. Now he knows how we live, what we eat, how we work, and he knows the life of the mountains. Your son, ma'am, has learned to read from our book.

> Don José, peasant farmworker speaking
> to the mother of his literacy teacher
> (quoted in DiMontis 1980, 2)

I don't believe, like some people say, that they wanted to domesticate us with the literacy campaign. I think the revolution wants us to educate ourselves so that we can define what we, the Nicaraguan people, want, otherwise we wouldn't be conscious of our actions. It's when we don't know how to read and write that we're domesticated.

> Ricardo Lopez Cerda, bottling plant
> employee (quoted in Gayo 1980, 29)

Now that we've finished the course and passed the exams, that doesn't mean that we're necessarily going to be doing a whole lot of reading. But we've discovered that we are able to learn. That big thing—reading—

that only city people were able to do—is no longer such a big thing. For the first time in my life, I feel able to walk with my head up."

> new literate
> (quoted in Barndt 1982, 5)

Previously, all we knew of people in the cities was that they [the National Guard] came and killed people. Now we know that city people and country people can live together.

> peasant from Chinandega
> (quoted in Barndt 1982, 4)

The literacy crusade taught us two things. One, what our own children are capable of doing and of becoming. Two, what our country is like and how gentle and how poor our people are in the countryside.

> Mabel Somarriba (1980)
> mother of three *brigadistas*

I was a snob before I went off to teach literacy. I didn't greet or talk to peasants who came into town; I fussed a lot about dressing up and making up my face, and before I put on the new boots the Crusade gave me, I filed and painted my toenails. Now that I know people from the surrounding valleys, people are always stopping by to greet me and I love it. My old worries just bore me now.

> Julia, a *brigadista*
> (quoted in Trueman 1981, 14)

We take our malaria medicine twice a week, and we're supposed to use our water purifying tablets. . . . The sicknesses among the children are many. Eight children in the next valley died last month of measles, three from the same family. It's unbelievable, the inhuman conditions these people live under. I feel indignation and rage at not being a doctor. How I want to study these things, to learn how to stop this from happening.

> Gabriela Selser (1980), a *brigadista*

In San Pablo . . . on the border with Honduras there was a squad of women. There were many characteristics of the area which made it inappropriate for women to be assigned there. There were incursions of counter-revolutionary bands because of the nearness of the border and of the fact that it was mountainous—and it was very mountainous. The area is almost impenetrable, there are snakes, vipers, everything imaginable. But, those women, they stayed there until the end of the Crusade. They sparked the growth of the mass organizations and such things, although some compañeros (male brigadistas) refused to go there because they were afraid since it was on the border. . . . In those districts I tell you without exaggerating you have to walk eight or ten hours to get there in the rainy season—with sharp cliffs and everything. But those women got there and stayed. I tip my hat to them. We all agreed, "Those women, they have balls."

> Omar, a seventeen-year-old *brigadista*
> (quoted in Flora et al. 1982, 25)

Returning from the literacy crusade I had certain conflicts with my family; they wanted me to remain a little girl, an object. In the crusade we women felt liberated; we all worked, we helped out in everything, and we were not under the thumb of our parents. We survived for five months alone and that gives you the experience to know how to run your own life.

> Josefa, a sixteen-year-old *brigadista*
> (quoted in Flora et al. 1982, 33)

The crusade has been carried out by the kids of Nicaragua, the wonderful kids who under the leadership of the *Frente* fought the tyrant—intelligent kids, sacrificing, determined—idealists and realists all at the same time. For me, the principal lesson of the campaign is that now Nicaragua knows that it can count on this treasure for its future. Not all the best children died in the war. With the living, we can carry out the other necessary wars to be fought, the war against social injustice, the war against poor health, the war against disease. The crusade is over. The people of Nicaragua and the commitment of the *Frente* made it possible. Thanks to their efforts, Nicaragua will be totally different in the future. It will be a better nation, a nation that all Nicaraguans deserve. If that's not a triumph, excuse me, but then what the hell do you call a triumph?

> a priest, teaching supervisor
> (quoted in Von Rechnitz 1982, 3)

The pride and accomplishment felt by the Nicaraguans involved in the campaign were reflected internationally. Their sense of triumph and victory was recognized: "The panel of judges designated by the director general of UNESCO to grant the 1980 prizes for distinguished and effective contribution on behalf of literacy . . . has unanimously chosen for first prize—the National Literacy Crusade of Nicaragua" (UNESCO 1980).

7

Conclusions and Appraisal

The ultimate success of the literacy crusade depended on a commitment of the spirit—a commitment of a people and a government born of a liberation struggle. Only that kind of creative force could generate and maintain the levels of sacrifice and dedication required to accomplish such a task. For when all is said and done, the crusade is not a story of complicated techniques or complex cost-benefit analysis. It is a story of people and the extraordinary potential for liberation and creation that exists within nations.

—Father Fernando Cardenal, S.J. (1981)
National Coordinator
Nicaraguan Literacy Crusade

The conclusions and insights presented in this chapter focus principally on the educational aspects of the literacy campaign, especially issues related to curriculum, methodology, and training. In a varying degree of detail, other issues are also examined, such as the social context in which the campaign evolved, the crusade's organizational structure, its transition to an ongoing adult education program, its use of international assistance, and its effectiveness in reaching its overall goals. In order to determine and analyze major program conclusions, this discussion draws upon the critical reflection undertaken by the planners themselves, both during and after the campaign. Certain issues have been selected because they may provide insights to other nations that might consider such an endeavor in a similar moment of transition and transformation. An appraisal of the campaign's overall accomplishments concludes the study.

The first three topics addressed in this chapter relate to Nicaragua's particular social context and its effect on the crusade. Both the liberation struggle and the process of transformation had a far-reaching impact on the development of the campaign's educational program and the follow-up plan, as did, to a lesser degree, the response of those people who opposed the revolution and its changes.

Social Context: Struggle and Transformation

Confrontation and Creativity

The fact that Nicaragua was engaged in a process of profound transformation created a social climate in which confrontations were common and the possibilities for creativity and change were great. The society was in a state of transition between systems, immersed in a revolutionary process of nation building. One social order had been categorically rejected, and the new order was still a vision, a system to be forged in the process, the pathway not yet clear. The Somozan system of inequity, repression, and corruption, which many Nicaraguans associated with capitalism, was to be transformed. Some form of socialism was the commonly accepted alternative. Even the Catholic church hierarchy and the more conservative members of the junta who had wealthy business interests rhetorically supported this position.

So even though the exact details of how the new Nicaragua would be established had not been defined and there was a continuing ambiguity as to the specifics and implications of the changes, the general outlines of the society were clear and were widely supported. In contrast to the marked inequities of the old system, the new Nicaragua was to be egalitarian in nature, founded on citizen participation and the redistribution of power and wealth. The challenge was to give life to this vision. Creativity and conflict characterized the transition. Confrontation between old and new provoked problems and contradictions, but it also promoted tremendous opportunities for growth and learning. Responsibilities were given, and effective results were expected. This situation encouraged people to work to their maximum potential. The problems and contradictions that accompanied the process were considered natural products of change, sometimes anticipated and sometimes not, but always providing new grist and material for the work mill and always expanding people's knowledge and understanding.

The design and implementation of the crusade took place amid this creative conflict. The tension between old and new, between the vision of the future society and the search for practical means to reach it, gave a special urgency and dynamism to the process. Within this context, the campaign confronted the program planners and personnel with several interrelated challenges—personal, political, and pedagogical—all revolving around the creation of an educational program that would be consonant with the new conception of society. How these people responded to such challenges was related to their own composition as a staff, a composition probably representative of many countries undergoing such transitions. The staff members themselves were an amalgam of old and new. Teachers and Ministry of Education employees from the old system were incorporated into the program alongside new people who were especially chosen for their professional expertise, potential for growth, and commitment to the process.

On a personal level, the challenge of planning the campaign affected the entire staff. In grappling with design questions, its members faced the contradictions and prejudices of their own upbringing and social background. The vast majority of them came from urban settings, were members of middle- or upper-class families, and products of higher education and years of formal study that sometimes had taken place outside of Nicaragua. The rural areas and people were largely unknown to many of them except through textbooks or servant relationships. Sometimes this narrow, isolated upbringing affected the ability of the planners to empathize with the rural people or to see them in their full human dimension as intelligent, creative, and skilled individuals, albeit sometimes superstitious or ignorant of city ways. Despite the desire to overcome such paternalistic feelings, inbred attitudes of superiority remained. Out of this situation arose tensions between staff members of different class backgrounds as well.

The personal affected the political. In order to meet the political goals of the campaign, in terms of redistribution and popular participation, the planners had to do battle with these personal values and attitudes. Beliefs and behavior that had been spawned by past upbringing were strong in everyone. Although the new, specially selected staff members were profoundly committed to the revolutionary goals, they found that personal and political transformation was not just a matter of desire or will. It was difficult for them to shed their years of socialization and isolation under the former system. For the old guard, those who had been longtime bureaucrats under Somoza, it was even more difficult to do so. For both old and new, the challenge and meaning of the crusade inspired them to a dedication and spirit of cooperation that had been previously unknown in Nicaraguan public servants. But dedication to the task and cooperation seemed easily attainable in comparison to overcoming the more intangible attitudes that were embedded deep in the psyche—attitudes toward the poor, toward change, toward education. The crusade became the crucible in which changes in these attitudes could be forged.

The confrontations, and the subsequent learning and growth that they fostered, perhaps can best be seen in the response to the educational challenge the group faced. Rhetorically, everyone agreed that the old educational system was bankrupt—authoritarian and oppressive—although long-standing members of the ministry were not quite as detailed or lengthy in their criticism. The question before the staff was how to create an educational program for adults that would be congruent with the egalitarian and participatory goals of the revolution. The difficulties of this challenge were compounded by the fact that many of the planners had professional expertise in primary school education but were unfamiliar with the principles of adult education or consciousness raising. Staff members, especially the old guard, tended to resort to the familiar traditional modes of education, which only repeated the authoritarian model of the past and did not allow for the creative participation called for by the revolutionary leadership. With no knowledge of or practice with alternative approaches, even the specially selected staff fell back into former power relationships of total teacher authority and student passivity.

This problem, which was to be expected in such a transition, was seen vividly in the confrontation that occurred during Workshop 1. In order to present the literacy primer to the participants, the woman responsible for its development gave a lengthy speech. A professor and senior ministry official, she was an expert in the writing of children's textbooks. Her traditional formal presentation and academic attitude were a striking contrast to the participatory, innovative style of the training program, and this difference in approach provoked considerable conflict and debate. However, the experience served as a rich source of learning for the entire group. The process was painful, yet productive. People increasingly realized that the old ways, which relegated students to passivity, needed to be unlearned, and new ways, which promoted learner creativity and participation, needed to be forged. However, that realization was no automatic guarantee of a change in approach. The new was sometimes resisted, and the belief in people's full capacity to handle complexity unconsciously questioned. This tendency can be seen, for example, in the initial doubts expressed about the relationship between dialogue and transformation, and about the use of art, sociodrama, and community-action research.

Problems of this kind were not related just to the participatory methods being attempted, but they also reflected a certain technocratic, formal orientation that was held by some of the planners. For example, one important learning game was initially discarded from the program because the planners were unable to see its practical application. A word-building game, it involved the use of small squares, each containing different syllables, which were put together to form words. The game was rejected because some people felt that the only way to print it would be on special cardboard paper at a printing press—too costly a proposition. The suggestion by others that the teachers or participants could make their own game by handprinting the squares on whatever paper was available was vetoed. It was argued that such writing would be sloppy or perhaps illegible and the squares too uneven to be used. However, the practical experience of the campaign revealed the problems with the old approach and technocratic orientation. The direct confrontation with reality proved the potential of some of the new approaches, and in certain cases led the planners who had questioned their viability to reconsider their previous objections. For example, the syllable game was rescued and introduced after the first month of the campaign in its handwritten, homemade version.

The key factor in determining how planners viewed the more participatory, practical approaches, and how effective they were in designing and implementing those approaches, depended in the final analysis not so much on their political commitment or educational skills but on their definition of self and on their personal view toward other people, especially the poor. Those planners who had a strong need to see themselves as professional elites providing highly specialized university-acquired expertise had a difficult time. Their narrow technocratic orientation limited their ability to accept practical solutions or to fully respect people who lacked any formal education. On the other hand, the planners who had developed a profound belief in the innate intelligence and curiosity of people and in their capacity for learning and creativity found it much easier to design and implement such participatory methods. The experience of the crusade helped affirm that belief in people and challenge the elitist, technocratic orientation of some planners. The learning program, with all of its modifications and adaptations, was a measure of the process of human change and growth—a product of the conflict between old and new.

During the actual campaign, the tension between old and new was also played out on another level, between the teachers and the students. There was a recurrent antagonism between the two groups, which stemmed from natural generational differences and, more important in this case, from their different experiences and commitments. The teachers had been socialized under the old system; the students, by the revolution. Many teachers were uneasy about the changes in society, while large numbers of students avowed their commitment to the goals of transformation. Moreover, teachers had a psychological stake in maintaining the former type of relationship with their students. To relinquish being the unquestioned authority and source of all knowledge in the classroom was terribly painful for many of them. Their very sense of self was threatened by the new participatory methods. Conflict was inevitable. Within the context of the crusade, in the more positive cases, this tension resulted in new appreciations and understanding of one another and of educational practices. In negative situations, mistrust and a reliance on authoritarian methods were deepened.

The conflict between the old and the new, as seen in the Nicaraguan campaign, is an inherent dynamic of the social transformation process. How it is resolved and played out in a short-term, initial program like the crusade depends on many factors, among them the political philosophy of the leadership, the educational expertise of the members of the planning staff, their joint commitment to and belief in the poor, and the attitudes of the implementers and the participants. In Nicaragua, the educational program was unusual in that it successfully incorporated the participatory goals of the revolution into many aspects of the learning activities—the training, methods, and materials. The process, of course, was not a smooth one and is one that continues, difficult and never-ending. It is a constant struggle, filled with contradictions and change, undertaken by people who are given the challenge and opportunity to excel and serve. Sometimes they fail; on occasion, they achieve greatness.

Design and Management Style

The campaign's educational design process and management style emerged in large part from the particular experience of the war of liberation and allowed for unusual flexibility, responsiveness, and participation. The liberation struggle served as an inspiration and a teacher. Its lessons were many—some pedagogical, some philosophical. Educational activities that had been carried out during the long years of fighting and community organizing had demonstrated the validity of a variety of teaching approaches and learning principles. Small study groups had met throughout the struggle to analyze, plan, and carry out war-related tasks; clandestine literacy efforts had been conducted as well. Learning in this context had been based on a process of action and reflection, and the lessons had had a direct, urgent, and immediate application to reality.

In pedagogical terms, a combination of methods and techniques had been used, such as experiential learning, dialogue, group discussions, and collective problem solving, and as a result, the importance of stimulating learner participation, initiative, and creativity had been proved. The war had also reaffirmed an understanding and a belief in human potential and popular participation as it had revealed the tremendous imagination and capacity for learning that existed within people regardless of their educational backgrounds. These experiences and this understanding provided the pedagogical and philosophical foundation for the crusade.

Working partly on the basis of these earlier experiences, the crusade's educational planners developed a design process and work style that were unusually flexible, innovative, and responsive in dealing with program problems and weaknesses. The process involved constant criticism and analysis, design and modification—learning from experience, identifying weak points, responding to ever-new problems and contexts, proposing alternative solutions, and analyzing their effectiveness. In the design process, problems and achievements were not traditionally defined as successes or failures but as continuing challenges. The staff members saw that their creative activity was not a static effort producing some immutable finished product, but a dynamic, never-ending process of change and development. For them, all aspects of the program, all problems, were grist for the mill. A permanent attitude of questioning and problem solving predominated, as did an energizing sense of humor and an ability to make jokes in the face of difficulties. In utilizing this approach, most of the planners demonstrated a high degree of self-criticism, humility, adaptability, laughter, persistence, and commitment to excellence. Their unusually close bond with field staff members also allowed the planners to obtain valid, reliable information and provided them with a critical sounding board and planning partner.

For some of the planners, the creative process was not an articulated, conscious one beyond the general notion that the crusade itself was a national process of learning and growth. For others, however, it was based on a carefully thought-out philosophical analysis, as can be clearly seen in program documents that emphasize learning by doing, knowledge building, and the relationship between theory and practice. But in either case, the process and its participants functioned with a high degree of responsiveness. This was due in large part to the fact that the crusade was run in a completely unique Nicaraguan fashion according to the management model that had been developed during the insurrection. The approach was not based on precise long-term planning but was rooted almost totally in being able to respond quickly to the moment. Without a precise vision of the future, except in very general terms, the strength of the approach lay in the planners' being in touch with the immediate situation. Since no detailed, long-term plan existed, reality became the only effective available guide for decision making. Up-to-date feedback was constantly solicited, and the staff always on alert. Responses to problems were provided quickly and, on the whole, quite effectively as a result. A model rare in management, it proved highly flexible and efficient in most circumstances because of the staff's close ties with the people who were carrying out the program and their knowledge of the day-to-day operational problems those people faced.

Some of the major examples of the staff's timely problem-solving efforts include the development of the dialogue process, learning games, comprehension exercises, Saturday workshops and the joint EPA-supervisor educational planning committees. Each technique demonstrated the ability of the team to respond effectively and imaginatively to program weaknesses.

However, in the process, the planners themselves faced internal problems and contradictions. One of the major difficulties facing them was their own fragmentation into small, isolated working groups—curriculum, research, training. Although the working style within each of the various groups was unusually dynamic and rich in debate and discussion, this separation from one another and the lack of systematic opportunities for joint team discussions affected the coherence of the program design and limited the creative process. Although informal discussions took place, the rich potential for interchange was hampered until after the crusade was in operation. Efforts were then made to work in a more interdisciplinary and cooperative fashion. Although the original divisions never disappeared, the members of the three groups increasingly worked together on joint activities in a closer system of coordination.

Another contradiction that became apparent involved the relationship between national planning and local participation. Despite the participatory goals of the revolution, the initial planning process did not actively involve the future program participants. It was true that community people did have input through the pilot project, but they did not have a direct voice in the actual design process of the learning materials. In part, this situation was the result of problems of time, limited staff, and the chaos of the moment. Some national planners were aware of the contradiction and suggested that literacy commission members take on this role. In addition to the resource mobilization and fund-raising activities of the commission, these planners proposed that member representatives become involved in the direct planning process by serving as a sounding board for campaign designers—making suggestions and critiquing the project's materials and methods. Although top officials recognized that this proposal was a good one, they did not consider it a priority. Other demands seemed too heavy. The inexorable deadlines imposed by the March starting date were causing almost intolerable pressure on the staff members, and new responsibilities, such as those that would be required for more participatory planning, seemed out of the question.

During the campaign, however, this contradiction was addressed. Participant input was constantly solicited through indirect channels, such as feedback gathered by crusade personnel, and through more direct means as well. Participants provided important contributions during the two national planning and evaluation congresses and the series of community and regional meetings that preceded them. As the campaign progressed, local literacy commissions also increased their effectiveness as vehicles for citizen participation. In the follow-up adult education program, materials were increasingly designed with the direct participation of the learners—personal stories, poems, songs, and interviews with participants providing the basis for study and reflection. Participants themselves also took on the teaching roles previously carried out by *brigadistas* and coordinated the learning of the follow-up study groups.

Class and Cultural Differences

As an integral part of the structural transformation process, the campaign helped many participants begin to overcome class and cultural differences, but it also, quite expectedly, engendered an antagonistic, violent reaction from certain sectors of the nation's wealthy elite and the ex-National Guardsmen who had fled the country after the dictator's defeat. By providing young people from the city, many of them from the middle or upper classes, with the opportunity to work and live side by side with the rural poor, the crusade made it possible for program participants to develop new friendships, commitments, and an appreciation of one another. These relationships and understandings crossed traditional class and cultural barriers and helped begin to lay the foundation for a society in which, over time, inequities and forms of discrimination might be decreased to a minimum. However, because the campaign was designed as part of a rapid process to redistribute power and wealth, it was to be expected that the program would provoke a strong response on the part of those sectors of society that felt most directly threatened by the changes being instituted.

As the enthusiasm for the campaign grew, and, by association, the legitimacy of the revolutionary leadership, the displeasure of certain wealthy business people and large hacienda owners grew as well. Their hopes to exert the economic and political power that they felt to be rightly theirs were being diminished. Some of them had assumed that they would be able to establish the same kind of control over Nicaragua that their counterparts throughout Central America maintained over their respective countries. In part, this assumption resulted from the support and encouragement they received from the Carter administration, which, prior to the dictator's defeat, did everything in its power to create a political structure that would hold the *Frente* in check. U.S. policymakers hoped that the new political system could be controlled by a coalition of businessmen, large hacienda owners, and the traditional political parties that had existed under Somoza. When this U.S. strategy failed, the Nicaraguan elites hoped that another similar approach would be taken that would lead to a political victory for their coalition. However, this group did not propose elections, because they knew the *Frente* would win overwhelmingly and thus guarantee the indisputable legitimacy and supremacy of the FSLN for many years to come. These elites,

Campaign momentun → to shift power away from old structure to The Sandinistas.

of course, grew increasingly concerned about each government measure that consolidated its power and established its credibility. The campaign was clearly one of the most dramatic and popular of those measures.

For example, during the first National Congress, which was held midway through the campaign, the representative from the Superior Council of Private Enterprise (COSEP), remained seated, quiet and grim-faced, amid the booming cheers, songs, and standing ovations of the enthusiastic audience and finally stomped out loudly in the middle of a speech. COSEP and opposition leaders like Alfonso Robelo who spoke out against the crusade tended to lose a certain amount of credibility with the general populace because the majority of Nicaraguans felt an extraordinary pride in and identification with the program.

Although some members of the upper class were condemning the campaign, spreading fearsome rumors about what would happen to those who participated in it, and generally working to undermine it, a significant number of wealthy families were participating actively in the crusade. In part, this support was due to the fact that many of the top government leaders came from the middle and upper classes. This blood relationship, the smallness of Nicaraguan society, and the popularity of the campaign helped moderate the inevitable class antagonisms during the first year of the revolution.

One group, however, acted beyond the law and drew the condemnation of the society at large—the ex-National Guardsmen who had escaped over the border into Honduras. As abhorrent as it was, their reaction to the campaign was predictable. They were trained and practiced in violence. Through murder, rape, and threat, they tried to cripple the popular government program. They, along with certain wealthy business people, recognized the power and the potential of the crusade—especially in political terms. Moreover, the ex-guardsmen must have been seriously worried about the inroads that the *brigadistas* were making in the North, in the very areas where the majority of the guardsmen had grown up and still had close relatives. The literacy volunteers, with their sincerity and youthful enthusiasm, often broke down barriers of strong mistrust in these villages, even among the immediate families of former guardsmen. For these political outcasts the direct threats that the campaign presented, of undermining their potential basis for support and of establishing the new government's legitimacy, were too great to ignore.

The constant danger the volunteers were in led to the passage of strict legislation on crimes against literacy participants, but the danger also led some *brigadistas* and teachers to the conclusion that they should be armed—a common, long-time practice among adults in the rural areas of Nicaragua. This tendency was difficult to control, and unfortunately, it only increased the probability of serious accidents. Despite clear instructions stating that *brigadistas* were not to have any type of firearm in their possession, several volunteers were wounded accidentally because this rule was disobeyed.

However, cases of great courage in the face of unknown danger were recorded as well. One teenage boy, crippled from birth by polio and with one leg several inches longer than the other, was part of a small contingent carrying campaign personnel and students by canoe to a meeting upriver to discuss plans for the national literacy congress. Fired upon by ex-guardsmen, three people were killed. As soon as the shooting began, the boy jumped out. Taking the canoe rope through his teeth, he swam to the opposite shore, saving an Indian woman and her child who barely escaped the bullets that had torn apart the boy's teaching supervisor who had been sitting behind them.

Problems of volunteer security haunted the staff. However, the fact that the campaign occurred during the first year of the revolution probably helped to lessen the extent of possible violence against the *brigadistas* while maximizing the potential for overcoming class and cultural differences among the participants. If the campaign had been postponed until 1981 or 1982, or implemented in a regional fashion as some government officials had argued for, the violence would have undoubtedly been worse, and some of the initial enthusiasm and spirit would have been lost because of fear or disenchantment.

By 1981, armed groups of ex-guardsmen in Honduras were being joined by other Somozan associates as well as by certain Nicaraguans who had become disaffected with the revolution. Some of these people received special guerrilla training in clandestine camps located in the United States, and despite explicit news and television coverage about them and their illegality, the U.S. government did not interfere with the functioning of the camps or their participants. In 1982, rumors began to spread about massive CIA support for these armed groups; in 1983, the rumors were confirmed. Murder, torture, and rape continued to be standard practice, and kidnapping was added. Among the most common targets were union organizers, Catholic lay activists, community militia members, and government development workers such as doctors, nurses, agronomists, and teachers. In 1983, some 750 people were killed by these groups. About fifty were personnel of the adult education program, often peasants and young people who had volunteered to serve their communities as learning coordinators so that people's study of reading, writing, and mathematics could continue after the campaign. In certain areas, these attacks severely crippled the program. Some people withdrew; others studied secretly, burying their books every day after class.

Educational Obstacles: Lack of Experience

The major educational obstacles that affected the literacy campaign's development were related to problems and deficiencies that had been inherited from the past. *Few people in Nicaragua had any background or experience in adult education programs, literacy projects, or participatory learning methods.* Those who did were often in demand elsewhere in the government. For example, one unusually innovative community educator and organizer, Jorge Vogel, was put in charge of rural education activities for the Ministry of Agriculture. A man loved and respected by his peasant colleagues and co-workers, he was assassinated by counterrevolutionaries three months after assuming the position. This lack of educational expertise was exacerbated by the fact that the nation's teaching force was conservative, both pedagogically and politically. Education, as practiced in Nicaragua, had been authoritarian and rigid. Teachers had been socialized into an educational system based on political graft, student submissiveness, and rote memorization—a system in which the teachers were considered the sole source and dispenser of knowledge and wisdom.

In practice, these obstacles were addressed by creating a support system and a learning environment within the campaign that allowed for an intensive amount of informal, on-the-job staff development. Responsibilities were assigned, demands were great, and expectations for achievement high. An unshakable belief that all was possible with hard work and commitment spurred people on to excellence. Foreign experts were carefully selected to work with the staff members. Some of the experts arrived in Nicaragua on their own, volunteering their services; others were sent at Nicaragua's request by governments and international agencies; still others were specially sought after on an individual basis by the crusade staff from universities, church organizations, and private institutions. In the national office, there were educational support personnel from Argentina (2), Canada (1), Chile (1), Colombia (4), Costa Rica (1), Cuba (4), El Salvador (1), France (1), Honduras (1), Mexico (2), Peru (1), Puerto Rico (1), Spain (4), the United States (3), and Uruguay (1).

The strong integration of this diverse group into the campaign's structure and the deep personal commitment of these people to the program were highly unusual and contrasted with traditional technical assistance relationships in which pay differentials are high, living is luxurious, and work hours are relatively easy. On the whole, the international experts did not consider themselves, nor were they thought of, as foreign advisers per se. Instead, with few exceptions, they were incorporated into the staff in a collegial fashion as one more member of the team, under the supervision of their Nicaraguan coordinators, with full responsibilities and opportunities to contribute but with certain different strengths and professional experiences to share. Those foreigners who did demonstrate any pretentiousness—a characteristic that is despised by Nicaraguans—or tried to impose preconceived plans or ideas on the staff usually lost their credibility and eventually left either on their own accord or as a result of an official request. In such cases, nationality provided no protection as Argentines, Cubans, and one Canadian were dismissed or asked not to return as a result of these concerns. On the whole, however, the international staff members provided support that was highly valued.

Addressing the problem of teachers who were isolated from the process, because they were antagonistic to social changes and the revolution, was more difficult. One of the main strategies devised by the educational planners involved placing students in positions of leadership as a counterbalance to the teachers. In the training program, teachers were to be paired with students, and in the first two phases, this strategy was quite successful. Some effective teacher-student training teams were produced. However, during the third phase, the pairing system did not function because university students were not included as participants, as had been originally intended, and the general dissatisfaction of the teachers was greater than had been anticipated. They resented being taught by nonprofessionals. The training teams managing Phase 3 were made up of one professional teacher and one university student, and often the teacher was from the primary school level.

Although the planned strategy was not implemented as fully as had been intended, the very participation of the teachers during the campaign itself, especially those who lived in and worked with peasant communities as *brigadista* supervisors, helped overcome some of their rigidity and authoritarianism. In some cases, they developed a new respect for their student charges, young people who were often showing a maturity and intelligence that were beyond expectation. Many supervisors refined the new teaching skills that had been presented to them in training and acquired a greater understanding of the country's needs and a commitment to the programs of national development.

However, the continued exercise of those new attitudes and methods would depend upon the effectiveness of the in-service training program the Ministry of Education provided as a follow-up. Without constant support and some practice in a dynamic exciting learning environment, the experience the classroom teachers gained during the campaign could easily dissipate. Although some attention was paid during ministry planning to the valuable lessons of the crusade, follow-up training for primary and secondary teachers did not seem to be organized in a way that would maximize the campaign's contribution to the formal education system. Crusade staff members did participate in the follow-up training in order to explain the lessons learned from the literacy effort, but they did not work on the design or coordination of the training program itself. The minister, Carlos Tunnerman, and his director of policy planning wanted to apply the lessons and methods that had been proved by the campaign but did not have the appropriate professional staff to direct the effort. Since most of the Ministry of Education trainers had not participated in the first two phases of the crusade's training program, the lessons that had been learned then were not applied to their fullest extent, and although the training content was varied, the process and methods were limited. Subsequently, however, one of the top international advisers—a significant contributor to the design of the campaign's training program—was chosen to become a special assistant to the Minister of Education. Such a choice could overcome this imbalance in the future.

Time Factor

Despite some disadvantages, the immutable target date that was fixed for the campaign's launching served as a positive force in the development of the program. The knowledge, among both the organizers and the population at large, that the date was firmly fixed motivated people to labor beyond their normal job hours or levels of endurance. Staff and supporters worked against the clock. There was little time for bureaucratic excuses and no room for the traditional eight-hour work schedules. Everyone knew they had to produce and produce fast. The fixed target date instilled an urgency in people. Amid the exhaustion, it also created a certain energy and vital bond as well. Although it is true that certain program aspects were weakened by the inexorable time pressures, without the firm target date, the campaign would probably have had to have been postponed until the following year and precious momentum and commitment would have been lost.

Educational Program

The discussion in this section will center on the formal learning program: curriculum, methodology, and training. The vast amount of informal learning that occurred during the campaign by volunteers and participants will not be addressed in detail.

Curriculum and Methodology

The pilot project, which was designed to test the program materials and teaching methods, provided some valuable insights, but the effort was not accorded the importance necessary for it to be fully effective. In part, this lack was the result of a structural flaw, which was recognized by the team itself. In its desire to replicate the different geographic and social conditions of the country, the team selected test sites that were at a considerable distance from one another and not always easily accessible. This situation, coupled with the short time line that the team was working under, made supervision and information gathering difficult. Even more serious was the fact that certain changes in the sequence of the curriculum, judged inconsequential at the moment, were made without testing their impact in the pilot project. Time pressures were too great. The untested changes, however, presented linguistic difficulties for many learners later during the campaign.

The main curriculum materials used in the program included a literacy primer and a math text. In addition, a teaching guidebook was provided for the volunteers. *The content of both the primer and its math text was national in scope and as such acquainted all learners with basic information about Nicaragua's history, development plans, and new social structures.* This simple transfer of information provided people with a common knowledge base, which was important to the nation-building and transformation process Nicaragua was engaged in.

The primer was relatively simple and innovative in design but problematic in linguistic sequencing. The lesson structure of the literacy text was similar in some respects to the Freirean type of primer that had been designed by Nicaraguans for a church-sponsored program in the early 1970s; in other aspects, it was similar to the Cuban primer of the 1960s. It expanded Freire's key-word concept and simplified the three-sentence structure of the Cuban model. Each lesson began with one short sentence or phrase that contained a key word from which an individual syllable family was selected for study. In the pilot materials, key syllables were printed in red, which greatly facilitated the learning of the participants, but this innovation had to be dropped in the final campaign version because of the high cost of printing.

Because no linguistic study was undertaken and modifications were made without pilot testing, the syllables presented in the primer were not taught in the most appropriate order. Adding further complications to this situation was the fact that complex syllables were also presented early in the text, so that the level of difficulty of the first lessons did not help create learner or teacher confidence.

The math text and number problems provoked great interest among the learners, frequently surpassing that for reading and writing. The personal motivation for studying mathematics seemed to be higher than for learning how to read and write. There are several probable reasons for this fact. Math skills may have more direct relevance to learners' lives, and they can perhaps lead to a greater satisfaction of people's perceived needs. The content of the math text included information about economic and social institutions that affected the learners' livelihood and welfare most directly, for example, the basic grain and food distribution program, ENABAS. Also, the text was introduced after students had completed the primer's seventh lesson and may have had the initial effect of being a novelty. However, the interest in mathematics seemed to remain strong throughout the rest of the campaign, so much so that in some instances, it had to be strictly regulated to no more than an hour and a half of study per week in order to guarantee that participants would complete their program of reading and writing. Mathematics continued to be studied and the text completed by students during the follow-up program.

The teaching guide provided basic methodological information to the volunteers, but the instructions were sometimes found to be unclear, and the information was not always complete. Although the preliminary versions were fairly lively, the language and graphic design of the final guide tended to be dry and formal. Its rather pedantic style did not seem appropriate for engaging the young volunteers in the teaching process. Little background material was given on the specific nature and characteristics of the adult learner or on the reading process. Those oversights were remedied somewhat during the campaign as separate pamphlets and flyers were distributed that helped clarify the ambiguities and provided additional information on adult learning and reading theories. They were designed in a more attractive style with illustrations, a variety of typefaces, and on occasion, a humorous comic-strip format.

The formal curriculum and methodology formed one important part of the educational process and the living-learning context the campaign participants were immersed in formed another. All of the individual components—materials, methods, participants, and everyday life—interacted in a dynamic, ever-changing way to form an educational whole. For example, when parts of the formal educational structure proved weak, whether in method or in text, the daily sharing of lives between volunteer teachers and students helped overcome these deficiencies. The desire to teach well and the urge to learn were mutually encouraged by this relationship. The common living experience, especially in the rural areas, enriched the formal learning sessions to a great degree. By far the most important ingredient in the crusade's educational program was the human bond that was formed as a result of living together and sharing community life.

In the context of specific lessons, the dialogue process was one of the weakest areas of the method, but it was still a significant advance over the rote memorization methods that had previously been used almost exclusively in the Nicaraguan educational system. The original guidelines designed to help *brigadistas* conduct the dialogue were too brief and not written in a way to provide adequate instruction about the process. When this weakness was discovered, it was immediately addressed, and a new, more complete set was distributed. Although these more engagingly written guidelines were a great improvement, the process itself suffered from one major flaw. It did not include a step specifically designed to elicit discussion about the learners' individual personal relationships to the situation being analyzed. As a consequence, the participants' sense of identification with the problem under discussion and feelings of responsibility for its solution were lessened. The potential for dialogue and action was limited. The danger of this oversight, according to some of the national staff, was that an awareness of the individual's relationship to self and to community—the dreams, aspirations, fears, and foibles of each person as they related to others—was never recognized in the formal dialogue process. As a result, the staff worried that the development of a selfless commitment to community and to building a new society would be weakened and that participation in programs of transformation would be mechanical. To promote revolutionary consciousness in the fullest and most creative way, the dialogue process needed to affirm an understanding of both the individual self and the society in which people lived and worked and to link learning directly with specific concerns of the participants. Given this problem and the young volunteers' inexperience in the dialogue process itself, most *brigadistas* found it difficult to move from a simple description of a photograph to actually engaging people in a thoughtful analysis of their lives that could lead to some sort of concerted community action. Given the minimal amount of training the volunteers received, the poor selection of discussion photographs, and the general unfamiliarity with the approach, expectations regarding the dialogue were unreasonably high. Instead of occurring within the context of the lessons, there were often lively dialogue and discussion outside the formal study time in the natural sharing of everyday life.

However, certain misapplications and misunderstandings regarding the dialogue process, which occurred at the beginning of the campaign, resulted in some learner resistance. When large numbers of volunteers found that they could get people to discuss a photograph only superficially, some began to add speeches and lectures to the process. This spontaneous addition undermined the method. Most participants did not become involved in critical dialogue during official study time, but at a minimum, they did have an opportunity to contribute some of their ideas in describing and discussing the general content of the photographs, an opportunity for participation and expression that most of them had never had previously.

In an attempt to simplify the literacy method certain important elements were eliminated; however later, during the campaign's operation, they were reincorporated, and other supportive methods were also developed. Originally, each lesson had a varying number of steps up to fifteen. For simplicity in teaching, the number was standardized at ten by collapsing some steps into one and eliminating others. In this reduction process, two relatively easy steps—comprehension and word creation—that would have contributed to building learner confidence were dropped, but these two skills turned out to be precisely the areas in which the people needed extra practice. Halfway through the campaign, a series of exercises and learning games were designed and distributed in order to correct this deficiency. Practical experience had shown that focusing on a standardized methodology was too limiting because people have different learning styles and therefore need a variety of approaches to accommodate their differences.

The original fear of some planners that an abundance of methods would detract from learning literacy skills was surmounted in this case, but a certain formalism of style was not overcome until much later during the adult education program. A vivid example of the struggle between the old and the new, this debate over style reflected differences in standards and learning theories. One of the fundamental aspects of the method involved the formulation of words, but the printed syllable chart that had been designed to help the volunteers teach this process failed. To solve this problem, the word-building game, which had previously been discarded because it was thought it would be too sloppy and illegible, was resurrected.

However, one critical aspect of educational methodology was largely ignored. A major goal of the transformation process was to affirm such attitudes and values as cooperation, creativity, selflessness, and initiative, yet few campaign planners realized the extent to which individual teaching methods promote or detract from such behavior. When developing methods, the value or attitude dimensions were not discussed, and as a result, the ability of the program to systematically meet this goal was lessened.

Community-action research was the most imaginative and potentially the most revolutionary aspect of the learning method developed for the campaign. This process helped bridge the contradiction that is prevalent in development work between the need for national planning and the need for local participation in decision making. It provided a concrete means of expanding community participation in development planning and transformation through a structured educational process. Although many organizations and participatory channels had been created to address this revolutionary goal, no systematic, structured learning or working methodology had been developed to engage the community as a whole in the process. The literacy session dialogues were supposed to stimulate critical thinking and action on the part of the crusade participants, but community-action research was the first step in the attempt to involve the entire community in transformation.

The initial results of the community-action research method were promising, and the commitment to it was enthusiastic. However, its power and strength as a coherent learning and transformation process fell victim to several program obstacles and deficiencies. Two in particular affected the outcome—time and a scarcity of resources. The strict schedule of precrusade planning activities made it difficult to hold joint team meetings, and although Father Cardenal supported the process, a common understanding of the concept of community-action research or its important benefits was never achieved. The limited number of trainers made the mobilization of the entire national educational staff necessary at a critical moment. National team members, including the designers and the experienced facilitators of the process, had to move to the rural areas in order to direct the regional training programs. Just a few days later, information from the printer revealed that publication costs were running high, and the decision was made to cut the number of pages in the teaching handbook. In the subsequent rush editing, much of the material on the community-action research process was eliminated, and in the intense seven weeks before the campaign began, there was neither the time nor the staff available to get it reinstated. However, once in the field, some teaching brigades developed a similar process naturally as a result of their own structured learning activities in field research.

Training Program

Of all of the aspects of the educational program the training component was the most effective in putting the goals of the revolution into practice. Decentralized in organization, it was participatory in structure and method and highly responsive and creative, especially in the first two stages. It laid the foundation for dynamic channels of decision making, information gathering, and team problem solving that are unusual in a government bureaucracy.

However, certain oversights and problems in training hindered some aspects of the campaign, but they were minor in comparison to the achievements that were attained as a result of the training program. First, in the initial phase of training, the practicum teaching experience was not accorded the importance it deserved in relation to curriculum development. The problems identified in the field were overlooked, and valuable information was lost that could have contributed to a further refinement of the materials and method. Second, the training was too limited on certain levels, and in some cases, it was fragmented. University students and professional teachers were given preparation to train literacy volunteers, but they received no training for the supervisory and management roles they were expected to assume once the campaign began. This oversight caused serious problems of coordination and supervision until it was addressed through an in-service staff development program during the crusade. Given the commitment to the dialogue and the concept of community-action research, the training program should have been extended on each level by about three days. Volunteers required more concrete practice in the method, and trainers needed more experience both in applying the process and in providing helpful feedback on it.

The fragmentation of the training affected program coherence. The only crusade staff members who received the complete training program were members of the regional pedagogical teams and the volunteer teaching force. Despite the training plan, which called for their participation, people in the other organizational divisions of the campaign never participated in the full process. The EPA leadership and representatives of the citizens' organizations did not take part in the official crusade training until the end, and in some cases, not at all. The training workshops, especially the first two, forged a common understanding of the dynamics of learning and participation in a process of social transformation. They also established a strong commitment among the participants to the new educational methods and cooperative working styles. The fact that about three-fourths of the campaign's staff and almost all the EPA leaders never fully took part in that rich process of shared experience and analysis limited their ability to understand the program and, hence, to work in and coordinate optimally with it. This situation would also limit the future development of the adult education program and its leadership.

The last-minute change in trainee selection for Workshop 3 probably created more problems for the training program than were fully understood at the time. Switching from training teams of teachers and university students to training teams of two professional teachers created resentment among many of the teachers who had not anticipated becoming involved in the crusade for yet another two weeks. The change also weakened the fourth tier of training because the political-pedagogical balance that had been provided by the teacher-student team was eliminated. In terms of promoting the new educational approaches, the students were considered more capable, convinced, and enthusiastic proponents. The same was true in the political realm, the students on the whole being more aware and committed, although clearly undisciplined. The fears of some government leaders that many university students were self-centered and prone to anarchy, and therefore potentially destructive of the training program, overlooked two key factors: the sense of commitment instilled by the training process and the maturity that young people gain when given responsibility.

A final problem that became apparent during the training program has special relevance for planners of national campaigns. It, too, was the result of a sudden, unforeseen change in plans and arose out of a desire to involve as many young people as possible in the crusade experience. The last-minute decision to include all secondary students in the training, whether they were going to be *brigadistas* or not, caused unnecessary tensions and a divisiveness in the final stage of the pre-campaign workshops. Because both potential *brigadistas* and other students not participating in the campaign were integrated into the same programs, discipline became a problem in some cases, and as a result, training was made more difficult.

Despite these problems, the training component of the campaign was successful in that it promoted some major goals of transformation—participation, redistribution, political awareness, and social integration. *The decentralized nature of the training process, even though it diminished the professional quality of the workshops, allowed for the preparation of the entire national teaching force in new, more participatory learning methods.* Teachers became acquainted with the new methods in their first workshop experiences, and then, as trainers in the next level of workshops, they had the opportunity to put those methods into practice. The training process served as the first national educational seminar for the country's professional teaching staff. It was a beginning step in introducing pedagogical approaches that were designed to help increase learner participation and break down authoritarian classroom relationships and teaching styles. Because the workshops employed a team-teaching approach, teachers also had the opportunity to develop more cooperative working relationships with their colleagues.

The organizational structure of the workshop promoted high levels of participation and provided concrete opportunities for leadership development and cooperative teamwork. The different sizes of the various levels of the educational structure—from the small nucleus study groups of four or five to the squadrons, of about fifteen, and finally to the General Assembly, which was made up of the entire workshop—allowed for ample discussion and learner involvement. The committee structures, which were designed to coordinate the workshops, gave participants responsibility for program operations and provided them with concrete experiences in teamwork, decision making, and evaluation. Practice in leadership was given as well because both coordination and educational structures operated on the basis of rotating officers—new group coordinators, assistants, and secretaries were chosen every three days.

Learning methods and activities were varied and highly participatory. The wide range of approaches employed in the training not only reflected the goals of the revolution but also provided the educational variety that is necessary in order to respond effectively to individual learning needs and styles. The approaches included utilizing role plays, debates, panel discussions, art, sociodramas, poetry, songs, research, evaluation, criticism/self-criticism, and microteaching. Consonant with the goals of transformation, they stressed cooperation, creativity, and critical thinking. The methods and activities promoted team building, experiential learning, shared responsibility, problem solving, and cultural affirmation. For example, in choosing names of fallen heroes as the study group symbols, participants affirmed the nation's history and increased their awareness of the past. In writing poetry or couplets to express the feelings of their group, they affirmed themselves as cultural beings and creators. In the panel discussions and study group sessions, they had an opportunity to hone their analytical skills and to practice public speaking.

More than any other pedagogical component of the campaign, the first two phases of training put the goals of the transformation into operation and consequently provided the most important lessons for other nations that are committed to participation and literacy. Workshops 1 and 2 prepared the crusade's national and regional educational personnel, and thus laid the pedagogical foundation of the entire effort. The effectiveness of these two phases of training is measured by the critical, honest, and dynamic working relationship that was established between the national and regional teams and by their joint ability to respond creatively and quickly to educational problems in the field. This relationship was one of shared decision making and mutuality. More than any other relationship or structure, it addressed the classic problem of control that emerges from sometimes conflicting priorities and needs of a nation and its communities. Like the community-action research process, it struck a balance between national direction and local participation.

The first two phases of training helped create an organizational structure within the educational division of the campaign that allowed for dialogue in decision making and high levels of initiative and responsibility. A good staff member was not judged on his or her ability to follow orders blindly but on the capacity to contribute imaginatively and critically and to act effectively in the face of problems. Decisions involving the campaign's educational aspects were not made from above to be followed mechanistically by obedient bureaucrats below. The pedagogical teams believed that such an approach would kill initiative, diminish an individual's sense of responsibility, and lead to dependency relationships. Rather, the educational personnel were active participants in the ongoing planning to improve the campaign's operation. They contributed suggestions and directions, analyzed and criticized proposals, and were given the authority to take initiative.

Without this kind of relationship and preparation, the campaign would probably have suffered serious setbacks, setbacks that could have easily put the entire crusade in jeopardy. The logistic problems facing the staff in the actual implementation of training almost crippled the program, but the initiative, enthusiasm, sense of responsibility, and skills in problem solving that were engendered by the first workshop helped the participants overcome many of the overwhelming obstacles in order to successfully complete the second training level. That same dynamism was communicated to the members of the second training workshop, and it allowed them to continue on in a similar spirit when confronting even more massive problems. The first levels of training, besides guaranteeing the success of the campaign workshops, also forged a bond between two groups—the students and the teachers—upon whom the success of the entire campaign rested, two groups that began by being highly suspicious of and antagonistic toward one another. The beginning phase of training was instrumental in building these relationships and structures because of its truly participatory design, the competence and commitment of the trainers, and the openness and balance of its first participants.

Organizational Issues

Questions of organization affected the operation of the campaign on many different levels and influenced the character of the follow-up program as well. *The campaign was incorporated under the organizational umbrella of the Ministry of Education, an arrangement that was designed to provide more efficient access to ministry resources and structures, but was often unnecessarily cumbersome, conflictual, and a potential obstacle to future innovative programming in adult education.* The logic of placing the crusade within the ministry seemed reasonable on the surface, however, unforeseen events later placed the desirability of that organizational relationship in question.

The campaign could have avoided some of the time-consuming and energy-sapping problems of "double bureaucracy" and overlapping lines of authority if the crusade had been established as a fully autonomous agency. As the campaign proceeded, the staff frequently behaved as if it were separate and was chastised as a consequence. Because of the inexorable time pressures on the crusade staff members, they often made decisions and took actions without going through the proper ministry channels, thus incurring the hostility of ministry officials and establishing a poor working relationship with them, which affected both immediate relations between personnel as well as future programming possibilities. If the organizational arrangement had guaranteed a direct application of lessons learned in the campaign to the formal education system, the bureaucratic difficulties might have been worthwhile, but it did not.

Despite these problems, the system occasionally functioned with flexibility, overcoming the obstacles inherent in such a bureaucratic marriage. For example, when provincial Ministry of Education directors were assigned to head up the literacy commissions, their lack of knowledge of and preparation in the new philosophy and practice of education meant that they were limited in their ability to function in the position. As a result, they were often replaced by the provincial-level coordinator for the crusade and transferred to other tasks. In practice, this arrangement worked more effectively and finally was adopted nationwide when, in the last two months of the program, ministry directors were reassigned to oversee the urban literacy work and were replaced officially by the provincial crusade coordinators as heads of the provincial commissions.

The most serious question related to the campaign's placement within the ministry's bureaucracy was one that involved future creativity and effectiveness and had possible consequences for the political consolidation of the revolution. The campaign had created the largest and most far-reaching organizational network in the country, one that extended to the most remote areas of the nation. Maintaining dynamic, responsive organizational support for that network was, therefore, important to the further building and strengthening of the new society. Being a part of the Ministry of Education was detrimental to this process for several reasons. Despite arguments by certain crusade staff members for a separate structure, the placement of the campaign within the ministry almost guaranteed that the follow-up adult education program would also be housed under the ministry umbrella—and it was.

The ministry traditionally dealt with the formal system of education, and principally with children, while the adult education program tried to address the special needs and interests of adults in a revolutionary society, newly literate people who were suddenly being given responsibilities and opportunities for social participation that had been unknown previously. Incorporating the program under the control of the Ministry of Education, with its child-centered focus and large bureaucracy, made it difficult for the adult education program to maintain the special character, creativity, and ability to respond to problems effectively and quickly that had been developed during the campaign. Ministry personnel were trained in the teaching of children in formal classroom settings over a gradual time period, and they had little understanding of the unique requirements of adult learning or how to respond to them effectively in a rapidly changing and demanding environment. They saw formal education for children as the ministry's natural priority. In such a context, adult education did not receive the attention, budgetary allocation, or autonomy it needed.

The weight of tradition, of bureaucracy, of formality, and of the poor history between the campaign and the ministry bore down upon the follow-up program and affected its development. For example, despite the possibility of international funding, efforts to create an autonomous center for the ongoing study and application of innovative adult education were discouraged by ministry personnel. Such a center, similar in concept to the Adult Education Institute of Tanzania, initially would have given a core group of educational planners the space and time away from the extraordinary pressures of the actual operation of the program to analyze and design adult learning programs in a more innovative, responsive way. It also would have allowed them to develop and implement in-service training for program staff and university courses for education students. Besides questions of budget and control, much of the ministry leadership was too preoccupied with the immense problems of starting the first full school year under the revolution to support an autonomous education program.

This situation was compounded by the fact that a certain ambivalence existed among the top government leaders as to what priority the ministry's adult education program actually had in the nation's political process or development strategy. Some believed the follow-up program should concentrate on the mastery of grammar and math skills and not on issues of political education or organizing. Although they recognized the presence of the campaign's nationwide network, the leaders generally believed that government ministry programs should not be concerned with political development and that the citizen and labor organizations would ultimately be more representative and therefore should be the central focus of all development work and political organizing. Because these organizations were in their infancy and had nothing comparable to the grass-roots reach of the campaign structure, development activities and political organizing did not occur as extensively or as quickly as they might have if the adult education program had been given the autonomy and authority to carry them out. Some members of the program staff lamented that oversight because they believed it would have negative repercussions on the political consolidation of the revolution and on the promotion of community development projects. They argued that isolating the acquisition of skills from political organizing and community improvement activities would eventually alienate learners and seriously hamper the development of personal initiative and commitment. This concern found expression in the educational methodology developed for the follow-up program. The method included an action step designed to involve people in solving community problems, but, in part because the learning groups were not conceived of or given support as action organizations, this step was rarely implemented effectively. By narrowly defining the parameters of the adult education program, the government clearly missed an important opportunity to strengthen the political and social foundations of the revolution at a critical moment of transition.

The campaign's internal organizational structure became more complex over time and was highly responsive to changing operational demands. However, its expansion and the lack of integration between the Pedagogical Division and the rest of the organization sometimes created inconsistencies during the crusade and affected the continuity of the follow-up adult education program. As the campaign expanded and new activities were undertaken, different organizational divisions, with their associated departments and work teams, grew in number. They were analyzed as to their particular function, then placed under the appropriate division and located in the organizational chart. In certain instances, departments and teams were later reassigned to other divisions when it became clear that either their tasks were not being performed satisfactorily, often because of already overloaded schedules, or those tasks were more appropriately the bailiwick of another part of the organization.

There were one or two cases in which, despite their advisability from an organizational standpoint, it would probably have been better if the changes had not been made. For example, the gathering of statistics on literacy learning was originally to be handled by the pedagogical staff in conjunction with the Bureau of National Statistics and Census (INEC), but since the Organizational Division was in charge of general crusade statistics, such as the number of *brigadistas* and the number of students, it was felt for purposes of efficiency that the organizational personnel should take on all work related to statistics. However, because of the pedagogical team members' strong commitment to quality and their need for accurate information in order to plan the follow-up program, higher standards of learning, clearer instructions to test givers, and a more useful analysis of data would probably have resulted if the gathering of statistics relating to literacy had been kept under the domain of the pedagogical staff. The fact that the EPA and ANDEN were placed under the sole authority of the Organizational Division limited their contact and their ability to coordinate with the Pedagogical Division in planning for the supervisory role they would be expected to assume once the campaign got started.

The most important long-term effect arising from the lack of integration between the Pedagogical Division and the rest of the organization was the result of differences in staff preparation and experience that would affect the future educational and political coherence of the follow-up program. The national and provincial pedagogical teams had extensive training in the new educational philosophy and techniques and participated in the campaign as educators working on problems of learning and consciousness raising. The rest of the crusade personnel, many of whom would become the staff members of the adult education program, participated in the campaign as administrators, supply officers, or statisticians, working on issues of logistics and organization, and as a result, they did not gain the rich practical experience and theoretical preparation the pedagogical staff received.

The initial follow-up materials and organization of the adult education program put into practice the participatory goals of the revolution, but the transition period was more difficult than had been anticipated. Besides being sound educational practice, reliance on local residents, often new literates themselves, to staff the adult education program strengthened the level of community participation, provided people with an opportunity to increase their leadership skills, and gave them a sense of belonging to the program as well as a sense of their own personal worth.

The initial study materials—a current-events type of magazine and a learning game similar to Scrabble—were developed especially for the harvest season from September to February, when migration is common and labor is intense. The materials were designed to stimulate creativity, consolidate skills such as word building, and continue themes of national and personal interest. The magazine contained articles on such topics as food production, home improvement, child care, poetry, history, and defense. In later issues, the curriculum designers introduced some innovations to the magazine, which increased both the team's enthusiasm for its own work as well as learner motivation for study. Program participants were interviewed by the pedagogical staff about their lives, families, communities, and work; sometimes they were photographed. Their words were then used in photo-stories for the magazine such as "How Nubia Sanchez Builds a Clay Stove" or "How Juan Saved His Village from Attack by the Guard"—stories that were illustrated with individual photographs presented in a sequence with handprinted sentences placed in square balloons—comic book style—for text.

Despite efforts to make the transition a smooth one and guarantee uninterrupted learning for new literates, the September to January program, which immediately followed the campaign, involved considerable obstacles. Designing the follow-up program, an activity that took place during the campaign, had been difficult because the initial team, with the exception of the UNESCO adviser, had had no experience in adult education or educational planning. A great deal of valuable time and momentum was lost as a result. It was not until late in the campaign, when the actual crusade staff members and other adult education experts were incorporated into the team, that the program began to take shape. Carrying out the program also proved difficult because many people migrate during that season of the year, which affected the levels of participation in the village-based learning groups. Attendance decreased dramatically in many areas of the country.

Another factor that affected the transition was the loss of Father Cardenal as director of the program. Exhausted from the demands of the campaign, he rejected the enthusiastic government offer to continue on in the same capacity for the follow-up program. Instead, he wanted to remain close to the young people who had been the backbone of the crusade—the *brigadistas*—and requested a transfer to the post of educational director of the Sandinista Youth Association. This rather abrupt shift in leadership disrupted the transition because the organization was not fully prepared to accommodate the change. Father Cardenal's quiet force and integrity had helped inspire staff members in moments of crisis; his common sense and belief in people had instilled good judgment and cooperation. The loss of such a leader during a time of change and insecurity was unfortunate, and it placed an awesome burden on the remaining staff, especially on the newly selected director, Francisco Lacayo, who had not expected to assume full responsibility for another six to twelve months. Although Lacayo proved to be an able administrator and an educator of great imagination and unusual sensitivity, he had not been prepared to take on the massive administrative tasks of a director immediately. As a result, his participation in the creative aspects of future program planning was severely curtailed, and the follow-up effort lost the innovative talents of a dynamic educator.

Internal bureaucratic obstacles further affected the transition. It took the Ministry of Education about two months to approve the organizational structure and staff requests for the adult education program. In the interim, many valuable campaign staff members were lost to other government agencies, despite a deep desire on their part to continue working in the adult education program. Unable to survive economically without the guarantee of a job, they had to seek employment elsewhere. The crusade therefore served as a source of seasoned educators for government development efforts, but campaign leaders were unable to retain all of the crusade staff for the follow-up program.

A Concluding Assessment

The Nicaraguan National Literacy Crusade was an important and successful beginning step in the process of social transformation and nation building. It immersed a significant sector of the population directly and quickly into a program that was specifically aimed at restructuring power relationships. By providing the poorest and most abandoned members of society with concrete literacy skills and a special awareness of their own potential and ability to express themselves, the campaign prepared people to be active, thoughtful participants in the new economic and political structures that were being formed. The campaign also helped strengthen the organizational capacity of some of these structures, thus further solidifying the new power balance on behalf of the poorer sectors of Nicaraguan society. The follow-up program, while consolidating the skills and attitudes that had been gained during the campaign, also gave these sectors specific leadership roles in which to use and practice their newly developed talents and abilities. Another significant accomplishment that was crucial for transformation was the development of the young people who participated in the campaign. Their new understanding of poverty and commitment to the poor and programs of social change increased the likelihood of their future involvement in the revolutionary process as public servants and committed professionals and workers.

However, certain undesirable, but natural, consequences of the campaign could serve as a drain on or an obstacle to the transformation process in the future. In the formal education system, such a consequence affected the reintegration of students and teachers back into school. Since the literacy brigades had been organized around the schools, teachers and students from the same institution often worked together during the campaign. Sometimes that relationship proved positive; in other instances, it did not. Generally, those teachers who demonstrated a commitment to the campaign earned the respect of their students, but in situations in which this was not the case, returning to the formal classroom was difficult, and discipline became a problem. ANDEN, the teachers' association, was instrumental in finding a workable solution to the conflict. When the conflicts were disruptive, teachers were allowed to transfer to other schools. On a personal level, parents sometimes found that their *brigadista* children had become more independent than the parents would have preferred, and new ways of relating to each other had to be developed.

Because of the massive nature of the campaign, its successful termination spawned great expectations among people for continued adult learning opportunities to better their living situation through job advancement. The increased demand for education in the cities could not be fully met because to do so would have placed a serious burden on the already stretched government budget. Urban technical night schools were flooded by newly graduated literates, and there was dissatisfaction when all applicants could not be accommodated. In the rural areas, there was a real possibility that as people finished the follow-up basic adult education program, they would migrate to the cities if no gainful employment could be found in the rural areas, thus increasing the already serious urban pressures for shelter, services, and employment. However, despite these present and potential difficulties, the literacy campaign contributed significantly to the creation of a new, more equitable social order. The participation of previously disenfranchised members of society—especially women and the poor—in positions of leadership marked a historic change in the country's power structures.

The overall effectiveness and success of the Nicaraguan National Literacy Crusade were a result of a very unique set of circumstances, circumstances which could not be replicated easily in other nations. The campaign emerged from a liberation struggle in which large sectors of the population had participated as combatants or active civilian supporters. This massive participation and ultimate triumph over the dictatorship forged a sense of national unity and pride that had been unknown previously. The high loss of life during the war instilled in the survivors a profound sense of responsibility and commitment to the dead. People wanted to honor the sacrifices that had been made and begin their lives again by working to build a better nation. The new government leaders shared this feeling and believed that in order to develop the country, citizens needed to be educated and to become actively involved in the changing society. As a result of the war, the leaders had a deep respect for people's capacity to learn, participate, and respond to difficult challenges. They saw the crusade as an integral part of national development, and it was out of this context that the campaign emerged. The integration of the program into the development plan, the strong government commitment to the campaign's efforts, their faith in people, and the creative energy of the citizenry that had been released by the struggle were key factors in the effectiveness of the crusade. The Nicaraguan literacy campaign tapped the extraordinary potential of a nation to confront basic inequities and serves as a tribute to the generosity of human spirit and the power of political commitment.

Appendix A: Methodology and Interviewees

Methodology

To understand the context of the campaign and to choose relevant program issues, I conducted a review of literature that included selections from the fields of education, sociology, political science, and development theory. I examined specific literacy campaigns such as those of Cuba, Guinea-Bissau, and Tanzania as well as UNESCO's international effort—the Experimental World Literacy Program (EWLP). This survey of literature and projects was made to determine key issues common to literacy work. I fully examined the Nicaraguan crusade's documents and files and observed participants for a period of one year. As a member of the central staff working on evaluation and future program development, my observations were mainly from a national planning perspective, but I also participated in activities in the field. The period of direct observation lasted from the planning stage to the operation phase through the implementation of the follow-up program. In addition to these procedures, I held open-ended and structured interviews with key Nicaraguan officials, program staff members, participants, international experts, and U.S. embassy personnel.

Asked to participate as a special adult-education consultant to the director, I had complete access to the program leaders, campaign staff members, and crusade files. This unusual level of access was granted in part because of my long association and experience in Nicaragua. Between 1971 and 1973, I served there in a variety of capacities: as a paramedic with a rural Baptist clinic organization, as a researcher with the Central American Business Administration Institute (a Ford Foundation- and USAID-financed graduate school modeled after the Harvard Business School), and as an educational consultant to several Catholic peasant institutions. From 1977 to 1979, I was an adviser on Central American issues to a church-sponsored human rights organization—the Washington Office on Latin America—which worked closely with Father

Fernando Cardenal, the then vice-rector of Nicaragua's Catholic University. Father Cardenal, who became director of the campaign in August 1979, was eager to have an experienced educator document and analyze the literacy program as objectively as possible so that the campaign might provide practical insights and lessons to other nations undertaking similar efforts.

Interviewees

The following is a list of all those people I interviewed, according to title or position:

National Office

Crusade director
Executive assistant
Organizational Division coordinator and adviser
Statistical Department coordinator
Internal Technical Secretariat coordinator
Citizen association coordinator
Pedagogical Division coordinator
Curriculum coordinator and three team members
Library/Museum coordinator
Research coordinator and two team members
Training coordinator and three team members
Financial coordinator
Administrative coordinator
Transportation Department coordinator
Communication Department coordinator
Logistical Support Department coordinator
Coordinator of national congresses
Executive assistant to the minister of education
Vice-minister of adult education

Provincial Offices

Five provincial coordinators
Three Organizational Division coordinators
Twelve Pedagogical Division coordinators
Four representatives of the Sandinista Youth Association
Five representatives of ANDEN
Two representatives of the ATC
One representative of the AMNLAE

Municipal Offices

   Seven municipal coordinators
   Four organizational coordinators
   Ten pedagogical coordinators and advisers
   Three statistical personnel
   Five Sandinista Youth Association members
   Four representatives of ANDEN
   One health *brigadista*
   Two representatives of the AMNLAE

Less-structured interviews were held with the following people as to why they participated in the campaign, what they learned, and what were their problems and accomplishments:

Community Level

   Twenty-three *brigadistas*
   Three health *brigadistas*
   Two cultural *brigadistas*
   Twelve GUAS
   Ten MOA members
   Fifty-eight literacy learners
   Fourteen parents of *brigadistas*
   Three priests
   Twelve teaching advisers

General interviews were also conducted with a variety of government officials, international advisers, private citizens, and international literacy experts to obtain important background information.

Secretary of the FSLN National Board of Directors
Chief adviser to the minister of planning and a ministry staff member
Representatives from the Ministry of Transport, the ATC, ENABAS, ANDEN, the Catholic Educators' Association, and the AMNLAE who served on the National Literacy Commission
President and members of COSEP, the Superior Council of Private Enterprise
President and secretary of the Nicaraguan Democratic Movement (MDN), an opposition party
Secretary-general of the International Council for Adult Education, Toronto, Canada
UNESCO adviser to the campaign

UNESCO director of literacy, adult education, and rural development, Paris, France

Two UNESCO literacy experts, Paris, France

Vice-minister of adult education, Cuba

World Council of Churches adviser to the campaign

U.S. ambassador to Nicaragua

Director of U.S. Agency for International Development in Nicaragua

Appendix B:
General Interview Format

A series of questions guided the interviews with key crusade staff members. A relaxed, informal, and collegial environment was maintained throughout the sessions. All interviews were conducted in Spanish, recorded on tape, and translated by the author, who is considered to be bilingual, having achieved a 4+ on the Foreign Service Institute Spanish language examination.

1. How and why did you become involved in the literacy campaign?
2. What were you doing prior to your involvement with the crusade?
3. What was your area of study and your experience in the field of education?
4. What was your position and what were your responsibilities in the campaign? What was the function of your section or team?
5. Trace the activities of your section or team and your participation in those events from the beginning of the campaign to its conclusion. Include any memorable vignettes that might help others understand the experience.
6. What were the major obstacles you and your colleagues encountered? What were their causes? How did you address them and how effectively do you believe they were overcome? Please illustrate with vignettes where possible.
7. What do you consider to be the major achievements of the campaign, both overall and in your area of work? To what do you credit these achievements? Please illustrate with vignettes.
8. What were the principal weaknesses and problems in the design and operation of the campaign, both with respect to your work area and with respect to the crusade in general? How were these difficulties addressed and how succesfully were they responded to? Please

illustrate with vignettes. If you had it to do again, would you address them differently? How?

9. What do you consider to be the major lessons learned from the campaign from a pedagogical point of view as well as from an organizational perspective? Illustrate with vignettes.

Bibliography

Adams, Frank. *Unearthing Seeds of Fire*. Winston-Salem, N.C.: John F. Blair, 1975.

Alemán, Luis. National Literacy Crusade, Managua, Nicaragua. Interview, 10 October 1980.

Alemán, Luis, et al. *Cuaderno de educación Sandinista para capacitadores*. Managua, Nicaragua: Ministry of Education, 1979.

Almond, Gabriel A., and Verba, Sidney. *The Civic Culture: Political Attitudes and Democracy in Five Nations*. Princeton: Princeton University Press, 1963.

Amin, Samir. *Literacy Training and Mass Education for Development*. Persepolis, Iran: International Symposium for Literacy, 1975.

Anderson, C. Arnold, and Bowman, Mary Jean. *Educational and Economic Development*. Chicago: Aldine, 1965.

Apter, David E. "Political Religion in the New Nations." In Clifford Geertz, ed., *Old Societies and New States*. New York: Free Press, 1963.

Arce, Bayardo. "Speech: Workshop 1." Frente Sandinista de Liberación Nacional, Tepeyac, Nicaragua, 5 December 1979. Mimeograph.

Arnove, Robert. "Nicaraguan National Literacy Crusade of 1980." *Comparative Education Review* 25 (June 1981).

Arnove, Robert, and Arboleda, Jairo. "Literacy: Power or Mystification." *Literacy Discussion* 4 (December 1973).

x Arrien, Juan B. *Nicaragua: Revolution and Educational Project*. Managua, Nicaragua: Ministry of Education, 1980.

Arrien, Juan B., et al. *Educación y dependencia: El Caso de Nicaragua*. Managua, Nicaragua: INPRHU, 1977.

Arruda, Marcos. World Council of Churches, Managua, Nicaragua. Interview, 16 March 1980.

Aurora Workshop 2. Managua, Nicaragua, Ministry of Education, 10 February 1980. Tape.

Barndt, Deborah. "The Nicaraguan Literacy Crusade." Toronto, Canada, 1982. Typescript.

Bhola, H. S. *Report of a Study Submitted to UNESCO: Campaigning for Literacy*. Toronto, Canada: International Council for Adult Education, 1981.

Bhola, H. S., ed. "Functional Literacy: One Approach to Social Change." *Literacy Discussion* 4 (December 1973).

Black, George. *Triumph of the People*. London: Zed Press, 1981.

Blaug, Marc. "Literacy and Economic Development." *School Review* 74 (May 1966).

Boorstein, Edward. *The Economic Transformation of Cuba.* New York: Monthly Review Press, 1968.

Bowles, Samuel. "Cuban Education and Revolutionary Ideology." *Harvard Educational Review* 4 (1971).

Cain, Bonnie. Creative Associates, Washington, D.C. Interview, 18 April 1982.

Campos, César, National Literacy Crusade, Managua, Nicaragua. Interview, 25 August 1980.

Campos, César, et al. "Research Methodology." National Literacy Crusade, Managua, Nicaragua, October 1979. Mimeograph.

――――. "Community-Action Research." National Literacy Crusade, Managua, Nicaragua, November 1979. Mimeograph.

Canales, Julio. National Literacy Crusade, Jinotega, Nicaragua. Interview, 29 April 1980.

Cano, Alonso. National Literacy Crusade, Managua, Nicaragua. Interview, 22 December 1980.

Cardenal, Fernando. "Objectivos de la Cruzada Nacional de Alfabetización." *Cuaderno de educación Sandinista para capacitadores.* Managua, Nicaragua: Ministry of Education, 1980.

――――. National Literacy Crusade, Managua, Nicaragua. Interview, 3 March 1980.

――――. "Cruzada Nacional de Alfabetización." *SIC* (Caracas, Venezuela: Centrol Bumilla) (April 1980).

――――. National Literacy Crusade, Managua, Nicaragua. Interview, 19 July 1980.

――――. National Literacy Crusade, Managua, Nicaragua. Interview, 2 September 1980.

――――. Sandinista Youth Association, Managua, Nicaragua. Interview, 10 November 1980.

――――. Sandinista Youth Association, Washington, D.C. Interview, 6 April 1981.

Cardenal, Fernando, and Miller, Valerie. "Nicaragua 1980: The Battle of the ABCs." *Harvard Educational Review* 1 (1981), pp. 1–26.

Carnoy, Martin, et al. *Cuba: Economic Change and Educational Reform 1955–1974.* Washington, D.C.: World Bank, 1979.

Carrión, Carlos. Speech before First Congress of National Literacy Crusade. Managua, Nicaragua, 17 June 1980. Tape.

Casco, Lourdes, Ministry of Planning, Managua, Nicaragua. Interview, 15 June 1980.

Cendales, Lola. National Literacy Crusade, Managua, Nicaragua. Interview, 16 August 1980.

Ciriano, Don. Nueva Segovia, Nicaragua. Interview, 10 June 1980.

Citlali, María, and Miller, Valerie. "Report to Fernando Cardenal." National Literacy Crusade, Managua, Nicaragua, July 1980. Typescript.

Couvert, Roger. *La Evaluación de los programas de alfabetización: Guía práctica.* Paris: UNESCO, 1979.

Crone, Catherine D. "What Are We Learning?" *World Education Reports.* New York: World Education, January 1979.

Cruzada Nacional de Alfabetización. "Capacitación I." Ministry of Education, Managua, Nicaragua, 1979a. Mimeograph.

———. "Proyecto piloto: Evaluación de taller." Ministry of Education, Managua, Nicaragua, 1979. Mimeograph.

———. "Proyecto." Ministry of Education, Managua, Nicaragua, October 1979. Mimeograph.

———. "Eduardo Lopez Brigada." Ministry of Education, Nueva Segovia, Nicaragua, November 1979a. Typescript.

———. "Enrique Lopez Brigada." Ministry of Education, Nueva Segovia, Nicaragua, November 1979b. Typescript.

———. "Preguntas: Taller Tepeyac." Ministry of Education, Tepeyac, Nicaragua, November 1979c. Typescript.

———. "Wiwilí Brigade." Ministry of Education, Wiwilí, Nicaragua, November 1979d. Typescript.

———. *Internal Bulletin.* No. 3, 27 December 1979.

———. *El Amanecer del pueblo.* Managua, Nicaragua; Ministry of Education, 1980.

———. *Internal Bulletin.* No. 4, 7 January 1980.

———. *Internal Bulletin.* No. 10, 18 March 1980.

Curle, Adam. *Education for Liberation.* New York: John Wiley and Sons, 1973.

→ Dawson, Richard E., and Prewitt, Kenneth. *Political Socialization.* Boston: Beacon Press, 1969.

Dickson, M. *A Chance to Serve.* London: Dennis Dobson, 1976.

Di Giovanni, Cleto. "U.S. Policy and the Marxist Threat to Central America." In *Heritage Foundation Backgrounder.* Washington, D.C.: Heritage Foundation, October 1980.

Di Montis, Lorena. "Los Brigadistas aprenden a leer de los campesinos." *La Prensa* (Managua, Nicaragua), 17 July 1980.

Dreyfus, Enrique. COSEP, Managua, Nicaragua. Interview, 29 May 1980.

Dumont, B. *Functional Literacy in Mali: Training for Development.* Paris: UNESCO, Educational Studies and Documents, 1973.

Fagen, Richard E. *The Transformation of Political Culture in Cuba.* Stanford: Stanford University Press, 1969.

Fals Borda, Octavio. *Science and the Common People.* Dubrovnik, Yugoslavia: International Forum on Participatory Research, 1980.

Food and Agriculture Organization (FAO). "The Declaration of Persepolis." *Ideas and Action* 10 (1975).

Faure, Edgar, et al. *Learning to Be—The World of Education Today and Tomorrow.* Paris: UNESCO, 1972.

Ferrer, Raul. "Cuba's Literacy Campaign." *Convergence* 6 (1973).

———. UNESCO, Managua, Nicaragua. Interview, 15 February 1980.

Flora, Jan, et al. "The Growth of Class Struggle in the Nicaraguan Revolution." Manhattan, Kans.: Kansas State University, 1982. Typescript.

Fonseca, Carlos. Speech rebroadcast October 15, 1980, on Sandinista Radio. Tape, National Radio Archives, Managua, Nicaragua, 1980.

Freire, Paulo. *Pedagogy of the Oppressed*. New York: Herder and Herder, 1968.

―――. "The Adult Education Process as Cultural Action for Freedom." *Harvard Educational Review* 40 (1970).

―――. *Education for Critical Consciousness*. New York: Seabury Press, 1973.

―――. *Are Literacy Programmes Neutral?* Persepolis, Iran: International Symposium for Literacy, 1975.

―――. *Pedagogy in Process: Letters from Guinea-Bissau*. New York: Seabury Press, 1978.

―――. "Minutes." National Literacy Campaign, Managua, Nicaragua, October 23, 1979. Mimeograph.

Frente Sandinista de Liberación Nacional. "Informe sobre cruzada." Managua, Nicaragua, November 1979. Mimeograph.

Galtung, Johan. *Literacy, Education, and Schooling—For What?* Persepolis, Iran: International Symposium for Literacy, 1975.

Garady, Roger. *Literacy and the Dialogue Between Civilizations*. Persepolis, Iran: International Symposium for Literacy, 1975.

Gayo, Carlos. "Entrevistas." *Ya Veremos*. (Managua, Nicaragua) no. 3 (1980).

Geertz, Clifford. "Ideology as a Cultural System." *Ideology and Discontent* (1964).

Gillette, Arthur Lavery. *One Million Volunteers*. Harmondsworth, Eng.: Penguin Books, 1968.

―――. *Cuba's Education Revolution*. London: Fabian Society, 1972a.

―――. *Youth and Literacy*. Paris and New York: UNESCO/UNCESI, 1972b.

―――. *Beyond the Non-Formal Fashion: Towards Educational Revolution in Tanzania*. Amherst, Mass. Center for International Education, 1977.

Goody, Jack, ed. *Literacy in Traditional Societies*. Cambridge, Eng.: Cambridge University Press, 1968.

Gorostiaga, Xabier. Ministry of Planning, Managua, Nicaragua. Interview, 12 July 1980.

Goulet, Denis. *Looking at Guinea-Bissau: A New Nation's Development Strategy*. Washington, D.C.: Overseas Development Council, 1978.

✕ Greenstein, Fred. "Political Socialization." *International Encyclopedia of the Social Sciences*, vol. 14.

Grisby, Kitty. National Literacy Crusade, Managua, Nicaragua. Interview, 12 October 1980.

Griswold, Wendy. "Transformation and Remembrance." *Harvard Educational Review* 1 (1982), pp. 45–53.

Habib, El. Arab Regional Literacy Organization, Udaipur, India. Interview, 9 January 1982.

Hall, Budd. "Adult Education and the Development of Socialism in Tanzania." Los Angeles, University of California, 1974. Dissertation.

―――. International Council for Adult Education, Managua, Nicaragua. Interview, 4 September 1980.

Hall, Budd, and Kidd, J. R., eds. *Adult Learning: A Design for Action*. New York: Pergamon Press, 1978.

Harmon, David. *Community Fundamental Education*. Lexington, Mass.: D. C. Heath and Company, 1974.

Harmon, David, and Hunter, Carman St. John. *Adult Illiteracy in the United States*. New York: Ford Foundation, 1979.

Harrison, Lawrence. USAID, Managua, Nicaragua. Interview, 13 January 1981.

Herzog, William A. *Literacy Training and Modernization: A Field Experiment*. East Lansing: Department of Communication, Michigan State University, 1967.

Hirshon, Sheryl. *And Also Teach Them to Read*. Westport, Conn.: Lawrence Hill and Company, 1983.

Horton, Aimee "The Highlander Folkschool: A History of the Development of Its Major Programs Related to Social Movements in the South, 1932–1961." Chicago: University of Chicago, 1971. Dissertation.

Hoxeng, James. *Let Jorge Do It: An Approach to Rural Nonformal Education*. Amherst, Mass.: Center for International Education, 1973.

Hurtado Lopez, Anselmo. "To My Literacy Teacher and Compañero." National Literacy Crusade, Managua, Nicaragua, July 1980. Letter.

Institut d'Action Culturelle (IDAC). *Guinea-Bissau: Reinventing Education*. Geneva, 1976.

International Council for Adult Education (ICAE). *The World of Literacy*. Ottawa, Canada: International Development Research Centre, 1979.

————. "Participatory Research: Developments and Issues." *Convergence* 14 (1981).

International Freedom from Hunger Campaign. "Rural Literacy." *Ideas and Action* 105 (1975).

International Institute for Adult Literacy Methods (IIALM). *Teaching Reading and Writing to Adults: A Sourcebook*. Tehran, Iran: International Institute for Adult Literacy Methods, 1976.

Jeffries, C. *Literacy—A World Problem*. New York: Praeger Publishers, 1967.

Kahler, David W. "As Educators We Are Artists and Politicians: A Look at Mass Literacy Campaigns in the Service of Political Processes." Center for International Education, Amherst, Mass., 1978. Mimeograph.

Kassam, Yusef. *Illiterate No More: The Voices of New Literates from Tanzania*. Dar es Salaam: Tanzania Publishing House, 1979.

Kindervatter, Suzanne. *Nonformal Education as an Empowering Process with Case Studies from Indonesia and Thailand*. Amherst, Mass.: Center for International Education, 1979.

Kozol, Jonathan. *Children of the Revolution*. New York: Dell Publishing, 1979.

Lacayo, Francisco. National Literacy Crusade, Managua, Nicaragua. Interview, 29 August 1980.

Lafeber, Walter. *Inevitable Revolutions: U.S. in Central America*. New York: W. W. Norton and Company, 1983.

Landez, Virginia. Letter to National Literacy Crusade. Managua, Nicaragua. July 1980.

Leiner, Marvin. "Major Developments in Cuban Education." In David Barking and Nita Manitzas, eds., *Cuba: The Logic of the Revolution*. Andover, Mass.: Warner Modular Publications, 1973.

Lernoux, Penny. *Cry of the People*. Harmondsworth, Eng.: Penguin, 1982.

Lorenzetti, Anna, and Niejs, Karel. *The Cuban Literacy Campaign*. Paris: UNESCO, 1964.

Macias Gomez, Edgard. *Alfabetización de adultos nicaraguënses*. Managua, Nicaragua: INPRHU-Caritas, 1972.

Mariño, Germán. National Literacy Crusade, Managua, Nicaragua. Interview, 18 August 1980.

Mariño, Germán, et al. *Guía de preguntas*. Managua, Nicaragua: Ministry of Education, 1980.

Mashayekh, Farideh. "Freire: The Man, His Ideas, and Their Implications." *Literacy Discussion* 1 (1974).

M'Bow, Amadou-Mahtar. Literacy Day speech. Paris, UNESCO document, 7 September 1978.

———. Letter to Fernando Cardenal, January 15, 1980. Managua, Nicaragua, National Literacy Crusade Archives.

McFadden, John. National Literacy Crusade. Managua, Nicaragua. Interview, 3 May 1980.

———. Washington, D.C. Interview, 10 November 1983.

✗Meiselas, Susan. *Nicaragua*. New York: Pantheon Press, 1981.

Merriam, Charles Edward. *The Making of Citizens*. Chicago: University of Chicago Press, 1931.

Mhaiki, Paul. UNESCO, Udaipur, India. Interview, 7 January 1982.

Miller, Valerie. Field notes. Managua, Nicaragua, 1980.

Millet, Richard. *Guardians of the Dynasty*. Maryknoll, N.Y.: Orbis Books, 1977.

Montenegro, Francisco. *Informe de censo*. Managua, Nicaragua: Ministry of Education, 1979.

Morales, Manuel. Managua, Nicaragua. Interview, 10 November 1980.

Nicaragua. Government of National Reconstruction. *First Proclamation*. Managua, Nicaragua, July 1979.

Nicaragua. Government of National Reconstruction. Ministry of Education. *Plan Waslala*. Managua, Nicaragua, 1978.

———. *La Educación en el primer año de la Revolución Popular Sandinista*. Managua, Nicaragua, 1980a.

———. *Tareas permanentes*. Managua, Nicaragua, 1980b.

Nicaragua. Government of National Reconstruction. Ministry of Education. National Literacy Crusade. *General Evaluation Report by Squadrons: Workshop I*. Managua, Nicaragua, 1979.

———. *Evaluation Report: Workshop III Carazo*. Managua, Nicaragua, 1980.

Nicaragua. Government of National Reconstruction. Ministry of Education. National Literacy Crusade. Research Section. *To Learn to Know Reality*. Managua, Nicaragua, October 1979.

———. *Research*. Managua, Nicaragua, November 1979.

Nicaragua. Government of National Reconstruction. Ministry of Planning. *Plan '80*. Managua, Nicaragua, 1980.

Nuñez, René. National Board of Directors of the Frente Sandinista de Liberación Nacional, Managua, Nicaragua. Interview, 4 February 1980.

Nyerere, Julius. *Education for Self-Reliance.* Dar es Salaam, Tanzania: Ministry of Information, 1967.

Openham, J. *Non-Formal Education Approaches to Teaching Literacy.* Ann Arbor: Michigan State University Press, 1975.

Parajón, David. Message to parents. Managua, Nicaragua, 3 April 1980.

Pastrán, Francisco. "Report on Mobilization." Ministry of Education, Managua, Nicaragua, 5 June 1980. Typescript.

Pearce, Jenny. *Under the Eagle.* London: Latin American Bureau, 1981.

Perezón, Mario, et al. *Borrador del manual de capacitadores.* Managua, Nicaragua: Ministry of Education, October 1979.

Perez-Valle, María. National Literacy Crusade, Managua, Nicaragua. Interview, 12 August 1980.

Pezzullo, Lawrence. U.S. embassy, Managua, Nicaragua. Interview, 30 May 1980.

Postman, M. "The Politics of Reading." *Harvard Educational Review* 2 (1970).

Prieto, Abel. "Report to International Council for Adult Education on the Cuban Literacy Campaign." Ministry of Education, Havana, 1981. Mimeograph.

Radio Sandino. Radio Broadcast. Managua, Nicaragua, 9 May 1980.

✕ Rahnema, Majid. *Literacy: To Read the Word or Read the World?* Persepolis, Iran: International Symposium for Literacy, 1975.

Ramirez, Julio. Letter to parents. Nicaragua, 5 July 1980.

Ramirez, Sergio. "Speech: March 24." *La Cruzada en Marcha* 4 (April 1980), p. 4.

Rivas, Auxiliadora, and Suazo, Asunción. "Conversation in Literacy Class." Managua, Nicaragua, National Literacy Crusade Archives, May 1980. Tape.

Rivera, Guadalupe. National Literacy Crusade, Valle Enoc Ortez, Nicaragua. Interview, 10 August 1980.

Robelo, Alfonso. Managua, Nicaragua. Interview, 30 May 1980.

Rogers, Everett M., et al. *Modernization Among Peasants: The Impact of Communication.* New York: Holt, Rinehart and Winston, 1969.

Román, José. *Maldito país.* Managua, Nicaragua: El Pez y La Serpiente, 1979.

✕ Rothschuh, Guillermo. *El Nuevo sol.* Managua, Nicaragua: Ministry of Education, 1980.

Saenz, Roberto. National Literacy Crusade, Managua, Nicaragua. Interview, 9 September 1980.

Saenz, Roberto, et al. *Cuaderno de educación Sandinista: Orientaciones para el alfabetizador.* Managua, Nicaragua: Ministry of Education, 1980.

Sandinista Youth Association. "Diario de brigadista." *El Brigadista* (July 1980).

Sandino, Augusto César. As quoted in Jose Román, *Maldito país*, p. 135. Managua, Nicaragua: El Pez y La Serpiente, 1979.

Selser, Gabriela. Letter to parents. Atlantic Coast, Nicaragua, 10 April 1980.

Selser, Gregorio. *Sandino: General de hombres libres.* Mexico City: Editorial Diogenes, 1978.

Somarriba, Mabel. Managua, Nicaragua. Interview, 27 August 1980.

Suarez, María. National Literacy Crusade, Managua, Nicaragua. Interviews, 9 and 18 September 1980.

Tefel, Reynaldo. *Infierno de los pobres.* Managua, Nicaragua: INPRHU, 1972.

Tjerandsen, Carl. *Education for Citizenship*. Santa Cruz, Calif.: Emil Schwarzhaupt Foundation, 1980.

✗ Trueman, Beverly, "Cultural Insurrection in Nicaragua." Boston, 1981. Mimeograph.

Tut, Thaung. *Curriculum Development for Peasants and Workers in the Socialist Republic of the Union of Burma*. Tehran, Iran: International Institute for Adult Literacy Methods, 1980.

Udaipur Conference. "Campaigning for Literacy: Proceedings." International Council for Adult Educaton, UNESCO, Udaipur, India, January 1982. Xerox.

United Nations. Educational, Scientific, and Cultural Organization (UNESCO). *Literacy as a Factor in Development*. Paris: Minedlit, 1965a.

_____. *World Conference of Ministers of Education on the Eradication of Illiteracy, Final Report*. Tehran, Iran, 1965b.

_____. *Literacy, 1967–69*. Paris, 1970.

_____. *Practical Guide to Functional Literacy: A Method of Training for Development*. Paris, 1973.

_____. *Experimental World Literacy Programme: Report and Synthesis of Evaluation*. Persepolis, Iran: International Symposium for Literacy, 1975a.

_____. *Literacy in the World Since the 1965 Tehran Conference: Shortcomings, Achievements, and Tendencies*. Persepolis, Iran: International Symposium for Literacy, 1975b.

_____. *Conferencia general, vigésima reunión*. Paris, 1978.

_____. "Literacy Award Declaration 1980." Paris, September 1980.

United Nations. Educational, Scientific, and Cultural Organization/United Nations. Development Program (UNESCO/UNDP). *The Experimental World Literacy Programme: A Critical Assessment*. Paris: UNESCO, 1976.

United Nations. Food and Agriculture Organization. *See* Food and Agriculture Organization.

United States. Agency for International Development (USAID). *Nicaragua: Rural Sector Development Loan*. Washington, D.C., 1975.

_____. *Latin American Programs*. Washington, D.C., 1978.

Vasquez, Luisa. National Literacy Crusade, Valle Enoc Ortez, Nicaragua. Interview, 9 August 1980.

Verba, Sidney. "Comparative Political Culture." In Lucian W. Pye and Sidney Verba, eds., *Political Culture and Political Development*. Princeton: Princeton University Press, 1965.

Verne, E. *Literacy and Industrialization: The Dispossession of Speech*. Persepolis, Iran: International Symposium for Literacy. 1975.

Verner, C. "Illiteracy and Poverty." *Literacy Discussion* 2 (1974).

Viscusi, Margot. *The Tanzanian Literacy Experience*. Paris: UNESCO, 1972.

Von Rechnitz, Alfredo. "Diario." *Barricada* (Managua, Nicaragua), 9 September 1980.

✗ Waksman, Daniel, et al. *La Batalla de Nicaragua*. Mexico City: Bruguera Mexicana de Ediciones, 1979.

χ Walker, Thomas W., ed. *Nicaragua in Revolution.* New York: Praeger Publishers, 1982.

Wallace, Anthony, "Revitalization Movements." *American Anthropologist* 63 (1956).

_____ . *Culture and Personality.* New York: Praeger Publishers, 1961.

Washington Office on Latin America (WOLA). "The Nicaraguan AID Program: INVIERNO." Washington, D.C., 1977. Typescript.

Index